ROUTLEDGE LIBRARY EDITIONS:
HISTORY OF EDUCATION

LANDMARKS IN THE HISTORY OF PHYSICAL EDUCATION

LANDMARKS IN THE HISTORY OF PHYSICAL EDUCATION

By

J. G. DIXON

P. C. MCINTOSH

A. D. MUNROW

R. F. WILLETTS

Volume 22

Routledge
Taylor & Francis Group

LONDON AND NEW YORK

First published in 1957

This edition first published in 2007 by
Routledge
2 Park Square, Milton Park, Abingdon, Oxon, OX14 4RN

Simultaneously published in the USA and Canada
by Routledge
270 Madison Avenue, New York, NY 10016

Routledge is an imprint of the Taylor & Francis Group, an informa business

© 1957 Routledge & Kegan Paul

Printed and bound in Great Britain

British Library Cataloguing in Publication Data
A catalogue record for this book is available from the British
Library

Library of Congress Cataloging in Publication Data
A catalog record for this book has been requested

ISBN10: 0-415-41978-6 (Set)
ISBN10: 0-415-43262-6 (Volume 22)

ISBN13: 978-0-415-41978-9 (Set)
ISBN13: 978-0-415-43262-7 (Volume 22)

Publisher's Note
The publisher has gone to great lengths to ensure the quality
of this reprint but points out that some imperfections in the
original copies may be apparent.

LANDMARKS
IN THE HISTORY OF
PHYSICAL EDUCATION

J. G. DIXON
P. C. McINTOSH
A. D. MUNROW
R. F. WILLETTS

'Then seemingly for those two elements of the soul, the spirited and the philosophic, God, I should say, has given men the two arts, music and gymnastic. Only incidentally do they serve soul and body. Their purpose is to tune these two elements into harmony with one another by slackening or tightening, till the proper pitch be reached.'

'The Republic' Plato p. 412 trans. A. D. Lindsay.

LONDON

ROUTLEDGE & KEGAN PAUL

First published in 1957
© by Routledge and Kegan Paul Ltd
Broadway House
68–74 Carter Lane
London E.C.4
Printed in Great Britain
by Lowe & Brydone (Printers) Ltd.
London N.W.10
Second edition 1960

CONTENTS

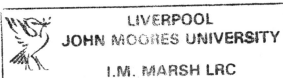

LIST OF ILLUSTRATIONS

PREFACE

WHEN, in 1946, the University of Birmingham first included physical education among those subjects which might be offered for the degree of Bachelor of Arts, a study of the history and principles of physical education became the core of the undergraduate course. The field to be covered was broad and a number of lecturers from the Departments of Greek, German and Education, from the School of History and from the Faculty of Commerce as well as from the Department of Physical Education itself, co-operated to plan the course of study and to give the lectures associated with it.

It was recognised that publications on the history of physical education in English were few and that even fewer attempts had been made to relate different systems of physical education to their social, economic and political background. This book, which is based on lectures on selected topics given within the University, has been written in the hope that the seven studies in the social history of physical education contained in it will be of interest not only to those professionally concerned with physical education but also to those concerned with other aspects of social history as well as to the general reader.

P. C. McI.

I

INTRODUCTION

∽∾∿∾∿∾∿∾∿∾∿∾∿∾∿∾∿

At a time when the first man to run a mile within four minutes is called upon to broadcast as the spokesman of his generation, when cricketers, climbers and a jockey receive knighthoods, when college football is big business in the United States and when, throughout the world, the Olympic Games have their diplomatic as well as their athletic importance, it may well seem that the study of physical culture as an aspect of culture in general has not received the serious attention which it deserves. The fact that the phrase 'physical culture' is usually associated with body building and muscular development and seldom bears the wider meaning given to it here is an indication of the narrow limits within which the subject has most often been studied. The chapters which follow are based on a broader conception of 'physical culture'; they postulate that physical culture is part and parcel of general culture and they try to show how several systems of physical education have developed, not *in vacuo*, but in different environments, moulded and shaped by those environments.

The first three chapters are concerned with physical education in the somewhat distant past, in classical Greece, in Imperial Rome during the first and second centuries A.D. and in Italy and England during the Renaissance.

The selection of these topics was based on three considerations. First, each period under review witnessed remarkable developments in the practice and theory of physical education. In classical Greece the city states had highly organized systems of physical education which varied from state to state and reflected the political organizations of those states. The Olympic Games and the other athletic festivals which drew competitors from many different states and which were the occasions for highly technical performances of athletic events, rested on a foundation of extensive physical education throughout Greece. A theory of physical education or 'gymnastic' was worked out by Plato and published in *The Republic*. This theory, even if it did not reflect the practice of Plato's day or the practice of any other day, was nevertheless significant and had a profound influence in later centuries.

In the second century A.D. the theories of Claudius Galen were, in their own way, as complex as those of Plato but, unlike the latter, they were closer to the practices of people living at the time. Galen worked out in some detail systems of exercise suitable for the vast population of Rome, and many citizens followed programmes of exercises like those which he recommended.

During the Renaissance the re-emergence of physical education was as significant as the earlier achievements of the Greeks and Romans. There took place, first in Italy, then elsewhere, a new synthesis of the ideas and exercises of earlier days. Under the influence of the humanists and within the city states of Italy during the fifteenth century the physical education of the ancients was translated and interpreted for the new aristocracy.

The second consideration which influenced the selection of topics was that the development of physical education in each period had, and still has, some significance for the modern world. Physical education in Greece became a form of initiation into citizenship. To-day it is not customary to think of physical education in schools as initiation into adult life, yet the fact that cricket and not baseball is widely taught in English schools while baseball and not cricket is taught in American schools shows that the pattern of adult physical culture still determines some features of the physical education of children. In the Greek city state this initiatory aspect of education was strongly emphasized. By contrast, Galen and his contemporaries in Rome were occupied with the problem of 'keeping fit' in an urban community from which both the necessity and the incentives to take exercise had disappeared. The problems of urbanization

2

are familiar enough to-day and many of Galen's theories have been echoed in the instructional manuals of the twentieth century. The Renaissance was marked by an admiration for physical prowess in the aristocracy, coupled with an etiquette of modesty, or, at least, a condemnation of ostentation. The etiquette or ethics of sport, the moulding of character and the conditioning of behaviour through physical education as well as the acquisition of physical skills as social accómplishments were studied closely by humanist educators.

The third consideration was the diversity of physical education in these periods both in motive and in application. While physical education in Sparta became closely related to military training, physical education for the great majority of the inhabitants of Rome was divorced from military training. There the army had its own specialized form of physical training. For the ordinary Roman physical education was recreational in that it was designed to give pleasure and relief and to provide enough exercise and exercises to maintain a sense of well-being in men and women who had little work and much leisure. During the Renaissance the military motive was certainly not absent but it was subordinate to the view of physical education as a necessary part of the education of the whole man. Mercurialis reproduced in detail the practices of the ancient world; Baldassare Castiglione in Italy and Sir Thomas Elyot and Richard Mulcaster in England, among others, re-interpreted them for their own communities.

Diversity has also been a characteristic of the development of physical education in Europe and America from the end of the eighteenth century onwards. The last four chapters trace the simultaneous development of physical education in different parts of those continents. Even when systems of physical education had a common origin, their subsequent development was often quite different. Both in Scandinavia and in Germany physical education in the early nineteenth century owed a debt to the writings of Rousseau and the paedagogics of Pestalozzi. In both countries the Napoleonic wars were a stimulus to physical education, but, as the century wore on, the Scandinavian system became more therapeutic and more pacific while in Germany physical education first acquired political ties and then became the instrument of aggressive nationalism. The

3

United States during a period of immigration imported first the German and then the Swedish system and rejected them both. In their place she evolved a pattern of physical education as varied as her forty-eight states and yet typically American. It became a unifying influence in a country of many races and creeds. Great Britain in her insular way developed a pattern of physical education in her Public Schools which was distinct and unique in the nineteenth century. Organized games, especially the team games of cricket and football, were the core of a system which not only produced stamina and other physical attributes but also sought to train boys, and later girls, in self control and self government and inculcated in them an ideal of sportsmanship. But this physical education was for the ruling classes. The physical education of the masses had to wait until near the end of the nineteenth century. When it came it proved to be an import from Sweden championed by women. This dichotomy of physical education had no parallel in Scandinavia, Germany or the United States. It reflected the peculiar structure of society in England.

In this introduction comparisons have been made between one system of physical education and another, but the chapters which follow are not comparative studies. Each one is an essay independent of the others but not irrelevant to them. The purpose of these superficial comparsons is to underline the differences between one system and another and to suggest that no development of physical education can be fully understood unless it is seen against the social, political and economic background of the country where it took place.

II

Social Aspects of
Greek Physical Education

R. F. WILLETTS

∞∞∞∞∞∞∞∞∞∞∞∞∞∞∞

1. INTRODUCTION

In the ancient Greek city-states, citizenship and civilization were closely connected. Civilization implied class societies, based on the exploitation of slave and serf labour, which afforded citizens their means of leisure. The citizens were themselves differentiated into richer or poorer groups, the more and the less leisured. Leisure was devoted, in varying degrees, to civic duties, peaceful and warlike, which, in more advanced communities, demanded qualifications which could only be provided by organized educational systems. These systems were developed from traditional, often quite primitive, forms which survived from tribal times; so that they included, from the beginning, physical education in varying degrees—from the almost exclusively physical education of Sparta to the more sophisticated and balanced composition of the Athenian system. Moreover, physical education continued to be closely connected with military training, so long as the city-state form of organization survived. Hence, physical education was considered to be of great importance by the various communities, so much so that the study of its composition and function cannot properly be understood apart from the study of its social environment.

Such a study is bound to bring to the fore certain aspects of the matter which have continued to be of as much importance

5

to later generations as they were to the Greeks; such as, for example, the relationship between physical and general education, between physical education and military training, or sport, or health, or social activities. For civilization implies that physical pursuits become systematized, playing their part in a general theory and practice of social behaviour.

The Greeks were conscious of their differences from barbarians, and it was apparent to them that civilization was distinguished from barbarism because civilized men lived together in cities, while barbarians lived scattered in villages or settlements. The basic social units of the Neolithic Age had been such scattered settlements or village communities. The end of the neolithic epoch was marked by the rise of urbanization, first in Mesopotamia and Egypt, later in Syria and Crete. The replacement of villages by towns was a revolutionary change in the conditions of social existence which implied much more than a mere expansion in size. The neolithic communities had been organized on the principles of the tribal system—the principles of kinship, common ownership and equality. The city-states were based on private ownership and the division of the community into classes.

In Mesopotamia the radical changes associated with urbanization began soon after 4000 B.C. and were completed by about 3000 B.C. In Crete the beginnings can be traced to the earlier part of the third millenium. From Crete urbanization spread to a number of centres on the mainland of Greece, such as Mycenae and Tiryns. Apart from these centres, people in most parts of Greece continued to live in village communities. Urbanization did not become at all dominant until after about 1000 B.C. Even then it was not uniform. Large areas of the Greek mainland were occupied by tribal or semi-tribal village communities down to 400 B.C. and even later.

Urbanization, then, began much later in Greece than it did in Mesopotamia. Though it began later, however, it progressed very rapidly. Within a few centuries the Greek city-states advanced to higher levels of political development than had been attained in Mesopotamia or the East. The older civilizations had ripened in the Bronze Age. The Greek city-states reached the climax of their development in the Iron Age. Iron was more abundant, more efficient and cheaper than bronze. Bronze Age

6

techniques had been organized as the monopoly of closed corporations or ruling classes; Iron Age techniques were much more widespread. Division of labour between different branches of production, agriculture, handicrafts, trade and so on, had been more extensively developed as industry and commerce made fresh advances. Populations tended to be much more markedly divided according to occupation into more or less permanent groups, each with bonds of common interest State institutions superseded tribal forms of organization, as the new groups formed by the ever-increasing divisions of labour, between town and country, between different sections of town labour, created new organs of officialdom to supervise their interests. The village settlements had been divided by lot into equal shares for all according to their needs. The city-states were towns governed by a landed nobility, surrounded by satellite villages inhabited by peasants.

As the landed nobility increased its economic and social privileges, appropriating first of all the arable land and then the pasture, there developed, in addition to the peasantry, a class of persons who had no land at all. These were encouraged to settle overseas; and consequently the Greeks became dispersed over the Mediterranean area. This process encouraged further developments in trade, which had previously been dependent on barter. Commodity production developed, and the invention of money followed. With the arrival of money there was nothing which could not be bought and sold. One of the first effects of money was to facilitate the alienation of the land. As commodity production developed, men began to cultivate the soil on their own account, a process which resulted in the individual ownership of land. Individual ownership and alienation went together. Many peasant families were driven off the land, reduced to exile, beggary or labour in the mines.

These developments brought a rapid increase of wealth to men of money, merchants and manufacturers. The nobility, in its turn, intensified the exploitation of the peasantry. The new men of money demanded political rights, the peasants demanded land. The ensuing struggles led to revolutionary changes in many states, culminating in the appearance of democratic forms of government. The conflict between the old landed nobility, resisting change, and a 'middle' class and a peasantry demanding

B   7

change, issued in the tyranny. The tyrant, representing the interests of these new forces of change, expropriated the landed nobility, centralized the administration, and reorganized the economy of the state to the advantage of those with whose support he had come to power. The confiscated estates were divided into small holdings, and the peasants thus settled on the land. Ambitious schemes of urban reconstruction and public works were embarked upon, and trade was encouraged. Consequently, expanding employment was assured for the artisans, and the obstacles were removed which the existence of the old nobility and their traditional economy had placed in the way of manufacturing developments. Under the protection of the tyranny, the owners of the new forms of wealth grew rapidly in power and influence, until their interest and the interests of the tyrant diverged, and the alliance between them broke down. The tyranny could then be overthrown and replaced by the political power of the new dominant class of property owners. Such a change resulted in the democratic revolution.

Democracy was new and typically Greek. The movement which culminated in the democratic revolution had its origin in Ionia, on the eastern shores of the Aegean. From there it spread along the trade routes to the mainland of Greece and also to the Greek colonies in southern Italy and in Sicily, promoting change and fresh vitality in every sphere of social life, and effecting, directly or indirectly, important advances in science, medicine, literature and education. But not all the city-states underwent the series of changes from monarchy to aristocracy, from aristocracy to tyranny, and from tyranny to democracy. Sparta and Crete were least affected by the democratic movement, both tenaciously adhering to aristocratic forms of government, and the former even retaining its peculiar form of double kingship. The revolutionary changes associated with democracy reached their highest point in Athens.

The Athenians were justifiably proud of their democracy. But ancient democracy was based on slave labour. The free citizen was expected to devote part of his leisure to political affairs, in the Assembly, the Council, or in some elective magistracy. The leisure of the free classes was ensured by the surplus wealth deriving from the exploitation of slave-labour. The slaves were 'live tools' who had no civic and human rights. The contradic-

8

tion which typifies ancient democracy is that the freedom of the citizens was based on the lack of freedom of the slaves.

The degree of development of the educational systems of the Greek city-states roughly correspond with the degree of development of their social systems. But even in the most advanced communities there remained marked traces of the more primitive forms of social organization of the youth associated with tribal society.

Physical education is, in a general sense, as old as human society. The adaptation of the body to organized work and to organized methods of warfare implies the transmission of skills through social training, as a means of ensuring the livelihood and survival of the group through its relative mastery over nature. Hunting, for example is a highly skilled occupation. Primitive warfare among tribes has often demanded systems of training the body to the extremes of physical endurance. In the same way, tribal dances are, not so much ends in themselves, as social activities designed to adapt the group to the labour of the harvest or the movements of actual warfare.

In a primitive hunting tribe there is division of labour according to sex, and the members of the tribe are distinguished according to their age-grade, as children, as adults and as elders. Children help the women to gather food, the hunting and fighting are men's work, and the elders are the tribal councillors. The individual passes from one grade to another by undergoing rites of initiation. The most crucial transitional stage is reached at puberty, when the boy is prepared for full tribal status and also for marriage. The initiation of girls follows a similar, but less elaborate pattern.

If we bear in mind such considerations, it is not surprising that physical education continued to be a major, and often a dominant factor in Greek education, even at its most sophisticated. This is explained by the survival of the traditions of primitive initiation of the tribal systems from which the city-states had, in varying degrees, relatively recently emerged and with which they remained in contact beyond the bounds of Hellenic civilization. In order to appreciate this survival it is necessary to understand the purpose of initiation in its primitive form. It has been thus explained:[1]

9

The function of initiation—to admit the child to the status of adult—is expressed in primitive thought as a belief that the child dies and is born again. To understand this conception, we must discard modern notions of the nature of birth and death. In primitive society, the newborn child is regarded as one of its ancestors come to life again. That is why, in many parts of the world, including Greece, it is or has been the custom to name the child after one of its grandparents. At puberty the child dies as a child and is born again as a man or woman. The adult is transformed in the same way into an elder, and at death the elder enters the highest grade of all, that of the totemic ancestors, from which in due course he re-emerges to pass through the whole cycle again. Birth is death and death is birth. They are complementary and inseparable aspects of an eternal process of change, which includes not merely birth and death as we understand them but also the growth and decay of the power to beget and to give birth.

Primitive forms of training were more conspicuously retained in those more backward Greek states where education remained, for the most part, physical education. But the continuing close relationship between intellectual education—whether rudimentary or advanced—and physical education, is typified by another characteristically Greek institution, the gymnasium. The gymnasium was an indispensable feature of the social life of the city-state. Larger cities often had two, or more, gymnasia, besides additional 'training-schools' (*palaistrai*). In the more advanced communities of the mainland, where intellectual education developed most rapidly, the parallel development of the gymnasium ensured that intellectual education did not become divorced from physical education. The relationship between gymnastic, music and philosophy was reflected in the social life, the arrangement and the architectural form of the gymnasium. Four periods can be defined in the history of the gymnasium.[2] In the first period, there was only a *dromos*, a running track or sports ground; the second was an archaic period for which Athens provides examples; the third is the fourth century B.C. and the Hellenistic period; and the fourth is the Roman period. With the latter we are not immediately concerned; but the evolution of the gymnasium in the other

10

periods reflects a general educational development from more primitive to more advanced forms. Even in the Classical period of the fifth and fourth centuries B.C., the Spartan, the Cretan and the Athenian systems reveal successive stages of development existing contemporaneously.

2. *SPARTA IN THE CLASSICAL PERIOD*

In the Spartan society of the Classical period there were three social classes, consisting of the ruling class of Spartans, the serfs, who were called Helots, and an intermediary class who were called *perioikoi*. The physical education of Helots and *perioikoi*, in so far as it could be described, would not be particularly significant for the present survey. But the physical education of the ruling class of Spartans is markedly significant. It was in many respects unique, and its primary military character is explained by the historical conditions in which the Spartan state arose.

The end of the Bronze Age and the beginning of the Iron Age coincided roughly with the end of the second millenium B.C. The radical changes in Greek society whose course has been briefly sketched were based on the application of Iron Age techniques. But the aristocratic phase of city-state development was, in certain areas, of a distinctive and enduring type, associated with the economic, social and cultural traditions established by a Dorian ruling class.

The Dorians were the latest arrivals of the several branches of the Greek race, and they have left the most complete evidence of their tribal traditions. They came from the highlands of Doris in Central Greece and moved into southern Greece at the end of the second millenium. They spread over the east and south of the Peloponnese and also overseas to the southern Cyclades, Crete, Rhodes and the Carian coast. When they came into Greece they were a league of three tribes. When they settled, in the Peloponnese or overseas, they were successful in maintaining their tribal forms of organization, however modified by subsequent developments. Although they were relatively few in numbers, the Dorians who settled in Sparta achieved a position of social and military supremacy. Hence their tribal system became the means whereby a ruling oligarchy of landowners imposed its domination over the other classes and sections.

11

Among themselves they tried to preserve their tribal rule of common ownership. Having established themselves on the banks of the Eurotas, the Spartans took possession of the whole of Laconia and later conquered Messenia. They divided the land into family estates which were inalienable. The serfs who tilled the soil, the Helots, were part of the estates. They were compelled to hand over 50 per cent of their produce to the landowners, who were thus provided with their contributions to the collective food supply. For the male members of the ruling class continued to eat in common, maintaining their traditional system of 'common meals' (*pheiditia* or *syssitia*). Hence, although an adapted tribal system perpetuated a system of equality for a minority, it now really functioned as an instrument of state power, the security of the state being guaranteed by the appropriation of an adequate food supply by the dominant class through the exploitation of serf labour. Once securely established, the economic system was directed on rigidly conservative lines; and the development of trade and commerce was consciously restricted.

Inequalities did develop among the rulers however, and in time there were Spartans who owned no land. The upper class of landed proprietors were called 'Equals' and the other citizens 'Inferiors'. In addition to the Helots there was also another subordinate class. These were the *perioikoi*, the free inhabitants who enjoyed their own civil rights, but had no share in the political privileges of the Spartan citizens. They outnumbered the Spartans and there were even greater numbers of Helots. Holding an intermediate position between the Helots and the Spartans, the *perioikoi* occupied a fairly extensive territory, scattered about the countryside or forming compact groups in a few townships. They could engage in trade, manufacture and fishing.

The Helots, descended from the original inhabitants, were serfs bound to the soil, deprived of political rights and freedom of movement, and always feared. For they never lost their spirit of independence and organized revolt when opportunity presented itself. They paid a fixed amount of rent in kind, and had to provide their own seed and the food for their own families. Not only had they to cultivate the fields, but they were also liable to military service. We are informed that the Ephors—the

12

five annually elected Spartan magistrates who assumed the chief administrative power—formally declared war upon the Helots every year. This traditional practice was a symbol of their position in the State.

The ruling Spartans were therefore dependent on the Helots for agriculture and on the *perioikoi* for their rudimentary trade and industry; and they were thus free to devote themselves to the administration of the state and the pursuit of arms, so as to defend the state against revolt from within and against any threat to their system from without. Therefore, respect for authority, physical fitness and military skill shaped the course of Spartan education, which was regulated by the state; and this education was, predominantly, physical education.

As soon as a child was born it was taken before the elders of its tribe. If it was considered to be a weakling, it was exposed. If approved, it was handed over to the parents. The male Spartan in particular was subjected to state-regulated discipline from the end of his sixth year until he was sixty. For the first six years the child was under the care of his mother, but very early on he was taken to the men's club-house by his father and sat near to him. After his sixth year the boy began his progress through a number of different age-grades. As soon as they were seven all boys left home to live in a disciplined and supervised communal system. Many of the details of the organization of their training are still obscure, but it seems likely that boys of different ages lived under the supervision of a young man called an *eiren*, eating and sleeping together as members of a community called a 'herd' (*agela*), corresponding to the communities of the adult males. These communities crossed those of the age-classes, each age-class being divided into 'herds of oxen' (*bouai*) headed by 'leaders' (*bouagoi*) of the same age. Instruction in gymnastics was given by the *eirenes*. Two or more 'herds', each commanded by its 'leader', took part in contests under the supervision of an *eiren*.

During the six-year period which lasted until the completion of his twelfth year the boy entered upon the first stage of the severe Spartan training, but did not take part in competitive exercises in music, dancing or athletics until he was ten. At the end of the twelfth year, the boys shaved their heads, wore only one cloak in a year, summer and winter, and were not allowed

13

to bathe or anoint themselves except on special occasions. In the summer they slept on rushes plucked by hand from the Eurotas. In winter they were allowed to add leaves of wolf's-bane to their bedding. At this age the boys were allowed the society of 'lovers', from among young men of repute. These relationships were often life-long. The boys attended to their own living-quarters, and the theft of fuel and food without being detected was encouraged. If a boy was caught stealing he was flogged, not because he was a thief but because he was an unsuccessful one.

The period of adolescence, from 13–18, marked the third six-year period. At the age of 18, the young Spartan acquired the status of *melleiren*. He was now a candidate for the rank of *eiren*, reached in the nineteenth year. A severe test of physical endurance is a not uncommon feature of rites of initiation into manhood among primitive peoples, and the public scourging of the *melleirenes* at the altar of Artemis Orthia was an institution of this general type. Plutarch tells us that he had frequently seen youths die under this ordeal. There is some reason to believe that this ceremony, which lasted until the fourth century A.D., acquired its more brutal characteristics in Roman times.

With the completion of his twenty-fourth year the Spartan ceased to be an *eiren* and became a first-line soldier. When he was thirty he became a full citizen and a member of the Assembly of citizens. He could now live with his wife and family. Marriage was not encouraged immediately after manhood was reached, but, on the other hand, those who remained bachelors after an unspecified time were subject to a variety of penalties. The marriage ceremony was ancient and took the form of abduction without a dowry. The young husband continued to live with his male companions and sometimes children were born before the married couple saw each other by daylight, since they continued for a long time to meet furtively only at night.

The practice of 'common meals' for the men was another survival of earlier tribal institutions. The place of these 'common meals' was still called in Crete the 'Men's House' (*andreion*) and this had also once been the name of the Spartan 'common meal', according to Aristotle. Xenophon several times refers to these groupings as 'tent-communities'.

14

The boys had their own equivalent of the 'common meals', whose established etiquette was probably the model of their communal meals. These were presided over by the *eiren*, who stayed with the boys after their meal, teaching them songs, asking questions about public affairs and biting the thumbs of those who gave wrong answers by way of punishment. (Analogous practices elsewhere suggest that this curious form of punishment had a magical significance, biting the thumb being a means of imparting wisdom.) At the age of about twenty the young man became eligible for election to an adult association. Election had to be unanimous and members had to make their monthly contributions to the common store under penalty of forfeiting their rights of citizenship. Excuses for non-attendance were limited to sickness, absence on hunting expeditions, or attendance at public sacrifices. On occasion the boys were admitted to the adult 'common meals' to listen to the conversation of their elders on political affairs and Spartan customs and to endure jokes at their expense.

Their early forms of military training prepared the young men for service with the *krypteia*, perhaps between the ages of eighteen and twenty. The word *krypteia* is sometimes translated as 'secret police' or 'secret service'. The atmosphere of secrecy implicit in the word probably derived, however, from the fact that the *krypteia* formed a distinct part of the series of initiations from boyhood to manhood. A period of withdrawal from the tribal settlement, spent in hiding in the bush and living on whatever nature and cunning may provide, is a common feature of tribal life in various parts of the world. But the Spartan authorities adapted the institution to their own purposes. According to Plutarch, groups of young men were sent out into the country districts armed with daggers, hiding by day and killing by night any Helots they caught. He adds that it was not uncommon for them to go into the fields where the Helots were working and kill the most sturdy of them.

Since its primary objects were to inculcate obedience to authority, the endurance of hardship and supreme fortitude in battle, formal education consisted mainly of physical education. Boys learnt a minimum amount of reading and writing, of which they had little need. For even their laws were learnt by heart, set to music; just as they learnt songs in praise of dead heroes

15

and deriding cowardice. They were encouraged to speak only briefly and to the point. Spartan music, however, flourished, and Plutarch describes the Spartans as 'most musical as well as most warlike'. The same writer tells us that they had three choirs at their festivals, a choir of old men, a choir of younger men and a choir of boys. The Spartans were also much given to dancing, to the accompaniment of flutes or lyres. Often their dances took the form of complicated drill movements or sham fighting. At the famous national festival of the *Gymnopaidiai*, which lasted for several days, three large teams of old men, younger men and boys performed such gymnastic evolutions, singing songs at the same time.

Though much of their time was taken up in gymnastics under the supervision of their elders, the boys were also taught to ride and to swim. Boxing and the *pankration* (an exercise combining wrestling and boxing) were forbidden. No professional trainers were allowed for wrestling, emphasis being placed not so much on technical skill as on strength and self-reliance. No spectators were allowed in the gymnasium and the oldest man present had to see that everyone took sufficient exercise. The boys had a physical inspection every ten days, carried out by the Ephors, and their dress and bedding were inspected at the same time.

Fighting was encouraged from an early age and older men promoted quarrels among the boys to see who was the pluckiest. There was an annual fight of the youths, which perhaps had a ritual origin symbolic of the victory of spring over winter. The playing field was surrounded by water; each team did its utmost to drive the opposing team into the water. They fought with their hands, feet and teeth, even tearing out one another's eyes. There was also an annual ball-game which apparently took the form of a straight fight for possession of the ball.

The girls too were organized in 'herds'. They took their meals at home but were encouraged to live an outdoor life and to train their bodies so that they might bear strong children. They participated in gymnastic and musical training, in wrestling, running, swimming and throwing the javelin and discus. At some festivals they danced and sang before the young men, praising the brave and deriding misbehaviour. Until they were married the women wore no veils and mixed with the men.

After the failure of Athenian democracy, historians and philo-

16

sophers with aristocratic sympathies tended to idealize the Spartan system. Even so this idealization was tempered by criticism based on the reality of Sparta's own decline. 'Compulsion and not persuasion will have controlled their education', wrote Plato,[3] 'because they have neglected the true Muse, who is accompanied by reason and philosophy, and have honoured gymnastic above music.' And Aristotle wrote:[4] 'The whole system of their laws was directed towards that aspect of right conduct relevant to military skill, since it served the end of conquest: so that, while warfare was their means of self-preservation, the hegemony they achieved occasioned their decline, because they were ignorant of the use of leisure and had mastered no higher form of training than the art of war.'

3. CRETE IN THE CLASSICAL PERIOD

Though similar in many important respects to the institutions of Sparta, the Dorian institutions of the cities of Crete reveal no less important differences. The legacy of the previous Minoan culture, the long-established tradition of urbanization, the development of commerce and the codification of law, including detailed rules relating to property, and the existence of a coinage from the beginning of the fifth century B.C.—all these factors contributed to the growth of more typically city-state institutions within the general aristocratic framework. Consequently Dorian tribal traditions in Crete had been more strictly adapted to centralized control by the apparatus of state than was the case in Sparta.

Nevertheless, it is clear from the evidence of the Law Code of Gortyna (perhaps the most important Cretan city of the historical period), and from other sources, that Cretan institutions still depended on their original tribal structure, though this had been transformed, just as in Sparta, into a coercive apparatus of state in the various cities. The primary feature is economic, political and social inequality. There were four main classes of the population; the slaves, the serfs, the *apetairoi* and the free citizens, who composed the ruling classes.

The slaves, like other movables, could be bought and sold. The serfs, less harshly treated than the Spartan Helots and probably not subjected to the same degree of economic exploitation,

17

were, like the land they lived on, inalienable, as in Sparta. The slave proper was a commodity, and formed the lowest social class, a product of urban economy. The serf lived in the country, as a part of the landed estate, which he cultivated for his master. He was allowed his own possessions, money and cattle; he also had his own family and (unlike the slave) could marry and divorce.

The *apetairoi* were a class of free persons excluded from the privileges of citizenship, occupying a social position midway between citizens and serfs. They can be compared with the Spartan *perioikoi*. The *apetairos* was so called because he did not belong to a *hetaireia*, a grouping analogous to the Athenian phratry. The clan, the phratry (a group of clans), and the tribe (a group of phratries) are organically related, as the ancient authorities testify and as the anthropological evidence elsewhere confirms.

The tribe is named in the epigraphic evidence as a still active institution and women were enumerated in it. The body of chief magistrates, known as the *kosmoi*, were drawn from certain clans, which had taken on the form of privileged kinship groups. Tribal organization generally, of course, had become restricted to the class of citizens within the overall structure of the state. The phratry, in the form of the *hetaireia*, had become an exclusive association of male citizens, preventing women and all non-citizens from exercising political rights. The aristocratic governments reflected these economic and social divisions. The states were headed by the boards of *kosmoi*, selected from the privileged hereditary groups, and a council of elders made up of former magistrates. The Assembly of citizens seems to have exercised little power in this period, though there is evidence to suggest that its powers revived, for various reasons, in the Hellenistic period. In Aristotle's time, the Cretan cities were well-known as centres of strife resulting from the disputes of aristocratic factions.

Whereas the administrative, judicial and executive power of the Spartan state was wielded by two kings, twenty-eight senators and five ephors, assisted by a very small number of minor officials, the apparatus of state in the Cretan cities was more highly developed, so that it allowed of a centralized system of control of tribute from the serfs. 'The Cretan admini-

18

stration of the *syssitia* is better than the Spartan', wrote Aristotle.[5] 'For, while in Sparta each citizen pays a fixed contribution, failing which he is legally deprived of a share in government, in Crete the system is more communal; since, out of all the crops and the cattle produced from the public lands and the tributes paid by the serfs, one part is devoted to the worship of the gods and the upkeep of public services, and the other part to the *syssitia*, so that all the citizens are maintained from common funds, men, women and children.'

The names of a fair number of Spartan age-grades have been preserved, but this is not so in Crete, except where puberty and the period of transition from youth to manhood are concerned. The importance attached to foot-racing is indicated by the terms *dromeus* and *apodromos*. *Dromeus* means 'a runner' and was the term applied to an adult, a citizen in his own right. Although the exact age at which a youth became a 'runner' is uncertain, it must have been at about twenty. The term implies the right to exercise in the public gymnasium; also, that, having now passed out of the 'herd', the young man could become a member of the 'Men's House'. The term *apodromos* was applied to a minor, one who was not yet allowed to take part in the public athletic exercises.

Our chief source of information about the organization of the Cretan youth is the account given by Strabo.[6] One of the most remarkable features of this account is the implication that Cretan marriage was a state-controlled and public ceremony, comprising all those who belonged to the same age-grade, thus preserving a tribal custom of great antiquity, though under state supervision. For Strabo says that those who were promoted from the 'herd' were obliged to marry at the same time.

The boys, continued Strabo, had to learn their letters and also lays from the laws and certain forms of music. Those who were still younger were taken to the 'common meals', or 'clubs', where they sat together on the ground to eat their food, wearing the same shabby clothes in summer and winter, and tending to the men as well as to themselves. Grouped according to 'clubs', each group under the charge of an 'instructor' (*paidonomos*), they contested with each other and with other 'clubs'. The older boys were taken into the 'herds', which were organized by the most influential notables among them, each collecting as many

19

boys as possible. The leader of each 'herd' was generally the father of the organizer, who was responsible for taking them to the hunt and to the foot-races, and for punishing the disobedient. Their food was provided at public expense. On certain appointed days, the 'herds' contended with each other in sham-fights, accompanied, as was the custom in actual warfare, by the music of flutes and lyres.

Strabo also gives details of the peculiar custom whereby boys were abducted from their homes by initiated adults. After giving warning of his intention, the abductor and his friends carried the boy away to the 'Men's House' of the abductor. He was then given presents and taken away into the country. After feasting and hunting with the abductor and his friends for two months, he returned to the city, receiving the gifts of a warrior's costume, an ox and a drinking-cup. These gifts indicated that the boy had entered upon the first stages of manhood. Boys who had been abducted by 'lovers' in this way were given the position of highest honour in dances and races, and they were allowed to dress in better clothes than others. Even after they had grown to full manhood they still wore a distinctive dress.

Despite the antiquity of the rule relating to marriage, the lapsing of ancient custom owing to the increase of individualism is apparent from the fact that the Cretan 'herds' were partly of a private character, since their organization had become dependent on the influence of a social *élite*. Moreover, education during childhood was no longer as systematic as in Sparta, and the youths did not form their independent communities until they were seventeen. Nevertheless, the inscriptions of the Hellenistic period show that the institution continued to flourish, not least, as we shall see, because of the oath of loyalty which the youths had to swear when they left the 'herds'.

4. ATHENS IN THE CLASSICAL PERIOD

The high level of Athenian civilization in the fifth century B.C. was achieved within the framework of political democracy. The economic foundation of this political democracy—primitive forms of ownership of land having completely disappeared with the earlier development of aristocracy and tyranny—was small-scale peasant agriculture combined with independent handi-

20

crafts. The new form of moneyed wealth associated with the rise of democratic institutions allowed the majority of the Athenians access to forms of private ownership, making it possible for the citizen labourer to become the private owner of his own means of labour, the peasant of the land, the artisan of his tools. An important feature of the democratic re-organization of Athenian society, which began with the reforms of Kleisthenes in the last decade of the sixth century, after the collapse of the tyranny, was the introduction of a new tribal system which gave political expression to the economic domination of the country by the city. The primitive tribal system, which the Athenian aristocracy had perpetuated and modified in its own interests— as had happened, in different conditions, also in Sparta and Crete—was abolished. The powers of the phratry, maintained by the aristocrats as a closed body, in order to restrict the citizenship, and likewise the restrictive powers of the hereditary clan, were broken. The new system restored to the wider citizen body, at least temporarily, the forms of its ancient tribal rights in a wholly new political context.

Private ownership was the pre-requisite of personal freedom, and since private ownership was developed by men, Athenian women were denied political, social and educational rights, even in the Athenian democracy of the early and best period. (Hence, while the physical education of boys and men in Athens was no less important, in its way, than in Sparta, there was, in marked contrast with Sparta, virtually no physical education for Athenian women.) And not many decades were to pass before slavery began to seize on production. For, although slaves had existed in Greece from early times, their usefulness, and therefore their numbers, were strictly limited while the economy remained agrarian. With the development of coinage, of a money economy, of trade and manufacture, there was an increasing demand for slave labour in workshops, mines, quarries and in transport.

The slave population of Athens grew rapidly once the economic basis for its expansion had been laid. Although estimates must be conjectural, it is likely that the citizen population of Athens was, in 431 B.C., about 170,000, compared with a slave population of about 115,000. Just over a century later, when a census was taken, in 313 B.C., there were 84,000 citizens and

21

400,000 slaves. Slaves were private property, and wealth in the form of slaves tended to concentrate in the hands of a minority. It was this minority which enjoyed leisure for educational pursuits, including the pursuits of various forms of physical training. Whereas wealthy citizens might own hundreds of slaves, poorer citizens, a growing majority, might own one slave, or perhaps none at all. As slave labour developed, the value of free labour declined, and the citizen population increasingly used their democratic rights to compel the state to increase its payments to them for performing their civic duties. The cost of these subsidies was met partly by trade and taxes, partly by revenues from the empire into which Athens, in the middle of the fifth century, transformed the league of free cities which she had led against the Persian invaders some thirty years earlier. A policy of suppression and expansion abroad led to war. At the end of the protracted Peloponnesian War with Sparta (431–403 B.C.) the Athenian empire was overthrown. From this time on the word democracy began more and more to assume the meaning of republican government, as opposed to monarchy, and to lose its radical associations with that early form of Athenian democracy which had given such impetus to the development of Hellenic civilization.

There were three main classes in Athenian society, the citizens, the metics or foreign settlers, and the slaves. All citizens could participate in the Assembly, and form part of the Council, and had to fill a whole number of major and subordinate offices and to perform a variety of public services. Payment for such public service became essential. The state also assumed obligation to provide public assistance for invalided workmen and for war orphans. In times of distress corn was sold cheaply or distributed free. Cultural and intellectual interests of the citizens were also encouraged. On feast days, citizens went to the religious ceremonies, processions and sacrifices, and they patronized the great dramatic festivals.

The citizen population was itself divided into four grades, based on income. Though the development of democracy increasingly broke down the distinctions between these grades and made it possible for poorer citizens to become eligible for the higher offices, social differences continued to exist, and the landed nobility long continued to be highly influential.

22

The citizens alone possessed political rights and they alone possessed the land. Rich citizens invested money in business and in banking concerns, and poorer citizens worked as artisans. But the greater part of industrial and commercial work was performed by the metics and the slaves. The metic class was of cosmopolitan origin. Metics went into every industry, and, through the import trade, controlled shipping. Though encouraged by the government, the metics, as foreigners, were excluded from political rights.

In theory, the system of citizenship enabled the citizen to have leisure sufficient for the exercise of civic duties, for education and for gymnastic. But since a large number of the poorer classes of the community had to work with their hands, they required technical instruction. Trades tended to be hereditary, craftsmen learning their skills from their fathers. There were also various systems of apprenticeship.

Since Athenian womenlived in seclusion, education in Athens, as was usual in most Greek states, with the exception of Sparta and Crete, was mainly for boys. There were three stages of formal education, a primary stage from the age of six to fourteen, a secondary stage from fourteen to eighteen, and a third stage from eighteen to twenty. The third stage was made compulsory by the state, and is, in this respect as in others, comparable with the Spartan and Cretan systems. The second stage was available only to the wealthy. Some form of gymnastics was taught over the whole educational period, a requirement that was occasioned by the liability of all citizens to military service. There is some reason to believe that there were schools in Athens early in the sixth century. These schools developed as private enterprises without endowment by the state. Parents selected a suitable school according to their means and also according to the subjects which they wanted their sons to learn. It may be that poor boys had little formal schooling, and merely learnt what they could from their parents, though elementary instruction in reading and writing was not expensive.

In the primary stage the 'schoolmaster' (*grammatistes*) was responsible for instruction in reading, writing and some arithmetic. He also taught his pupils to recite Homer, Hesiod and other poets. The 'lyre-player' (*kitharistes*) gave instruction in the seven-stringed lyre and in singing the works of the lyric poets

c   23

to its accompaniment. Wrestling, boxing, the *pankration*, running, jumping, throwing the discus and javelin, and other such exercises, were supervised by the 'trainer' (*paidotribes*).

Thus, the two main branches of education were 'music' and gymnastic, 'music' implying any art over which the Muses presided, more especially lyric poetry and music proper. Physical education was conducted either in a gymnasium or a 'training school' (*palaistra*). The *palaistra* was a training school for boys or part of a gymnasium specially devoted to wrestling or boxing. It often took the form of an enclosed space, if possible near a stream and open to the air, so that the trainees could be accustomed to endure the heat of the sun. They cost very little to erect and were to be found in the smallest villages and were often attached even to private houses. The gymnasia were large public buildings, costly to build. There were only three of them in Athens in the fourth century, and smaller towns could not afford to have them. They were open to citizens of all ages, either taking exercise themselves or watching other people: and they were used as a sort of club, frequented by sophists and philosophers.

The training master who was responsible for the instruction of the boys in the *palaistra* was called a *paidotribes* (from *pais* = 'boy' and *tribein* = 'to rub'). He owed his name to the rubbing with oil or various kinds of dust so commonly used in athletics. This training master was an expert in his own field. He was required to know which exercises were suitable for different types of constitution and he was in the habit of prescribing diets. His symbol of office was a long forked stick.

The roofless *palaistra* ensured that the exercises were performed in the sun and the open air, but little caps could be worn if the sun became too hot. The floor was of sand and, before taking any strenuous exercise, it was customary for the boys to break up the floor with pickaxes. Professional flute players were a normal attachment to the staff of a *palaistra*, since most exercises were done to the accompaniment of a flute.

Young trainees were at first taught deportment and easy exercises, and what was called 'gesticulation' was included in this early training. 'Gesticulation' chiefly exercised the arms but also included a series of movements of all the limbs, and was thus preliminary to the various dancing systems as well as to

24

more advanced gymnastics. Rope-climbing, leap-frog and perhaps ball-games would also be included in the early stages of training.

When the boys were older and stronger they participated in the regular and more advanced curriculum—wrestling, boxing, the *pankration*, running, jumping, throwing the discus and the javelin. (The traditional 'contest of five exercises' (*pentathlon*) consisted of wrestling, boxing, running, jumping, throwing.) Each exercise was designed for a specific purpose. Thus, the different kinds of wrestling were considered to strengthen loins, arms and legs; running improved lightness and speed, as well as providing a salutary exercise for the lungs, jumping made the lower leg vigorous and supple; throwing strengthened the muscles of arms and wrists. Later, such other exercises as ball-games, boxing, and the *pankration* would contribute further to the suppleness of physique acquired in the basic exercises.

In Greek wrestling, three throws were necessary for a victory. The combatants had their bodies oiled, which added both to the difficulty and the value of the sport. Various trainers would elaborate their own individual systems, with set forms of opening the bout and with different means of countering the opponent. Training in boxing was also reduced to formal systems. Boys used light gloves, consisting of thongs of leather wound round the fists.

The *pankration* combined wrestling and boxing, similar sort of gloves being worn as for boxing, except that the fingers were unfastened. Both boxing and the *pankration* normally continued until an opponent acknowledged his defeat. However, the *pankration* was not considered a proper form of sport for boys, except in the training-school, where the trainer could stop the bout if it showed signs of becoming too fierce.

The usual distances in running were two hundred yards, quarter-mile and long-distance, varying from three-quarters of a mile to about three miles.

In the long-jump (*halma*), weights like dumb-bells were held in the hands. To judge from pictures on vases, the jump appears to have been preceded by a few steps, the swing of the weights being used to assist the spring, with the arms thrown forward before the jumper took off and swung back before he landed. The floor was prepared to show the marks of the jump and to

25

break the jar of landing, and the jump was measured only if the jumper landed evenly on the prepared surface, leaving a clear impression.

Throwing the discus was often illustrated on vase paintings and by statues. The discus thrower would stand with right foot slightly advanced, holding the discus in his left hand. Transferring it to his right hand and swinging it back as far as possible, he would release it by an underhand throw, using all the weight of his body. The left foot would be brought forward to support the weight of the body as the discus was thrown. Long, unpointed rods were used to practise throwing the javelin and the spear.

Since cavalrymen were recruited from the wealthier sections of the community, riding seems to have been a much less common accomplishment than swimming or rowing. Cavalrymen were relatively few, but practised oarsmen were required to man the triremes.

Dancing was closely associated with religious ritual, and choral dancing, based on stylized systems analogous to those employed in physical education, was a common feature of many festivals. Skill in athletics, in 'music' and in dancing, were fostered by the festivals which played such an important part in civic life. At Athens, for example, festivals occupied about seventy days in the year. The most important Athenian festival was the Panathenaia, in honour of the goddess Athene, held in the third year of each Olympiad. Besides a great procession and sacrifice, this festival included musical and athletic contests, warlike exercises, a torch-race, and boat-races. There were four major Hellenic festivals, common to all Greeks, which were celebrated with games. These were the Olympian, the Pythian, the Isthmian and the Nemean. The four games differed in their origin, and in the details of their organization, but they were, in the main, conducted on the same principles.

During the first three quarters of the fifth century there was no provision for secondary education, and when it did become established it was largely open only to a wealthy minority. Many primary schools started secondary courses, but such higher education was chiefly supplied by a special body of instructors who came to be known as sophists. For higher education came into being as the result of a number of factors

26

which determined its special character. Democratic systems of economy and government created more or less leisured groups of citizens with special social responsibilities and official duties which they could not properly fulfil without some oratorical training. At the same time Greek science had undergone a remarkable development. During the course of the sixth century, in Ionia, Greek science reached a high level within the lifetime of Thales and Anaximander of Miletos, who concerned themselves with the problem of change. Later, in the fifth century, scientific thought was developed by Empedokles of Akragas and Demokritos of Abdera. The latter originated the atomic theory, which could not as yet, however, be tested by experiment.

Scientific advances brought about new forms of systematized knowledge, new ways of looking at the world generally, which conflicted with older established traditions of thought and training. Therefore the second half of the fifth century was an age of scientific treatises. Not only oratory, but such subjects as cookery, were systematized; and political institutions and moral systems were examined in the spirit of scientific inquiry. As the Greeks sought information about other lands and peoples, enlightenment began to spread.

In this environment of critical inquiry and scientific investigation, the growing demand for higher education was supplied by the sophists, who were in the habit of travelling from place to place. They gave instruction in the arts of rhetoric, of reasoning, and in all kinds of more specific subjects. They were not only teachers but also men of affairs, writing treatises, promoting discussion, spreading knowledge and stimulating an informed and critical public opinion. They were, in the main, rationalist in outlook, but held many diverse doctrines. Sokrates of Athens was their most famous representative, and most of our knowledge of him derives from the dialogues of his pupil Plato. Early in the fourth century established secondary schools arose and the great age of the sophists was over. The two most famous of these schools were those of Isokrates and Plato.

Plato, in his *Republic*, describes his ideal of an ancient city-state based on slave-labour, a hierarchy of social classes and the acceptance of the inevitability of war. He argues that education should consist, as it has always done in Greece, of 'music' and

27

gymnastic. The members of the ruling class are to be carefully trained in both throughout their lives from their earliest years. Since they must expect to endure such hardships in their campaigns as frequent changes of diet and climate, they must not be of delicate health. Hence a gymnastic system suitable for such warriors must be simple, and unlike the regimen of the ordinary trained athlete who falls a prey to illness whenever he departs from his accustomed diet.

Just as simplicity in music produces temperance in the soul, so simplicity in gymnastic produces health in the body. Every sort of valetudinarianism is to be discouraged, so that the person who has undergone the prescribed education in 'music' and gymnastic can be independent of medicine except in cases of extreme necessity. Unlike the athlete, who diets and exercises himself to acquire bodily strength, he will undergo the rigours of gymnastic training in order to add stimulus to the spirited part of his soul. For the traditional purpose of the combined education in 'music' and gymnastic was not that the soul should be tended with 'music' and the body with gymnastic. Rather, both together were intended to benefit the soul. If men devote themselves exclusively to gymnastic, they become unduly fierce and surly, rather than brave; just as, if 'music' is exclusively cultivated, they become enervated. Hence, the twin arts of 'music' and gymnastic were bestowed on men for the spirited and philosophic elements of their souls. But the service of these arts to soul and body is incidental. Their real purpose is to tune the two elements into harmony by a process of adjustment until the proper pitch is attained. The ideal is to be the most proper mixture of 'music' and gymnastic applied in the best possible proportion to the soul.

Although Plato's theories were never applied in practice, his views on physical education reflect the important part which it played in the social life and the formal education of the leisured classes of his time. Plato's pupil, Aristotle, although he does not idealize the possibilities of gymnastic in the same way, fully agrees with its practical educational importance. In his *Politics*, he points out that it is the business of gymnastic science to study what sort of gymnastic exercise is beneficial to what sort of constitution, and what exercise taken by all is best for the largest number; and also, if required, to produce a physical bearing

28

and an athletic skill that are not those most naturally suited to a particular physique.

He also argues that education by habit must precede education by reason, and that training of the body must likewise precede training of the mind. But premature and disproportionate athletic development, to the detriment of natural growth, is an error. While the Spartans have avoided this particular error, their system of physical training nevertheless produces brutality rather than the manly courage which is its aim. Consequently, he recommends that, until puberty, lighter exercises should be adopted, without hard diet and severe forms of training, so that growth may not be hindered. For when people train strenuously in their youth, they can be robbed of their strength. But if the three years after puberty have been spent on other studies, then the next period can be spent in hard exercise and a strict training diet. Since the development of the mind is hindered by physical toil, and that of the body by mental toil, strenuous mental and physical exertions should not be pursued at the same time.

The theoretical attention paid to the systematic training of the youth—including the purpose and proportion which were to be assigned to physical education—was rooted in the actual historical development of the Greek states and must have been much influenced by the prevailing Athenian system, culminating in the ephebic training.

For two years, from the age of eighteen, the youths of Athens formed a special category of the population and were called *epheboi* (youths). The system of ephebic training was reorganized in the latter part of the fourth century. Although the relevant evidence is chiefly late, the probability is that some of its essential features derived from earlier times, as is indicated in some of the archaic traces of the oath which was taken by the novices, and more generally by the parallels between the Athenian and the Spartan and Cretan systems. For, as in Sparta and Crete, the ephebic training was organized by the state; and it was certainly not organized primarily for intellectual pursuits— at least in the Classical period. Whatever its earlier forms may have been, it was developed by the state as an organized system of military training and only later became inseparable from the general educational system.

29

When he was eighteen, the Athenian youth entered upon the first stage of his enrolment and training as a citizen. If there was no doubt about his age and his parentage, his name was entered upon the roll of his deme, or parish. He then became legally an *ephebos* and he took the oath of allegiance, but not before, in all probability, he had been instructed in the laws of the city. The various tribes each selected three men over the age of forty, one of whom was finally chosen by the assembled people to supervise the *epheboi* of each tribe. The supervisors were called Censors or Moderators (*sophronistai*), and they were made responsible for morality and discipline. Military training was supervised by military officers. In the late fourth century general supervision of the *epheboi* was entrusted to a specially selected official, the *kosmetes* ('director').

After their supervisors had been appointed, the *epheboi* were taken round the temples, put into garrisons and started their training. They were taught the use of arms and they must have spent much time also in gymnastic training. The *epheboi* of each tribe took their meals together. Though discipline may have been strict, the *epheboi* had their full share of holidays and amusements. They took part in festivals and a special place in the theatre was reserved for them. After completing the first year of their training, they had to demonstrate the skill they had acquired at a public review in the theatre. Afterwards, they received a spear and a shield from the state, and these arms were looked upon as sacred. The second year was spent in patrolling the frontiers and manning the forts.

While they were *epheboi* the youths wore a special cloak, originally dark or black, later white. Since emphasis is laid by ancient writers on the rough cloaks of the Spartan and Cretan boys, and since black or dun was the traditional mourning colour in Greece—except in Argos, where it was white—it may be that, in all three cases, the wearing of this special garment was originally connected with the primitive belief in the death of the child at initiation.

5. THE HELLENISTIC PERIOD

The conventional limits of the Hellenistic period embrace the three centuries from the death of Alexander in 323 B.C. to the

30

foundation of the Roman Empire by Augustus in 30 B.C. At the time of his death the empire of Alexander included Macedonia, Egypt, most of Asia from the Aegean to the Punjab, south of a line through the Caucasian and Caspian region, with the exception of Arabia, Armenia, and the north of Asia Minor. Apart from those on the Black Sea, the majority of the Greek cities in Asia were his allies, while the League of Corinth controlled relations with Greece itself. After his death there was a struggle for power among his generals. By 275 B.C., three separate dynasties, descended from three of the generals, were established. The Seleucids took over a great part of the former Persian empire in Asia, the Ptolemies Egypt, and the Antigonids Macedonia. After 212 B.C., Rome began to play an active part in the affairs of the Hellenistic world, and eventually established imperial rule over the entire Mediterranean region.

The sphere of common Hellenic civilization was thus enormously expanded. In an age where the absence of machines was as remarkable as the compensating size of its slave populations, common Greek speech and education promoted uniformity in Hellenic modes of life among the free classes. This cohesion, alike in business practice as in religion, depended to a great extent upon the education of the youth on the Greek model. This education centred around the Greek gymnasium, which was not only a school, but served as a social centre for adults, engaged in what were essentially Greek activities. Numerous associations of this kind developed.

In the third century, the numbers of Athenian *epheboi* diminished to quite small proportions, and since brothers are found serving together, the age qualification cannot have been so strictly observed. In the second century, foreigners were enrolled and in course of time the native Athenians were outnumbered. From the third century onward, as the city-state ceased to be autonomous, military training was superseded by athletics, and courses in literature, rhetoric and philosophy were established. At what later became the leading university of the Roman Empire, wealthy young men came from all parts to study in Athens. The ephebic training—with its still recognizably archaic features of the Classical period derived from tribal age-grades—thus later developed into a university system of advanced education.

31

The system of grouping by age classes continued. Most Greek cities, small or large, had a system of ephebic training. Since men and boys were in the habit of frequenting market-place, gymnasium and 'training-school', it was natural that the ties which were formed during the ephebic period should continue to be fostered. The ages of the *epheboi* differed from place to place, but their form of organization very much influenced the educational system of the Greek world throughout the Hellenistic period. The associations of *neoi*[1]-youths older than *epheboi* and of a minimum age of nineteen or twenty—though not part of the education system, followed the pattern of the ephebic organization.

The governing and executive body of an association of *neoi* normally consisted of a gymnasiarch, a secretary and a treasurer, and they formed, under this body, a corporate group, recognized as legally capable of taking corporate action. Both in political and in municipal life the *neoi* were more important and more influential than the *epheboi*. For in civic decrees, we often find the *neoi*, though rarely the *epheboi*, associated with the highest political bodies. Such associations flourished throughout most of the Greek world, and particularly in Asia Minor, as an aftermath of the ephebic training, and their members primarily devoted themselves to gymnastic and athletic sports. In fact, we never hear of *neoi* connected with any other building than a gymnasium. In some cases the gymnasium was shared with *epheboi* and other groups, but in other cities there was a gymnasium which was used exclusively by *neoi*. Such gymnasia were generally devoted entirely to physical exercises, the gymnasia of *epheboi* and boys being educational centres, where 'music' as well as gymnastic could be pursued.

A favourite sport of the *neoi* was the *diadrome*, which was perhaps some sort of team-race. At Samos there was a *diadrome* every month. In some places we hear of *diadromai* directed by the gymnasiarchs. Besides wrestling and running, inscriptions mention *neoi* as participating in such exercises as archery and throwing the javelin. Inscriptions also make it clear that considerable quantities of oil were used by the *neoi*, which in itself is sufficient to indicate the popularity of gymnastic pursuits among these associations.

[1] Literally 'Young Men', but more nearly equivalent to our 'Old Boys'.

32

Reli fs depicting physical education at Athens in the late 6th
century B.C.

Above : runner about to start, two wrestlers and a javelin thrower.

Below : ball game, perhaps *Keretizein.*

Journal of Hellenic Studies

[*face page 32*

Similar associations of young men existed under different names, some of them rather more concerned with military affairs than were the *neoi*. But in the main, where cities had lost their independence and were now ruled by monarchs who could command standing armies, military training as a dominant feature of the training of the youth was no longer required.

Crete, however, remained an exception to this general tendency. Though the island had become more and more subject to outside influences of all kinds, the Cretan cities were never joined into any complete federal union and maintained their separatism until the Roman conquest in the first century B.C. Though their aristocratic institutions underwent, in some respects, quite considerable modifications, others of their traditional institutions were maintained. Among the latter was the 'herd', training in which remained a necessary preliminary for entry into the citizen body. The enrolment of the youth in 'herds' is well attested by inscriptions throughout the Hellenistic period, which show that the authorities managed to retain, and even to extend, their firm control over the education of the youth, with a continuing marked emphasis on military training. For warfare was endemic in Crete throughout the period, the cities being constantly involved in internecine struggles.

One of the most interesting and important pieces of evidence relating to the organization of the Cretan youth is an inscription, belonging to the late third or early second century B.C., which contains the form of oath taken by the newly-created citizens of Dreros. The young men swear loyalty to their own city of Dreros and to its ally Knossos, and enmity to the city of Lyttos. At this oath-taking ceremony it seems likely that the young men, having now reached the final stages of their initiation into manhood on graduating from the 'herd', laid aside their boyhood garments, assuming instead the warrior's costumes which each had received as a gift following the period of seclusion away from the city. The inscription concludes with an archaic passage whose meaning remains obscure, but from which it can be inferred that the youths were involved in an ordeal of initiation, from which one of them emerged as victor, an ordeal which perhaps took the form of a race.

33

REFERENCES

1. G. Thomson, *Aeschylus and Athens*. 2nd edition, p. 97. London 1946.
2. Fougères in Daremberg-Saglio, *Dictionnaire des antiquités grecques et romaines*. Paris 1891–8, s.v. 'gymnasium'. *Cf.* R. E. Wycherley, *How the Greeks Built Cities*, p. 143. London 1949.
3. Plato, *Republic*, 548. Trans. Lindsay.
4. Aristotle, *Politics*, 127 i b.
5. Aristotle, *Politics*, 1272 a.
6. Strabo, *Geography*, 10. 4. 20–21.

See also

Section 2.

Cambridge Ancient History, passim.

H. Michell, *Sparta*. Cambridge 1952.

M. P. Nilsson, 'Die Grundlagen des spartanischen Lebens', in *Klio*, 12.

Section 3.

R. F. Willetts, *Aristocratic Society in Ancient Crete*. London 1955.

Section 4.

C. M. Bowra, 'Xenophanes and the Olympic Games', in *Problems in Greek Poetry*. Oxford 1953.

F. M. Cornford in J. E. Harrison *Thémis*, pp. 212–259. Cambridge 1912.

K. J. Freeman, *Schools of Hellas*, 3rd Edition. London 1922.

E. N. Gardiner, *Athletics of the Ancient World*. Oxford 1930.

P. Girard, 'Education' and 'Ephebi' in Daremberg-Saglio *Dictionnaire des antiquités grecques et romaines*.

A. W. Gomme, *Population of Athens in the Fifth and Fourth Centuries B.C.*. Oxford 1933.

G. Thomson, *op. cit.*

Section 5.

C. A. Forbes, *Neoi*. Middletown 1933.

W. W. Tarn and G. T. Griffith, *Hellenistic Civilization*. London 1952.

R. F. Willetts, *Aristocratic Society in Ancient Crete*. London 1955.

34

III

Physical Education and
Recreation in Imperial Rome

P. C. McINTOSH

∽∽∽∽∽∽∽∽∽∽∽∽∽∽

IT is not possible within the space of a single chapter to give an adequate account of physical education and recreation throughout the Roman Empire. This empire spanned many centuries in time and, in space, stretched from Scotland to the Sahara Desert and from the Atlantic Ocean to the Caspian Sea. It embraced the tribal societies of Gaul and Britain, the city states of Greece and the ancient monarchy of Egypt. Generalizations on physical culture would be as meaningless as generalizations on the physical culture of the British Commonwealth. The differences between the physical education of the English Public Schoolboy and the African tribesman to-day had their parallels in the Roman Empire of yesterday and, in spite of unifying influences such as the Roman Army, the differences remained so acute that any general account of Roman physical education must reach formidable dimensions.

On the other hand, physical education within the capital of the empire over a short span of time, from the middle of the first century A.D. to the death of Galen in A.D. 201 provides the subject for a compact study for which there is considerable literary and archaeological evidence available. Moreover, while there are significant differences between Rome of the second century A.D. and cities of the twentieth century, the problem of catering for the physical well-being of a large population concentrated in a heavily built up area—a problem which was ever present with the Roman Emperors—is not unknown

35

in our own day and the way in which it was tackled in Imperial Rome is therefore of some interest. Attention will therefore be centred upon Rome, and although much that happened there had its counterpart elsewhere in the empire, no attempt will be made to assess the currency of Roman practices outside Rome.

That Rome was heavily populated there can be little doubt, but it is not easy to judge the exact extent of the city or the size of the population. There were a number of boundaries which served military or other purposes at one time or another. There was, for instance, the 'pomerium', the old fortified perimeter of Rome during the Republic. By the first century A.D. this had been far outgrown, and, of the fourteen regions into which Augustus had divided the city, only five were wholly within the pomerium. The Aurelian Wall built in A.D. 274 and enclosing about 3,425 acres or $5\frac{1}{2}$ square miles was designed not to enclose all habitations, but only vital parts of the city. Nor could the line of toll posts enclosing some 6,000 acres or 9 square miles be regarded as the true city boundary. The city must have extended beyond all these boundaries. Nevertheless it is certain that the city of Rome in A.D. 150 covered nowhere near the same amount of ground as, for instance, the modern city of Birmingham which, in 1950, sprawled over some 57,000 acres or 90 square miles. Yet the numbers of people who lived in these two cities at these dates were comparable. Birmingham had 1,112,340 inhabitants in 1951. The population of Rome has been a subject for widely differing estimates, but Carcopino having examined the evidence and discussed different theories concluded that it was probably between 1,200,000 and 1,727,000. He added, 'It is clear that Rome's population approached that of our own capitals in size, without enjoying any of the benefits of improved technics and communications which facilitate life and intercourse in our modern towns. . . . Rome was as enormous for her day as New York is for ours.'[1]

Inevitably such a large population within so small a compass lived in grossly overcrowded dwellings. About 50,000 lived in houses, each of which was arranged around a central courtyard. The rest lived in some 46,000 apartment blocks. There was, in fact, about one private house for every twenty-six blocks of apartments. As conditions of space and transport limited outward expansion, Rome spread upwards and various imperial

36

decrees tried in vain to limit the height of private buildings to seventy or even sixty feet.[2] Dangerously lofty construction continued. Landlords were unscrupulous in effecting minimum repairs so that the risk of buildings collapsing was ever present;[3] so was the danger of fire.

Imposing as these edifices were on the outside, inside they were ill furnished and ill lit. As there was no glass in the windows the inhabitants could either live in the light and the draught or they could close shutters and enjoy some protection from the weather in an unnatural gloom. Heating and cooking were usually effected by a brazier; the water supply, in spite of the 222,237,060 gallons that arrived daily in the city,[4] was not piped above the ground floor; similarly, sanitation upstairs was of the most primitive kind. Public conveniences, both elaborate and decorative, have survived and the network of sewers in the city excites the greatest admiration even to-day, but the complete absence of plumbing and drainage in most of the living quarters of the city led to an accumulation of filth and to personal habits, which, to judge from literary allusions, were not only unhygienic but also positively dangerous to passers-by.[5] So crowded together were the dwellings that a traffic problem arose which must surely have been the most acute of all time, for it became necessary to ban all wheeled traffic in daytime. There was no moment of quiet in the streets, for the noise of traffic at night followed fast upon the noise of daily life.

These, then, were some of the physical conditions of life in the city of Rome, conditions that helped to shape the pattern of education and recreation. Even more important than the city's physical structure in determining that pattern was the structure of society.

Both the archaeological remains and also literary evidence show that there were extremes of wealth and poverty in Rome. Above everyone stood the Emperor to whose tastes and appetites the whole empire ministered and to whose wealth not even the richest senator could approach, or indeed was allowed to approach. Below the Emperor were the two orders of senators and knights, with property qualifications of 1,000,000 sesterces and 400,000 sesterces. They enjoyed the privileges of a share in the administration of the empire and of preferential treatment before the law. The rest of the citizen population was an under-

37

privileged proletariat, many of whom would not have been able to scrape together the bare means of subsistence but for public assistance.

In the course of the second century the number of those receiving public assistance rose from 150,000 to 175,000. With their dependent families they represented a total of between 400,000 and 700,000 people fed at the public expense. Carcopino [6] has estimated that, taking account of soldiers and slaves who were provided for in other ways, there were less than 150,000 heads of Roman families who were sufficiently well off not to need the state's largesse, out of a total population of 1,200,000. On the other hand the rich were very rich, possessing extravagant town houses as well as country villas and having enormous concentrations of invested capital.

Wealth was not without its responsibilities and the distribution of largesse by wealthy individuals was expected and perhaps even enforced by public opinion. Wealthy patrons were the victims of a continuous series of demands upon their generosity. The response which Pliny the younger made to these demands is well known. A sum for the foundation of a library and an endowment to maintain it, a substantial gift for the provision of public baths, a gift of one-third of the cost of a high school and a substantial fund for the welfare of his freedmen were but a few of his benefactions. Those who held high office in the state, and above all the Emperor, were lavish in their provision of food, amusements, recreations and amenities for the population. The motives for this generosity were mixed, and perhaps some wealthy men were prompted by a humane charity without ulterior motive. Nevertheless it is difficult to escape the conclusion that the Emperors and the wealthy in general would not have gone to such lengths as they did to provide lavish festivals, spectacles, public baths and other buildings, even in times of treasury shortages, if they had not feared the political consequences of disappointing public expectation. The provision of facilities for physical recreation, especially at the Baths, made no small contribution to the problem of keeping the have-nots at a subsistence level of contentment.

No account of the structure of Roman society could of course be complete without mention of slavery. In the second century slaves numbered about 400,000 or approximately a third of the

38

total population of Rome. Their terms of service were not for the most part unduly harsh nor were they interminable. The process of manumission by which a slave was freed became so common that a legal limit had to be fixed upon the number of slaves that could be freed at any one time.[7] Once freed, the ex-slave or 'freedman' remained legally bound to his former owner or 'patron' by certain ties. His descendants of the third generation enjoyed full political rights. However, the regulations were often relaxed and full citizenship was granted prematurely to freedmen for services rendered to patrons or the state. Curiously enough, as gaps appeared in the upper classes of the Roman hierarchy they were constantly being filled from the slave classes and Tenney Frank [8] has estimated that 80 per cent of the population of Imperial Rome was descended from emancipated slaves. Many of these attained positions of great responsibility under the Emperor and amassed great wealth. Until the time of Hadrian, the most important posts in the Imperial Cabinet were held by 'freedmen' and to many it seemed better to be a rich man's slave than a poor man free-born. The contrast between rich and poor by no means corresponded to the distinction between citizen and freedman.

The whole economy of Rome came to depend on slavery and the demand for a fresh supply of slaves was a constant one. Part of the demand was met by prisoners of war. After Trajan's second Dacian campaign on the Northern frontier 50,000 prisoners were auctioned as slaves. The majority of slaves, however, probably came from the sons and daughters of those who were already in subjection.

The labour at the disposal of the Roman entrepreneur was therefore immense. Slaves provided much of the labour in the establishments of knights and senators as well as in trade and industry. Pliny the Younger, who did not account himself a rich man, cannot have had less than 500 slaves, while the emperor himself must have had about 30,000. Within the non-citizen population there was a hierarchy ranging from the Emperor's freedmen at the top, down to the 'aquarii' or water carriers who were considered one of the lowest forms of human life. Nevertheless slaves enjoyed a fair degree of personal liberty; there was nothing in their dress to distinguish them from citizens,[9] and although they were not eligible for public assistance they shared

D   39

in the recreations and amusements of the citizen population and enjoyed the same facilities at the baths.[10]

It is not surprising to find that the sharp distinction between the plutocracy and the masses was reflected in the educational system. Most children went to primary schools, 'Ludus literarius', where they were taught reading, writing and arithmetic by a master who subsisted on such fees as he could extract from the children's parents. Schools, which were usually housed under some awning in front of a shop, opened at dawn and continued until noon and teaching methods were brutal, not to say unimaginative.[11] Physical education did not figure in the curriculum of these schools at all.

Secondary and higher education was given by the grammarians and rhetoricians to the sons of the privileged few. The emperors, especially Hadrian, although they showed little interest in primary education, gave encouragement and support to these teachers. The most famous of them, Quintilian, has given us his views on education in 'Institutio Oratoria'. His conception of education was narrow in that he believed that its function was to produce the barrister-politician. As his ideal accomplishment was rhetorical composition, there was little room for physical education. It is true that Quintilian paid lip-service to the general education or care of the body, but only in so far as it affected the power of reasoning, and when he came to examine the function of physical education in detail he confined it to the training of gesture and posture in public speaking.

> I will not blame even those who give a certain amount of time to the teacher of gymnastics. I am not speaking of those who spend part of their life in rubbing themselves with oil and part in wine bibbing, and kill the mind by over-attention to the body: indeed, I would have such as these kept as far as possible from the boy whom we are training. But we give the same name to those who form gesture and motion so that the arms may be extended in the proper manner, the management of the hands free from all trace of rusticity and inelegance, the attitude becoming, the movements of the feet appropriate and the motions of the head and eyes in keeping with the poise of the body. No one will deny that such details form a part of the art of delivery, nor divorce delivery from

40

oratory; and there can be no justification for disdaining to learn what has got to be done. . . . In my opinion, however, such training should not extend beyond the years of boyhood, and even boys should not devote too much time to it. For I do not wish the gestures of oratory to be modelled on those of dance. But I do desire that such boyish exercises should continue to exert a certain influence, and that something of the grace which we acquired as learners should attend us in after life without our being conscious of the fact.[12]

Schools and teachers may not have recognized the value of physical education, but for the young man of means there were plenty of physical activities in which he could develop his skill, and there were incentives for doing so. Whether he were knight or senator, his political career would involve a period of military service for which he was expected to equip himself physically. His tasks may not have been as arduous as those of the legionaries, but horsemanship and physical stamina for campaigning had to be acquired and it was left to his initiative to acquire them. The life of the young knight or senator was by no means confined to Rome and in the country he might, like the young Hadrian,[13] indulge his passion for hunting or find an outlet for his physical energy in rural sports, while within the city itself he had at his disposal all those facilities for recreation which had been provided by private enterprise or an anxious despotism. Rome was a cosmopolitan city and high and low brushed shoulders in the streets and in the public buildings.

The problems of leisure were very pressing for people living in Rome. Some Romans were wholly unemployed, but even those who pursued a regular occupation or trade finished work at the sixth or seventh hour.[14] The length of an hour varied according to the time of year, but if it be assumed that the Roman worker stopped work at the sixth hour in summer and the seventh in winter his working day would never have been more than seven hours long. Because they started work at or before dawn, whenever it happened to be, they always had freedom to amuse themselves during the greater part of the afternoon. Martial [15] tells us that even at the fifth hour unwashed slaves were already off duty and on their way to the baths.

The only people who did not have the equivalent of seventeen

41

or eighteen out of every twenty-four hours free were the bureaucrats, administrative officials and professional men. This, however, is not the whole of the picture. Throughout the year there were a number of days fixed as holidays on which work and business were relaxed or suspended. At the time of Claudius the Roman calendar contained one hundred and fifty-nine such days. To these must be added such holidays as were decreed at the caprice of the reigning emperor and Carcopino has calculated that in the first century Rome had one day of holiday for every working day.[16] To overcome the 'ennui' which this state of affairs would have caused and to provide an outlet for the desires and passions of a populace debarred from political activity, entertainment was provided at the public expense. Out of one hundred and fifty-nine public holidays in the year, ninety-three were occupied with 'games' provided by the state.

The entertainments were closely associated with the buildings in which they were held, the circus, the theatre and the amphitheatre. The Circus Maximus, the largest of its kind, was similar to the Greek Hippodrome. In its final form it measured six hundred by two hundred metres. Unlike the Greeks, who stood or sat on the ground to watch their races, the Romans were provided with seats. Even in the time of Julius Caesar there were seats for 150,000, while the 'Regionaries' of the fourth century assess the total capacity as 385,000. Allowing for exaggeration, we can still hardly find a modern stadium to compete in seating accommodation with the Circus Maximus of Trajan's day. The horse races and chariot races which were put on with professional riders and drivers were interspersed with trick riding and acrobatics. A 'ludus' at the Circus had something of the atmosphere of Derby Day, something of the thrill of dirt-track racing, and something of the amusement of a modern circus. The 'ludus' programme grew to include as many as twenty-four races a day for as long as fifteen days, and the organization of trainers, veterinary surgeons, grooms, stable police, jockeys and the rest was quite as intricate as that of modern times.

The shows at the circus gained in popularity as theatrical performances declined. The total seating capacity of the three largest theatres in Rome amounted to some 50,000. Tragedy and comedy in these theatres sank to miming of the basest kind

42

in which actresses were permitted to undress entirely, and in which a condemned criminal might be substituted for the real actor, and put to death at the end in the appropriate manner. However, the worst excesses of butchery and human sacrifice occurred in the amphitheatres. The largest of them, the Flavian Amphitheatre, later to be known as the Colosseum, measured 584 yards around its oval circumference and was capable of accommodating 50,000 spectators for the 'shows' held within. These shows were of various kinds but nearly all were designed to excite or satisfy the most ignoble of human appetites. The most innocent of these shows was probably the 'lusio' in which trained gladiators fought with muffled swords. There were also 'venationes' in which wild beasts from all parts of the empire were pitted against each other or against professional baters and slaughterers. The beasts were also used to effect the public execution of criminals, real or supposed, who were condemned 'ad bestias' and thrown defenceless before the animals and before a holiday crowd that revelled in the scene. Perhaps the most popular spectacle was the 'hoplomachia' in which trained gladiators, recruited from slaves purchased for the purpose, from starving beggars, or from renegades of noble birth, and trained in barracks managed by the Emperor's procurators, fought to the death. Their only chance of survival was to inflict death on their opponent or occasionally, though worsted in the fight, to excite the sympathy of the crowd or the Emperor. Some games, however, were specifically designated as combats from which none might escape alive. Trajan himself was responsible for a show lasting one hundred and seventeen days in which no less than 4,941 pairs of gladiators took part.[17]

The commercialization of slaughter for public entertainment contrasts fiercely with the Greek dramatic and athletic festivals. Greek tragedy admitted of no act of violence on the stage and in the athletic contest there was nothing more brutal than the pancration, and even that was governed by humanizing regulations. The Greek athletic festivals of the sixth century B.C. came as near as the ancient world ever came to 'strife without anger and art without malice'. They were, moreover, at that time the recreations of the citizen body, not shows of professional entertainers, employed by government officials.

Three attempts were made to introduce the Greek athletic

43

and dramatic festival into Rome. Augustus had revived the ancient Roman Lusus Troiae in imitation of the Greek festival and youths of noble family gave displays of horsemanship and military prowess. The Lusus Troiae only survived for a few years. A second and more ambitious attempt to introduce the Greek festival was made by Nero. There had been Greek athletic contests in Rome before the reign of Nero, but for them athletes seem to have been brought over from Greece. Nero, however, tried to establish a cult of Greek athletics, not for Greeks but among the young men of Rome, and he built for them a gymnasium after the Greek model but his efforts to establish Greek athletics in Rome were not successful. The Emperor Domitian was more successful, and the Agon Capitolinus which he founded in A.D. 86 was celebrated every four years even as late as the fourth century. There were contests in running, boxing, discus throwing and javelin throwing as well as in the Arts. The Agon Capitolinus, however, appealed to a limited public and did not compete with the Ludi in the circus and the amphitheatre. Athletic festivals on the Greek model had few attractions for the citizens of Rome. Inevitably public participation in athletic or dramatic performances was associated with what were then vassal states. The very name Greekling (Graeculus) was a term of contempt and Juvenal in his third Satire poured scorn on the Greeks living in Rome in his day. Moreover, the Greek athletic festival which would be known to the Romans of the first and second centuries A.D. was not that of the Olympic Games in the late sixth century B.C. and the age of Pindar. By the time Rome came to dominate the Mediterranean world the Greek athletic festivals had been usurped by professional performers and in the process of commercialization they lost much of the dignity and idealism which had been such noble features in earlier years.

Public athletic contests and performances were not entirely absent from Rome in the first and second centuries, but they were the province of the professional, and it would have been impracticable and socially undesirable for the Roman citizen to compete. The professionals were organized in a union, the Synod of Rome, which received numerous favours from the emperors in return for the organization of athletic shows. Hadrian granted them premises for a permanent headquarters

44

and these contained a gymnasium and a council room. A diploma of membership was granted on payment of a subscription. The training programme of the professional athlete was intensive and time-consuming; this has been attested by Quintilian and other contemporary writers; and, if the mosaic portraits of trainers and athletes found in the Baths of Caracalla are to be relied on, the athletes career attracted men muscular in body, coarse of feature and of mediocre intelligence.

Were a survey of recreation in Rome to be confined to the circus, the theatre, and the amphitheatre, Gibbon's dictum that 'the most eminent of the Greeks were actors, the Romans were merely spectators', would ring true; but there was another side to Roman life. Strabo writing in the principate of Augustus describes athletics on the Campus Martius as one of the sights of Rome, while the many Thermae or Baths throughout the city made ample provision for a wide range of physical activities. The Baths were much more than instruments of hygiene; the larger public Baths contained shops, refreshment booths, gymnasia, courts for ball games, running tracks, gardens, libraries and conference rooms. It is now once more possible to trace the plan and construction of the Baths that Trajan built in Rome. The total area excluding projections was a rectangle measuring 280 metres by 210 metres, and it embraced three main features. The central complex of buildings included the cold room and swimming bath, the central hall, the warm room and the hot room, in that order from north-east to south-west, so that the hot room benefited from the full strength of the midday and afternoon sun. On either side of these main rooms were dressing-rooms and small bathrooms and two large open palaistrae surrounded by colonnades. Around three sides of this central complex there was open ground laid out with gardens and perhaps a running track.[18] Outside this open ground, forming the outside wall of the building, ran the peribolus containing libraries, reading rooms, gymnasia, ball courts and administrative offices. The Baths of Trajan thus provided extensive facilities, not only for cleansing and feeding the body but also for exercising it. They were among the largest in Rome but others, large and small, seem to have provided

45

similar facilities. The Stoic philosopher Seneca once had rooms above one of these establishments and in a letter to Lucilius he described the sounds that he heard.[19]

> I have lodgings right over a bathing establishment. So picture to yourself the assortment of sounds that are strong enough to make me hate my very powers of hearing. When your strenuous gentleman is exercising himself by flourishing leaden weights, when he is working hard, or pretending to work hard, I can hear him grunt; and whenever he releases his imprisoned breath I can hear him panting in wheezy and high-pitched tones. Or perhaps I notice some lazy fellow content with a cheap rub down and hear the crack of the pummelling hand on his shoulder, varying in sound according as the hand is laid on flat or hollow. Then perhaps a professional (pilicrepus) comes along shouting out the score in the ball game; that is the finishing touch. Add to this the arresting of an occasional roysterer or pick-pocket, the racket of the man who always likes to hear his own voice in the bathroom, or the enthusiast who plunged into the swimming tank with unconscionable noise and splashing. Besides all those whose voices are good imagine the hair plucker with his penetrating shrill voice—for purposes of advertisement— continually giving it vent and never holding his tongue except when he is plucking the armpits and making his victim yell instead. Then the cake seller with his varied cries, the sausage- man, the confectioner and all the vendors of food hawking their wares, each with his own distinctive intonation.

It was in the Baths that the Romans took their physical education and recreation. There they ran and jumped, performed exercises with weights, wrestled and played their ball games. They followed their exercise with a massage or a bath. The exact form of their games is difficult to determine, but their ball games in particular were varied and intricate.[20] The various activities seem to have had attendant instructors. It is not clear whether the 'pilicrepus' referred to by Seneca was a scorer, a ball boy or a coach, but in another letter Seneca referred to players taking orders from slaves who seem to have been employed as instructors.[21] Some habitués of the baths carried the culture of their bodies to excess, developing their

46

strength and physique for its own sake to the exclusion of other interests. Seneca said that 'their day passes satisfactorily if they have got up a good sweat and made good their loss of moisture with huge draughts of liquor'.[22]

Nevertheless, all Romans seem to have been concerned to some extent with the problem of keeping fit. Even Seneca who despised the cult of the body on the ground that however strong your sinews were you could never be a match for a first class bull,[23] found it necessary to recommend for general well being some 'short and simple exercises which tire the body rapidly and so save time'. Running, exercises with weights, high jumping, long jumping, and jumps known as 'The Priest's Dance' were the activities which he recommended.

The number of Baths in the city of Rome grew from one hundred and seventy in 33 B.C., when a census of baths was taken, to eight hundred and fifty-six in the fourth century when the 'Regionaries' were compiled. Some were privately owned or attached to private residences, others were built by contractors as commercial speculations and entrance fees were charged. Others, again, like Trajan's Baths and the Baths of Caracalla were provided by the Emperor and probably entrance was free, at least at certain times. Even where entrance fees were demanded the charge was only a quadrans, about a farthing, and children were admitted free. The facilities for personal hygiene and recreation at the Baths were available to men and women from the highest to the lowest. In many of the public Baths there was no separation of the sexes until the reign of Hadrian. Then it was decreed that the outer buildings and gardens should be open to all, but that the inner rooms, including the bathing facilities should be available for women only at one time of day and for men only at another time. For the vast majority of Romans a visit to the Baths became a matter of almost daily routine. Nero may have failed to graft his interpretation of the Greek festival on to Roman life, but within the walls of the Baths much of the life of the Greek palaistra and gymnasium was still carried on.

The public Baths were not skimped in any way, and their elaborate construction and decoration helped to compensate the poorer citizens for the tumbledown apartments in which they lived. Water, which was not supplied to private buildings

47

above the ground floor, was abundant in the Baths and was even filtered before it was supplied for use. The decoration of the Baths was as elaborate as their construction was efficient. Seneca tells us that:

> A man feels poor and shabby unless the walls are alight with large and precious circular mirrors, unless there are slabs of Alexandrine marble picked out with overlay of humidian, unless the marbles themselves are treated everywhere with elaborate surface colour designs as variegated as fresco, unless the ceiling is masked with glass; unless the basins into which we plunge our sapless over-sweated bodies have kerbs of the Thasian marble that once was only a rarity in some temple; unless the nozzles from which the water spouts are silver. And yet I am still speaking of mere plumbing for the million. When I come to the freedmen's baths, what then?[24]

Many Romans spent one part of their day in conditions of great squalor, but another part was enjoyed in precincts of palatial splendour. Had Seneca's letters been lost to posterity, the remains of the Baths constructed by Nero, Trajan, Caracalla and Diocletian would still have borne witness to the imperial policy of state aid for health and recreation. The facilities provided by the government at Rome to keep the populace clean and contented have hardly yet been surpassed in the modern world.

The facilities for physical recreation in Rome were lavish and they were in constant use, but the extensive and unprecedented urban development of Rome did not merely produce facilities. Rome was also the setting for a significant and original contribution to the theory and practice of physical training. The Romans devised and classified exercises and activities to produce specific and foreseeable effects upon the body in ways that had not been explored before. Greek athletics may have produced the physiques that Pheidias and other sculptors reproduced in stone but they had not been worked out for that purpose. The Romans, however, saw the specific needs of their own environment and worked out exercises to meet them. Quintilian's suggestion for the use of gymnastics to train gesture in public speaking was an instance of this genius; other spheres in

48

Girls exercising at the baths (thermae). A mosaic from the Roman villa at Piazza Armerina in Sicily, probably dating from the third century A.D.

Photo Balbo, Piazza Armerina

"Il Civettino, a game or posing practised by young men of noble birth in the squares of Florence in the fifteenth century. Their movements partook of the graceful steps of the minuet and the elegant postures of the gymnasium." E. Staley, *The Guilds of Florence*.

which the Romans did the same thing most successfully were military training, athletic training and medical gymnastics.

There were in Rome during the reign of Trajan about 12,000 troops and they underwent a specialized form of physical training which was probably uniform throughout the imperial armies. An account of recruit training has been handed down in the work of Vegetius, *De Re Militari*, written about A.D. 390. The date of publication is considerably later than the epoch of this study, and during the third and fourth centuries profound changes took place in the organization, composition and tactics of the Roman army. Vegetius's work would be almost valueless for a study of Trajan's army, were it not that he was describing things as they had been and as he thought they ought to be, but not as they were in his day. Sir Charles Oman has pointed out[25] that Vegetius was not describing the army of A.D. 390 with its small legions and large numbers of light armed troops but he persisted in describing the army of the early empire, when the heavy armed legionaries still formed the most important element. Vegetius's account of recruit training agrees with this hypothesis and it may be assumed that Trajan's soldiers underwent very much the kind of training that Vegetius described.[26]

The training of the Roman soldier was realistic and purposeful and Josephus, who fought against them, stated that the effusion of blood was the only circumstance that distinguished a field of battle from a field of exercise.[27] First the recruits were trained to maintain the military pace by persistent practice; summer marching was at the rate of twenty miles in five hours and quick marching was at the rate of twenty-three miles in five hours. As the Roman mile was only ninety-five yards shorter than the English mile, the pace required of the Roman soldier in summer marching was a little less than 4 m.p.h., and at this speed he had to do at least three ten-mile marches every month.

The correct pace was of fundamental importance both in cross-country marching and in maintaining the legions formation in battle, but the recruit was also trained in running, in jumping and in swimming. Vegetius maintained that every soldier whether in the infantry or the cavalry should learn to swim.

49

Weapon training was carried out under instructors called 'campidoctores'. A third or a quarter of the younger soldiers learned the use of bow and arrow, but all were trained in the use of stones and leaden balls as well as in handling the sword and shield and the spear. The underlying principle of weapon training was 'weight training'. The recruit had to learn his art with sword and shield twice the weight of those that he would use on active service: his spear too was heavier than his fighting weapon. Each recruit had a stake set in the ground and twice every day, in the morning and afternoon, he practised attacking it from every angle with his heavy equipment. Thus he built up a reserve of strength and stamina which stood him in good stead in the thick of battle. The same principle was applied to marching. So that the troops might be able to carry arms and provisions they were trained to march under weights of sixty Roman pounds or fifty-five pounds avoirdupois. Whether this figure included the weight of the armour and arms is not known. Vegetius said that it was not difficult when you became used to it.

Both recruits and experienced soldiers were required to practice mounting on horseback and dismounting until they could do it without having to think. In order to make continuous practice possible a wooden horse was constructed. In the winter it was kept under cover and in the summer it was set up on the campus. On this ancestor of the modern vaulting horse the Roman recruit first practised mounting unarmed, then armed, then from the left or the right side; after that he had to leap on and off again and finally he was required to mount and dismount armed with an unsheathed sword or a pike.

In addition to this recuit training there were the inevitable field reviews and manoeuvres: in peace time too the legions were occupied upon public works according to the ideas of their commanders. They constructed roads, bridges and harbours, they built amphitheatres, they dug canals, they even fought a plague of locusts.

Similarly, in professional sport and in medicine, gymnastics and artificial exercises were devised and developed to achieve specific effects on the human body. In athletic training, exercises were devised to produce particular physiques, and the conditions which produced this professional approach to training have been hinted at in discussing the failure of the Greek

50

athletic festival to find favour in Rome. In the Greek city state of the sixth century B.C. athletics, gymnastics or physical training were approved and encouraged and in some states, notably Sparta, their military value was undoubted. Nevertheless in many Greek gymnasia physical activities were largely spontaneous in their particular manifestations. Greeks ran and wrestled, swam and threw the discus because those activities appealed to them. There was a tendency for citizens to participate in different activities and there was little specialization. Nor was there a highly developed technique of training consciously balancing this exercise against that exercise and developing now this part and now that part of the body.

Early in the fifth century, however, the 'pot hunter' began to appear and Theagenes of Thasos was said to have won some 1,400 prizes at different athletic festivals. Athletics then began to become a full-time occupation for the gifted performer, and then, under the stress of competition, special training methods were devised to improve natural ability. About the year 456 B.C., boxers and wrestlers began to experiment with a meat diet to produce the body weight necessary for their sports, and special exercises were invented to produce this or that type of athlete.

Corresponding to this trend in practice was a parallel change in the use of words. In Homer there was no mention of gymnastics or of the gymnast or physical trainer. (The Greek word is literally 'gymnast' but it means gymnastic teacher not gymnastic performer.) In Plato there was some mention of gymnastic but there was still no mention of a gymnast or trainer. The art or science of gymnastics was in Plato's time part of the stock in trade of the 'paidotribes' (see Chapter II, page 24). The word gymnast was first used, not by Plato, but a little before his time, when the preparation and training of athletes for competition became an established practice. From then on the word gymnast was used to denote the specialist trainer or coach. So the word gymnastics, which for Plato had a very wide application and embraced a vast number of physical activities, came to have a more specific and less general connotation. It was limited to mean little more than 'applied exercise'. This new conception of gymnastics, especially gymnastics in the service of sport, was highly developed at Rome during the second century A.D.

The third sphere in which 'applied exercise' was extensively used was in medical gymnastics or therapeutic gymnastics. Our knowledge of developments along these lines is derived from Claudius Galen, a doctor and a prolific writer, many of whose works have luckily survived.

Galen was born at Pergamos in A.D. 130 to parents of the professional class. His father was an architect. At an early age he turned to the study of medicine and worked at it in Smyrna, in Corinth, in Alexandria, and elsewhere in the Middle East. He returned to Pergamos in A.D. 158 and became medical officer to a school of gladiators in order to gain practice in surgery and an opportunity to study anatomy. Cadavers were not available for dissection and all Galen's anatomical knowledge was gleaned from live human beings or dead animals. Later he went to Rome where he gained a considerable reputation and in A.D. 170 was engaged by the Emperor Marcus Aurelius as physician to his son Commodus. He became Physician to the Imperial Household and died in A.D. 201 at the age of seventy.

Galen was an avid student of all things medical, and of many things outside medicine, such as grammar and philosophy. About one hundred of his works survive, many of them written on medical subjects. Galen's books are particularly valuable because so few books upon medicine and gymnastics before his day have survived.

After the Hippocratic writings of the fifth and fourth centuries B.C. no medical work earlier than Galen's treatises has survived. His writings provide evidence that in the intervening period the Alexandrian medical school flourished and that Theon, an Alexandrian, produced a comprehensive work in four books on gymnastics. Galen distilled some of the works of his predecessors and contemporaries, and three of his works are directly concerned with two topics already mentioned, sports gymnastics and medical gymnastics.

The longest of these works consists of six sections or books and is called 'Hygiene'. It is usually referred to by the title of its Latin translation, 'De Sanitate Tuenda'. Here Galen maintians that skill in caring for the human body has two main divisions: one is concerned with modifying the condition of the body—therapeutics; the other is concerned with maintaining the body

52

in health—hygiene. From this beginning Galen ranges over a very wide field from breast feeding to senility and from constipation to sex relations. He discusses the work to be done by the physician, the health educator, the gymnast and the masseur. As in his shorter works he often anticipates modern theory and practice in physical education. He suggests, in a rudimentary form, the type of physical education that is suitable for children in different age groups, from birth to seven, from seven to fourteen and from fourteen to twenty-one.[28] He advocates exercise rather than drugs as a cure for constipation.[29] He issues a warning on the danger of strains and ruptures if vigorous exercise is taken without preliminary warming up.[30] He is a firm believer in massage both before and after vigorous exercise.[31]

Perhaps the chief interest of the work is a technical one and is to be found in the classification of exercises and activities according to their effect on the body. Galen classifies exercise into three groups. The first group contains exercises which give the muscles tone without involving them in violent movement. He calls them vigorous exercises. In modern terminology they would more accurately be called strengthening exercises and Galen so nearly anticipates the modern theory of producing strength by overload that his description of this group of exercises is worth quoting:

> Now we must discuss the individual and particular qualities of the exercises, first, however, having made it clear that there are many differences between them. For some exercises work different parts of the body at different times, one part more than another and some are slow movements while others are very fast; some are done in a state of tension, others in a state of relaxation, and, yet again, in addition to these, some are done vigorously and others gently. By a tense exercise I mean continuous and forceful work without speed, but by a violent exercise I mean working forcefully with speed. It will not matter whether we say forcefully or robustly. Digging, then, is both tense and robust. Similarly, holding four horses on the reins at the same time is a fairly tense exercise, but it is not at all speedy. In the same way lifting some heavy weight and either staying still or moving forward

53

a little is an exercise of the same kind; so is walking up hill. Certainly, the organs of the body that move first, raise and carry up all the other parts as though they were weights. The same applies to climbing a rope—an activity which they give boys in the palaestra, introducing them to tension exercises. Similarly anyone who takes hold of a rope or a high beam and hangs from it for as long as he can, is performing a robust and strong exercise, but not at all a speedy one. So is anyone who lifts his hands forward and upward with clenched fists and keeps them still for as long as he can. And if, then, he stands beside someone and asks him to pull his hands down while he resists, he produces still more strength in his muscles and nerves. For such are the specific effects which these exercises have. The effects are much greater if a person grasps a weight in each hand like, for instance, the halteres in the 'palaestra', and keeps them motionless stretched out in front of him or above him. If, in addition you were to tell someone to pull them down or bend them forcibly while he remained motionless and rigid, resisting not only with his hands but with his legs and back, he would be doing an exercise involving no small degree of tension in the organs of his body.[32]

The second group consists of exercises which, Galen thought, train quickness or speed. Running, sparring, using the punch ball, ball play, rolling on the ground either alone or with others and many arm and leg movements fall into this category. The formulation of this group of exercises is based on a conception of an individual's speed of movement or on the shortness of his reaction time which can be trained and improved in one activity and the improvement can then, in Galen's view, be transferred to another activity.

The third group of exercises which Galen calls violent exercises consists of all the exercises in the other two groups when they are done in a different way. Exercises in group one fall into group three if they are done rapidly and without interruption: those in group two fall into group three if they are performed with weights or in heavy armour. The general purpose of group three would appear to be the training of stamina and endurance.

There is a second and subordinate classification of exercises

54

according to the parts of the body which are worked. There are leg exercises, arm exercises and trunk exercises, and there are running and marching exercises. Many of them have reappeared in the nineteenth and twentieth centuries such as leg swinging forward and backward and skip jumping; also marching on the toes and running in ever decreasing circles until the runners double back on their own tracks.

Galen's two shorter works, 'Whether Health is the Concern of Medicine or of Gymnastics' and 'Exercises with the Small Ball', like the longer work, show the extent to which the technique of prescribing particular exercises had been developed. They also show the social conditions which had made this technique valuable. The former treatise begins with an attempt to define the terms 'medicine', 'health' and 'gymnastics'. Out of the ensuing confusion a central theme does emerge: it is that there is one art which is concerned with the health of the body and it cannot properly be called either medicine or gymnastics but needs a new name. Both gymnastics and medicine are part of the 'art of health' and gymnastics needs to be closely linked with medical knowledge and practice.

Two subsidiary themes of great interest also emerge. Galen draws a hard and fast distinction between normal fitness or well being and athletic fitness, and then emphasises several times that athletic fitness is dangerous and socially useless. It is dangerous to health and the athlete's training actually prevents him from performing socially useful tasks such as rowing, digging, ploughing or road making, whether in war or in peace. His conclusion is that since the state of athletic fitness is evil so must be the training which produces it. Gymnastics devoted to this end is a perversion of true gymnastics. It is a disreputable occupation. The broad implication of this conclusion is that gymnastics, or exercise for a specific object, can be applied both for good and ill. Gymnastics itself is good or bad according to the end which it attempts to achieve.

The second theme which emerges is that gymnastics is essential for the maintenance of normal health and well being. Galen says that the body can be affected and changed by four factors, surgery, medicine, diet and gymnastics. One of these is useless to the sick and two are useless to the healthy. The sick man needs medicine, surgery and diet but not gymnastics; the

E   55

perfectly healthy man needs gymnastics but not medicine or surgery. Physical exercise is necessary to maintain health from a functional or physiological point of view.

The second of Galen's minor works relevant to physical education is a brief monogram entitled 'Exercise with the Small Ball.' It is not a list or description of activities or games; it is merely a special plea for the use of 'small ball activities' of various kinds in physical education and the plea is based on several interesting arguments which again anticipate modern theories.

The first argument is this: 'The best gymnastics is that which not only exercises the body but which also delights the spirit. This is especially true of small ball gymnastics.' This statement has had its echo in modern manuals of physical education. The Syllabus of Physical Training for Schools published by the Board of Education in 1933 states, 'Enjoyment is one of the most necessary factors in nearly everything which concerns the welfare of the body, and if exercise is distasteful and wearisome its physical as well as its mental value is diminished.'

Galen was one of the first to say, or even to think it necessary to say, that gymnastics must be enjoyable. Neither Aristotle nor Plato who wrote so fervently in favour of physical education felt it necessary to stress the need to make physical exercise attractive. In the Greek city state of the sixth century B.C. gymnastics consisted either of activities which were indulged in because of their intrinsic and immediate appeal to the bulk of the citizen population, such as running, wrestling, throwing the discus; or it consisted in activities not immediately attractive, but obviously and clearly relevant to survival; such were the disciplinary and toughening activities of military training. Under the Roman Empire a very different state of affairs had come into being. Running, wrestling and other branches of athletics had been usurped by the professional performer, while the ordinary citizen tended to become a spectator; and the citizen army had given place to a professional soldiery so that again the ordinary man had no need to indulge in the rigours of military training. Galen moreover, on his own admission was writing not so much for the masses as 'for Greeks and for those who, though born barbarians by nature, yet emulate the culture of the Greeks.'[53] He was writing for the cultured and leisured

56

classes. Complete physical idleness, however, could not be tolerated, for health's sake, as Galen himself said and even Seneca admitted. Therefore, many people still continued to take exercise, not because they wanted to, but in order to 'keep fit'. It was because a concentrated effort had to be made to 'keep fit' that it was necessary to say that enjoyable exercise was better than tedious exercise. Galen was in fact trying to find forms of exercise which men would do for their own sake, just as in the twentieth century the trend has been away from formal 'P.T.' which very few people do for its own sake, and towards activities and skills which make their own appeal and need no special advocacy.

Small ball gymnastics are recommended by Galen too, because they are economical of equipment. Hunting, for instance, is beyond the reach of the man who has little money and little leisure; all that is needed in this special form of gymnastics is a ball and a small ␣␣␣␣␣␣ all ball gymnastics also has ␣␣␣␣␣␣ inastics because it trains not ␣␣␣␣␣␣ ie mental faculties and helps ␣␣␣␣␣␣ ard of Education's Syllabus ␣␣␣␣␣␣ ias, or should have, a two- ␣␣␣␣␣␣ :al effect and on the other a

referred to other forms of of the body equally instead ile other parts remain idle. development of the body of Swedish gymnastics, in gives a simple instance of be exercised according to tanding position with the y are exercised. By com- ver parts of the body are is exercised. In this way cessive leanness can both ent is that harmonious health but must also be

rcise with the small ball tem of exercises suitable

for different physiques and different aged people. Galen says, 'It is inferior to none in its use of violent exercise, but it can also be used for gentle exercise where this is needed for old people or the very young or for invalids. When combined with massage and hot baths it is most potent in the restoration of strength and health'. Galen summed up this treatise thus, 'The best gymnastics is that which produces health of body, harmony of its parts, and mental excellence. These come through the use of the small ball.'

It is not possible to say how far Galen's principles and theories were put into practice, how far his work reflected current usage, or how far he was advocating a new and original system. Probably his work represented a critical and progressive attitude towards the systems of physical training which he saw around him in the Roman world. His books were in some ways the greatest of the contributions of the ancient world to the science of medicine and of physical education. Yet Galen was also the first of the modern writers on physical education. When he died in A.D. 201 there was a gap of some twelve hundred years when little progress was made; but when the renaissance of learning and science took place, Galen's work provided the model and the basis for the further development of therapeutic gymnastics and systematic exercise.

REFERENCES

1. J. Carcopino, *Daily Life in Ancient Rome*, p. 14. London 1941.
2. Strabo V., 3. 7.
3. Juvenal 3. 190 *ff.*
4. Frontinus, *De Aquaeductibus*, pp. 65–73. The gallonage is taken from Carcopino. *Op. cit.*
5. Juvenal 3 269 *ff.*
6. J. Carcopino, *Daily Life in Ancient Rome*, p. 65. London 1946.
7. A. M. Duff, *Freedmen in the Early Roman Empire*, p. 31. Oxford 1928.
8. *American Historical Review XXI* (1916).
9. Appian B.C. 11. 120.
10. Martial VIII. 67.
11. Quintilian 1. 3. 16–17.
12. Quintilian, *Institutio Oratoria*, Bk. I, xi. Trans. H. E. Butler.
13. B. W. Henderson, *The Life and Principate of the Emperor Hadrian.* Methuen 1923.

58

14. Martial IV. 8 3–4.
15. Martial VII. 67.
16. J. Carcopino, *op. cit.*, pp. 205–206.
17. *Année Epigraphique*, 1933, No. 30. 1–2, 13–14.
18. The baths of Caracalla which were modelled on the Baths of Trajan and opened in A.D. 216 bear the unmistakable remains of a stadium along the south-west side of the peribolus. v. *A Topographical Dictionary of Ancient Rome* by S. B. Platner and T. Ashby. Oxford 1929.
19. Seneca, *Epistles* LVI. Trans. R. Gummère.
20. For a comprehensive account of Roman Ball games see Daremberg & Saglio, *Dictionnaire des Antiquités*, Vol. IV, p. 475 *ff.*
21. Seneca, *Epistles* XV.
22. Seneca, *Epictles* XV.
23. Seneca, *Epistles* XV.
24. Seneca, *Epistles* 86. Trans. E. P. Barker. Oxford 1932.
25. Sir Charles Oman, *A History of the Art of War in the Middle Ages*, p. 17. London 1924.
26. For an account in English of Vegetius's recruit training see Gibbon's *Decline and Fall of the Roman Empire*, Vol. I, Chap. I. There is also an English verse paraphrase written in the fifteenth century and published by the Old English Text Society No. O.S. 201 under the title *Knighthode and Bataile*.
27. Josephus *De Bello Judaico*, III. Chap. 5.
28. C. Galen, *De Sanitate Tuenda*, Bk. I, Chaps. 7, 8, 12. *Corpus Medicorum Graecorum*, Vol. V. Ed. K. Koch, Leipsig 1923.
29. C. Galen, *op. cit.* Bk. I.,Chap. 14.
30. C. Galen, *op. cit.* Bk. II., Chap. 2.
31. C. Galen, *op. cit.* Bk. II., Chaps. 2–7.
32. C. Galen, *De Sanitate Tuenda*, II, Chap. 9. Trans. P. C. McIntosh. *Corpus Medicorum Graecorum*, V. Ed. K. Koch. Leipsig 1923.
33. Galen, *De Sanitate Tuenda*, I. 10.

See also

Allbutt, C. *Greek Medicine in Ancient Rome*, Chap. XV. London 1921.
Barrow, R. H. *Slavery in the Roman Empire*. London 1928.
Dill, S. *Roman Society from Nero to Marcus Aurelius*. London 1925.
Dobson, J. F. *Ancient Education and its Meaning to Us*. London 1932.
Gardiner, E. N. *Athletics of the Ancient World*. Oxford 1931.
Green, R. M. *A Translation of Galen's Hygiene*. Springfield U.S.A., 1951.
Gwynn, A. *Roman Education from Cicero to Quintilian*. Oxford 1926.
Moore, R. W. *The Roman Commonwealth*. London 1942.
Smail, W. M. *Quintilian on Education*. Oxford 1938.
Wilkins, A. S. *Roman Education*. Cambridge 1905.

59

IV

Physical Education in Renaissance Italy and Tudor England

P. C. McINTOSH

IN 1396 Chrysoloras was appointed Professor of Greek at the University of Florence. At the end of the fourteenth century Greek was almost an unknown language in Italy. Vergerius, writing at that time, was complaining that 'it is hard that no slight portion of the history of Rome is only to be known through the labours of one writing in the Greek language; it is still worse that this same noble tongue once wellnigh the daily speech of our race, as familiar as the Latin language itself, is on the point of perishing even amongst its own sons, and to us Italians is already utterly lost unless we accept one or two who in our time are tardily trying to rescue something—if it be only a mere echo of it—from oblivion.'[1] The appointment of Chrysoloras as Professor of Greek at Florence is significant of a new interest in the language, literature and life of classical Greece, which in turn led to a new appreciation of the practice and theory of physical education in the Greek City State.

The preceding centuries had not been barren of knowledge of Greek life and thought. If the Greek language was not widely known, yet the works of many Greek authors had been available in Latin translations. The revival of Roman Law in the twelfth century was succeeded by an Aristotelian renaissance in the thirteenth. The views of Aristotle cannot have been unknown in the monasteries, schools and universities of the 12th, 13th or 14th century. Plato's philosophy was also

60

known at second hand.[2] Some of the ancient theories upon the cult of the body were doubtless rejected and others were adapted to the monastic and ascetic life. What was new in the fifteenth century was not the actual study of the classics but rather the attitude and approach of the 'humanists' to them.

Nor were the Middle Ages devoid of physical culture. The tournament, which by the fifteenth century had become stylized and decorative, in earlier centuries was a war-game between teams. Denholm Young [2] has shown that in the thirteenth century, the tournament, in spite of opposition from the Church, had a real function to perform—training for war. The ideals of knighthood certainly embraced an ideal of physical prowess manifested particularly in skill at arms, and just as in later centuries the exercise of physical prowess was governed by an ideal of behaviour, 'gratia' in fifteenth-century Italy and 'sportsmanship' in nineteenth-century England, so in the fourteenth century physical prowess was associated with 'loyautie' and its attendant qualities of 'largesse', 'franchise' and 'cortaysie'.[3] Indeed, the doctrine of 'courtesy' which was developed at the courts of Italian princes in the fifteenth and sixteenth centuries owed much to the age of chivalry.

In fifteenth-century Italy the age of Chivalry was passing away. The new interest in antiquity, characterized by the appointment of a Professor of Greek at Florence, was itself dependent on changing social and economic conditions. Throughout Europe the renaissance was preceded by an urban development; the burghers of the towns had steadily increased in wealth and in political power. In 1265 in England, Simon de Montfort had summoned two citizens from every borough to sit beside two knights from every county together with the barons and the ecclesiastics in parliament at Westminster; but whereas in France and Spain and England the towns were incorporated in a unified monarchy, in Italy a different situation had arisen. In that country there was a multitude of political units, republics and despotisms, whose existence depended solely upon their power to maintain it. As in Greece in the fifth century B.C. so in Italy of the fourteenth and fifteenth century A.D. the states had different constitutions and different political forms; Florence and Venice were republics, Milan, Mantua and Ferrara were despotisms. Nevertheless, the vitality

61

of all states depended on the growth of an economy based on money, the possibility of amassing great wealth and the existence of a class of 'property and intellect'.

In this situation the worth of an individual as distinct from the rank to which he had been born, tended to count for more than it previously had done. Aeneas Sylvius wrote in the fifteenth century that 'In our change-loving Italy, where nothing stands firm, and where no ancient dynasty exists, a servant can easily become a king'. The old order of Estates was superseded but the passing of the old nobility did not leave a vacuum. A new privileged class emerged, deriving its power from wealth and business ability.

As the new nobility emerged, the idea that gentility depended solely upon birth was forced to give ground, and during the fifteenth century and later, treatises were written which tried to reconcile the idea of a gentleman and of gentle birth with the claims of the new aristocracy.[4]

Characteristic of the new social organization was a new conception of physical education and physical virtuosity, but it was a conception of physical virtuosity for the privileged ruling class. Just as in Athens physical education was exclusive of slaves, of women and even of some of the male citizen body, so in the Italian city state it was in the education of the nobility that a new conception of physical education took shape.

At first the new nobility sought prestige by associating itself with the practices of the old nobility. Tournaments, now formalized, continued to be popular. 'It was in vain that from the time of Petrarch downwards the tournament was denounced as dangerous folly. No one was converted by the pathetic appeal of the poet: 'In what book do we read that Scipio or Caesar were skilled at the joust?' The practice became more and more popular in Florence. Every honest citizen came to consider his tournament—now no doubt less dangerous than formerly—as a fashionable sport. . . . It may be mentioned that a passionate interest in this sport was displayed by the Medici, as if they wished to show, private citizens as they were, without noble blood in their veins, that the society which surrounded them was in no respect inferior to a Court.'[5] Other opportunities for physical virtuosity were provided by the game of Calcio. This was a highly organized form of football which was popular

62

in the Italian states of the fifteenth century, and it appears to have been socially exclusive. An account of the game as played at Florence included the following regulation—'Moreover, even as every kind of man was not admitted to the Olympic Games, but only men of standing in their native cities and kingdoms, so, in the Calcio, all kinds of rascallions are not to be tolerated, neither artificers, servants nor low-born fellows, but honourable soldiers, gentlemen, lords and princes.'[6] This is a foretaste of the distinction between 'gentlemen' and 'players', and of the nineteenth-century British definition of an amateur in rowing and athletics as one who is not, among other things, 'by trade or employment a mechanic, artisan or labourer'. In Florence and other Italian states virtuosity at football was confined to the new nobility of soldiers, gentlemen, lords and princes.

It was not only in Florentine football that a social distinction was to be found; it was also exhibited in the general pattern of physical recreation. Educational writers of the time in general agreed that some physical activities were worthy of pursuit by the aristocracy and that others were not. They by no means always agreed which particular activities should be eschewed. One would have excluded the 'tourney' from physical education on the grounds that it was merely ostentatious. Another maintained that 'tumbling' and gymnastic tricks were unworthy of pursuit and should be left to the professional entertainer; yet 'Civettino', a handy pandy game, was played in the streets of Florence by young men of birth and manners. A third writer thought that dancing should not be indulged in. Nevertheless the principle of distinguishing between acceptable and unacceptable physical accomplishments was generally upheld.

It was among the aristocracy and at the Courts of the Italian Princes rather than at the universities that the new humanistic conception of education in general and physical education in particular grew up. Many of the educational tracts of the time were written in the form of letters to princes. Aeneas Sylvius, for instance, wrote *De Liberorum Educatione* for Ladislas, King of Bohemia and Hungary. Such works contained constant reference to what was necessary for the training of a prince or a courtier. In 1528 Castiglione published *Il Cortegiano*, which was translated into many languages and became a textbook for

63

the education of the aristocracy in Europe. Vittorino da Feltre, one of the most prominent of humanist educators taught for some years at Padua University and suffered under a sense of frustration there. It was not until he accepted in 1423 an invitation from the Marquis Gonzaga to go to his court at Mantua, that he was able to develop his own scheme of education, a scheme in which physical education figured prominently. It is, indeed, to the Courts that we have to look for the development of physical education. At Mantua and in the Courts of other Italian States, wealthy rulers like the Gonzaga and apostles of the New Learning like Vittorino, developed the education of 'L'uomo universale'—the whole man, the all sided man. It was there that 'humanism' developed. In this humanist conception of education, physical education held an important place.

At first the ideal of physical development was little more than the projection into a new social order of the old conception of a knight at arms. At a time when inter-state feuds were frequent and violent and when power passed into the hands of those who could seize it by whatever means they had at their disposal, the need for personal ability in the arts of war was obvious. P. P. Vergerius, called by Woodward,[7] 'the true founder of the new education', writing about the year 1404, apparently recognized little other purpose for physical education than to serve military needs 'so that if we be involved in arms we may be found ready to defend our rights or to strike a blow for honour or power. Especially must the education of a Prince accord a high place to instruction in the art of war, not less than to training in the arts of peace.'[8] Vergerius took Sparta as his model. He recognized that the means of waging war had changed and that training had to be adapted to the warfare of his own day in which cavalry played an important part. Nevertheless, war still involved physical endurance as well as skill in tactics and manoeuvre, and therefore boys should be gradually inured to privations and grave exertion so that they might be able to bear strain and hardship when they became men. It was for military efficiency that Vergerius would have boys learn the Greek pentathlon, swimming, horsemanship, use of the shield, spear, sword and club.

Aeneas Sylvius [9] too, maintained that children should be taught to use the bow, the sling and the spear and also to drive,

64

to ride, to leap and to swim, because it would be their destiny to defend Christendom against the Turk.

Military necessity has been pleaded in support of physical education in many countries and in many eras, and especially in times of turbulence and war. One renaissance scholar, J. L. Vives, strongly resisted this argument. J. L. Vives was born in Spain in 1492 and was educated in France. At one time he was University Reader in Humanity at Oxford. He was deeply moved by the violence of his time and his pamphlet *De Concordia et Discordia in Humano Genere* was a plea for universal peace among Christians. His fervent desire for peace influenced his whole educational theory. Realizing that many games and sports could be used for military training, he denied this function to physical education. Games, he said, must not be used to make boys wild and ferocious but their aim should be to promote the growth of the body. In arguing that the function of physical education should not be to equip Christians to fight each other, Vives does not seem to have commanded much support.

In Italy in the fifteenth and sixteenth centuries the importance attached to the military training of the aristocracy varied both from state to state and from time to time. At Urbino military distinction was a necessity and therefore held in high esteem; at Venice on the other hand, it was naval service which was held in high esteem, yet even naval service was subordinate in esteem to civic and diplomatic ability, and at Florence skill in arms was rated less highly than the techniques of finance, commerce and political organization. Moreover as time went on, the discovery of gunpowder, the use of artillery, the application of engineering to warfare and the employment of mercenary troops reduced the importance for the aristocracy of physical endurance of the Spartan pattern.[10] The power of money and technical knowledge were found to contribute more to the successful prosecution of war than skill with the bow and spear or the ability to stand up to grave exertion. Castiglione, whose book *The Courtier* was published over 100 years after Vergerius's *De Ingenuis Moribus*, did not attach nearly so much importance to military training. He still rated it highly, and this is not surprising since he himself accompanied the Marquis of Mantua in a war against the Spaniards for the Kingdom of Naples.

65

Nevertheless his book shows signs of the decline in importance of proficiency in arms. 'Now the French set a wrong standard in their choice of the interests of the Courtier. They have a mean opinion of all qualifications but that of arms.' Castiglione also recounts a conversation between a pseudo-courtier and a gentlewoman in which she invited him to dance. He refused to dance and to hear music and other entertainment 'always affirming such trifles not to be in his profession. "What then is your profession?" "To fight." Then said the gentlewoman, "Seeing you are not now at war nor in place to fight I would think it best for you to be well besmeared and set up in an armory till time were that you should be occupied, lest you wax more rustier than you are".'[11]

It is true that the courtier must be possessed of skill in arms, but he was not to be a professed soldier, for a fighting career was a very limited one. He would on the other hand devote himself to non-military sports and exercises. It was in fact the existence of professional soldiers that helped to make it possible for the aristocracy to develop their physical virtuosity in non-military ways.

At first physical education, apart from its military value, was allowed a place in total education chiefly as a means of relaxation 'because we are not so constituted that we are able to bestow ourselves all day long upon our ordered tasks'.[12] It was soon realized that physical education could also make a positive contribution to the development of the whole man. It was realized that physical skills could be used to express the personality and could add to the dignity of those who possessed them. Much of the credit for developing these ideas in theory and practice must go to two practising schoolmasters, Guarino da Verona and Vittorino da Feltre.

Guarino was invited by the Marquis Nicolo d'Este to Ferrara in 1429 as tutor to his heir Leonello. He remained as tutor until 1435. He then founded a school which later became a full university. Military training bulked large in the curriculum devised for Leonello. As well as specifically military exercises, riding, hunting, and even snowballing were taught for their value in warfare, but the inclusion of swimming and ball games had a different justification. Swimming was both healthy and useful in saving one's life, but it also provided for the aesthetic

66

enjoyment of the gleam of light upon the blue water, of the green banks of the stream and of the brilliancy of the sky.[13] Dancing was commended by Guarino as an aid to grace of carriage, and this view was a long way from that of Vergerius who maintained that 'to watch dancing girls, or to dance ourselves to music is altogether unworthy', although even Vergerius admitted that dancing might have a use as training, and as a means to an end, if not worthy of pursuit for its own sake.

Vittorino da Feltre was the contemporary and friend of Guarino and his career was somewhat similar. Vittorino went as family tutor to the Marquis of Mantua. He was placed in charge of the education of Gonzaga's children, four boys and one girl, together with the sons of Mantuan nobles and of his own friends. Not all were wealthy but Vittorino was allowed by Gonzaga to educate the poor at the expense of the rich. The inclusion of a girl and of poor scholars in Vittorino's school necessitated, or perhaps was the result of, a liberal view of education. A purely military conception of physical education was clearly out of place and in fact military training played little part in his scheme. He believed that the highest level of humanist culture could only be attained if the full personality were developed along the three channels, mental, physical and spiritual. To a large extent Vittorino's scheme for the physical development of his pupils reflected his own personality and way of life. Slight and frail of build, he had yet subjected himself to a rigorous self-discipline and to strenuous activity to develop his physical endurance. He thus became careless of cold and believed that artificial heat was the source of many 'humours'. He prescribed for his pupils a vigorous outdoor life and regular daily exercise in all weathers. In the hot weather he took them to Lake Garda or the Alps for a simple open-air life in order to induce habits of hardiness and the ability to bear fatigue.

Stamina may have been the primary objective of physical education but skill was not overlooked and Vittorino gave special encouragement to ball games, to jumping activities and to fencing. He regarded games and sports too as a sound corrective to self-indulgence, to effeminacy and to unsociability, and so recognized the part that physical education could play in developing socially valuable qualities and in training 'charac-

67

ter'. It is not without interest that by taking part himself in physical activities with his pupils he established a new relationship between pupils and teacher.

The view that the whole man had a physical side to develop as well as a mental and spiritual side gained ground steadily among the new nobility in Italy. Moreover, physical education was thought to embrace not merely the teaching of certain accomplishments. Everything that a nobleman did, whether intellectual or physical, must be done with ease, even with disdain (sprezzatura). He must be better than other men, but on no account must he vaunt or display his excellence. We have already noticed that Alberti advised against the 'tourney' because of its ostentation; public performance of any skill was decried for the same reason; in dancing, movements which were merely spectacular were to be avoided. It was for the dancing-master, not for the educated man 'to jump in the air and make lightnings with his feet'.

Ease and grace of movement were required in everyday activities as well as in games and sports, for every human activity was thought of as a means of expressing the personality; the contribution of physical education to the development of the whole man was not therefore confined to the teaching of specific social accomplishments. No writer was more emphatic on this than Matteo Palmieri. 'Every motion or attitude of the body which is out of harmony with the grace and freedom of natural activity must be avoided. ... Think how much is revealed through the hands; they help our expression, they are a language in themselves. ... And right training should imply always that the hands be used with grace conforming to our intention.'[14]

The education of the whole man became formulated in the doctrine of 'courtesy' and found its most complete expression in the work of Castiglione. *Il Cortegiano* was widely read both in Italy and throughout Europe. The conception of the courtier portrayed therein is an ideal one and was recognized as such by the author. It nevertheless provided a model for the education of the ruling class wherever social, political and economic conditions in Europe permitted. Castiglione considered the physical education of the courtier very important and he expressed most of the ideas which had been put forward already

68

by other humanist educators during the fifteenth century. The courtier was to undergo military training and also training in activities which were 'not directly dependent on arms but are akin to them, such as hunting, swimming, leaping, running and casting the stone'. The distinction was made between worthy pursuits such as 'tenyse' and 'vautyng', which he said was painful and hard but made a man lighter and quicker than anything else, and unworthy pursuits such as tumbling and rope climbing which were fit only for jugglers. The courtier too was to be better than other men at his skills but must not be ostentatious; and gracefulness must mark every activity in which he indulged. Castiglione even required his courtier to have certain physical qualities which could not be produced by training, such as medium stature. Tall men, he thought, were of a dull wit and inept at those exercises of nimbleness which he desired his courtier to have.

Women, too, were to share in the physical education of the courtier. They were not to join in hunting parties but they would enjoy riding and they would learn dancing which would enhance their carriage. As for games of skill, women would not apparently take part, but they should watch so that they might understand them, judge skill and converse intelligently about them.

The development of humanist education in Italy was primarily the work of laymen, but two books written by Cardinals in the sixteenth century show the extent to which humanist views of physical education were accepted by some leaders of the counter-reformation. Cardinal Sadoleto wrote *De Liberis Recte Instituendis* in 1530, two years after the publication of *Il Cortegiano*. Although he rejected the narrow asceticism of the Middle Ages he did not favour the development of specialized skills and physical accomplishments so much as the spontaneous, energetic, and open-air exercise to be had in running, riding, javelin throwing and ball play. Cardinal Antoniano, in *Dell' Educatione Christiana dei Figliuoli* published in 1584, advocated physical recreation for young and old, and argued that games could be used to train grace of body as well as qualities of character. There are, however, traces of an ascetic outlook, most noticeable in his absolute condemnation of dancing.

Castiglione's book and other educational works of the fifteenth and sixteenth centuries show that the physical education

69

of the privileged and ruling class was both accepted and systematized and that much of its inspiration, if little of its programme of activities, were derived from ancient Rome and the city states of classical Greece.

It is not possible to leave the study of physical education in Italy during the renaissance at this point. The revival of learning led to a renewed interest in the original Greek and Roman sources of medical theory and practice, particularly the works of Galen. Among these, few received greater attention than the six books *De Sanitate Tuenda* in which Galen had discussed the contribution of exercise to health and had classified particular activities and exercises by their effects upon the body. This was the first of Galen's works to be translated by Linacre from Greek into Latin. His translation dedicated to Henry VIII was published in Paris in 1517. During the latter part of the sixteenth century, at least twelve books were published upon medical gymnastics.[15] Two of these, by Italian doctors, deserve special mention because they ran into several editions and undoubtedly had an influence upon therapeutic physical education throughout Europe. The first was written by Girolamo Cardano, 1501–1576, and bore the same title as the translation of Galen's work, *De Sanitate Tuenda*. In fact, Cardano owed more than the title to Galen. His treatment of the hygiene of exercise and the classification of exercises into violent or light, rapid and slow, continuous and interrupted and the particular effects of special forms, were closely modelled upon his ancient authority. The second work was by Hieronymus Mercurialis entitled *De Arte Gymnastica*, in six books. Mercurialis was known throughout Europe as an authority on medicine and editions of his work on gymnastics first published in 1569 continued to appear at intervals during the next hundred years. While Mercurialis drew extensively upon Galen, the marginal references throughout the work show an extraordinarily wide range of reading and the third edition contained a list of one hundred and five Greek and Latin authors whose work he had consulted. The first three books were in the main descriptive of gymnasia and gymnasts and various games, sports and exercises both ancient and contemporary. Book four contained a general discussion of the physiological value of exercise and a refutation of the arguments against the health value of exercise, while books five

70

and six dealt in detail with the particular effects of dancing, of ball games, of swimming and of erect standing and other physical activities. Precise recommendations were made. Exercises were not only prescribed for those suffering from general or particular debility, but they were even prescribed for pathological conditions such as stones in the kidneys and varicose veins. More often, however, the suggestions for such cases specified the exercises that should not be taken rather than those that should. According to the title page the work was intended for others beside physicians and there is no doubt that this intention was fulfilled. By the time the work was published many of the humanist educators had already noted in general terms the therapeutic value of physical education. Vittorino da Feltre at Mantua devised special exercises for Allessandro, the delicate child of the Gonzaga family, when he was ill, and many general educational works stated that exercise was necessary to maintain health. Unfortunately, contemporary ignorance of physiology and anatomy made many of the precise statements about the effects of exercise erroneous and they must be put on a par with recommendations to preserve health by wearing a scarlet night cap and not sleeping on the stomach. Nevertheless, a physiological basis for physical education was recognized and the therapeutic value of physical education was never afterwards lost sight of.

Italy, then, was the origin and fount of ideas and practices in physical education during the renaissance. While the small republics and despotisms, where humanism grew up, were not reproduced elsewhere in Europe, the growth of a money economy, the breakdown of feudalism and the rise of a new privileged class of property and intellect were general features of European development; so too was the permeation of humanism and humanist educational ideals.

In England the new learning was slow to make itself felt in the fifteenth century. Chrysoloras visited London in 1409 and searched for ancient texts in Salisbury Cathedral, but he came on a diplomatic and not a teaching mission.[16] In 1418 Poggio Bracciolini, the Florentine humanist set out for England at the invitation of the Bishop of Winchester, and spent four years in this country, but, as far as finding opportunities to further the new learning went, they were disappointing years. It was after

F   71

Poggio returned to Italy that English humanism began. The patronage of Humphrey, Duke of Gloucester who enriched Oxford both with manuscripts and with buildings, did much to foster the early enthusiasm for the new learning. He attached humanist scholars to his household and commissioned new translations of the classics from Italy. Groups of scholars, including Grey, Free, Fleming and Tiptoft, Earl of Worcester, began to visit Italy and returned with valuable manuscripts for college libraries at Oxford. In spite of the enthusiasm of these early disciples the new learning made little impression upon English life until the very end of the fifteenth century and the beginning of the sixteenth century. At that time a group of scholars including Grocyn, Linacre and Latimer visited Italy and on their return settled down to teach at Oxford. The renaissance in England as in Italy coincided with similar and important changes in the older structure of feudalism. It is not surprising to find therefore that Italian humanism, together with its educational ideals and doctrine of courtesy, profoundly influenced the way of life of the ruling class in England, and that Italian concepts of physical education also found a home in this country.

The therapeutic value of exercise and physical education was appreciated as a result of the work of Linacre the distinguished translator of Galen. Books on health written and published in England emphasized the necessity of exercise if health was to be maintained.[17] While Linacre doubtless carried weight with the medical profession, the general educational system was much more strongly influenced by Erasmus and Colet. Here was a distinct contrast with the development of education in Italy. In that country the writers on education and the founders of schools such as Guarino da Verona and Vittorino da Feltre were laymen: in England the lead was taken by ecclesiastics, especially by Erasmus, and this seems to have restricted the influence of Italian views on physical education. In the new schools, except Merchant Taylors, there seems to have been little physical education and certainly no systematic physical education such as was advocated in Italy by Palmieri and put into practice by Vittorino. This is understandable if the life and educational views of Erasmus are examined, for he was associated with Dean Colet in founding St. Paul's School in 1510 and

72

influenced education throughout the country. He was brought up in the Low Countries and at the age of twenty became a monk in a monastery at Steyn. There he wrote an essay *On the Contempt of the World* in which he decries the body and places it in antagonism to the soul. 'The monks' he says, 'do not choose to become like cattle; they know that there is something sublime and divine within man which they prefer to develop rather than to cater for the body. Man's nature is more dignified than that of the beast. Our body, except for a few details, differs not from an animal's body but our soul reaches out after things divine and eternal. The body is earthly, wild, slow, mortal, diseased, ignoble; the soul on the other hand is heavenly, subtle, divine, immortal, noble. Who is so blind that he cannot tell the difference between body and soul? And so the happiness of the soul surpasses that of the body.'[18] Later in life Erasmus came to despise the monastic life but his views on education and physical education in particular were still coloured by asceticism. He found no place for physical education for a child beyond the age of six and the intellectual demands he made were so severe that he found it necessary to defend them and to defend also his omission of physical activities from his curriculum. 'We have to meet an argument against early training drawn from the superior importance of health. Personally I venture to regard the mental advantages gained as outweighing some slight risks in the matter of physical vigour.'[19] In the *Colloquies* there is a thumbnail sketch of a schoolmaster whose attitude to recreation was hardly one of encouragement. His boys chose one of their number to ask him for a holiday for games. The request was reluctantly granted with the words 'they that labour hard had need of some relaxation; but you that study idly and play laboriously had more need of a curb than a snaffle.' Erasmus thus was somewhat out of sympathy with the humanist conception of the physical education of 'L'uomo universale'. Erasmus may have been acquainted with that cult of the body in Germany which meant not the grace of Apollo or of the Epheboi at Athens, but a warlike ferocity of unparalleled coarseness. Whatever the environment that determined Erasmus's views, there is no doubt that, once formed, they were partly responsible for the neglect

73

of physical education in schools and colleges that were founded during the sixteenth century in England.

At the Court of the Tudor Monarchs asceticism had little influence and there the conception of the whole man and the doctrine of courtesy were readily accepted. In time these ideas came to be appreciated outside the court. Shakespeare in *As You Like It* revealed that he was fully alive to the need for the aristocracy to have certain physical accomplishments and to perform them with ease and without ostentation. In the opening scenes of the play, Orlando, the dispossessed son of the late Sir Rowland de Boyes, was required to reveal his nobility in an unmistakable manner and to enlist the sympathy of the audience. Shakespeare pitted him in a wrestling match against Charles, the Duke's wrestler, a professional thug, whom Orlando's brother Oliver had instructed to make away with his younger brother. Orlando belied appearances and Charles was overthrown. Both the wrestling match and Touchstone's discourse on lies later in the play were taken from an Italian book, Saviolo's *Practice on the Art of Duelling and Behaviour of a Gentleman.* Not only books, but teachers as well, were imported from Italy, and both monarchs and courtiers in Tudor England went to Italian masters for instruction in riding, fencing, falconry and hunting and other accomplishments which an educated man needed in society.

Castiglione's *Il Cortegiano* was translated by Sir Thomas Hoby and published in England in 1561, but Sir Thomas Elyot had already written a comparable work entitled *The Governour*, a treatise on the education of the ruling class. Several chapters in it were devoted to physical education,[20] and showed the influence of Italian ideas and the use of Greek and Roman authorities to justify the recommendations that were made. The games and sports that were prescribed for the governour were taken from English usage of Elyot's day but had classical authority to support them. Running was a favourite sport of Epaminondas and Achilles, swimming was popular with the Romans especially Horatius and Julius Caesar, while Greeks and Romans from Xenophon to Pompey enjoyed hunting. These sports therefore were worthy of pursuit. Not all sports were worthy of pursuit and Elyot, like the Italian humanists, made a clear distinction between what was and what was not fit for a

74

gentleman. 'Some men would say that in mediocrity, which I have so much praised in shooting, why should not bowling, claisshe, pynnes, and koytyng be as much commended? Verily as for the two last they are to be utterly abjected of all noble men, in like wise football wherein is nothing but beastly fury and extreme violence; whereof proceedeth hurt and consequently rancour and malice do remain with them that be wounded; wherefore it is to be put into perpetual silence.'

The difference in attitude to physical education between the court and the church is well illustrated in Elyot's discussion of dancing. He was a strong advocate of dancing but the opposition of the church could not be ignored and Elyot was at some pains to show that the condemnation of the church was based on a misinterpretation of a saying of St. Augustine that it were better to dig or plough on Sunday than to dance. St. Augustine was not condemning dancing out of hand but only dancing associated with idolatry and fornication. Elyot would have dancing as a part of liberal education from the age of seven to the age of twenty.

Perhaps the chief difference between the physical education of 'the Courtier' and that of 'the Governour' is that the latter was concerned not only with the training of character and the production of qualities which would be socially valuable, but also with the physiological effects of exercise. Elyot seems to have been familiar both with Galen's works and with the latest medical teaching and he claimed six specific physiological benefits that derive from exercise; exercise aided digestion, promoted long life, increased body heat, quickened the appetite, caused a more ready metabolism and cleansed the conduits of the body. He also classified exercises according to their effect on the body, or to be more precise he made a five-fold classification in which the first four categories were physiological. They were exercises that aid digestion, exercises that produce strength and hardness of body, exercises that produce agility and nimbleness, and exercises for celerity and speediness. The fifth category embraced all those exercises which he considered necessary in war and peace. Elyot was, in fact, concerned with three main objectives of physical education, enrichment of the personality, social success and physiological efficiency. His was the first book in English to pay equal attention to each of these objectives.

75

The interest of the upper classes in physical education in sixteenth-century England was general and Sir Thomas Elyot's book was not an isolated work. *The Schoolmaster*, by Roger Ascham, at one time tutor of Queen Elizabeth, was concerned with teaching methods in physical education, and three other works that have survived, *The Institution of a Gentleman* by an unknown author, published in 1555, *Queen Elizabeth's Academy* by Sir Humphrey Gilbert, 1572, and *The Institution of a Nobleman* by Cleland, 1607, all found a place in their systems for physical education.

All the writers on physical education in England noticed so far have been closely associated with the life of the Court and none were practising schoolmasters in the existing and newly founded schools and colleges. Nor was physical recreation encouraged in the older universities of Oxford and Cambridge. Football was forbidden in Cambridge in 1574, while at Oxford in 1584 any 'minister or deacon' convicted of this offence was to be banished and reported to his bishop; scholars over eighteen were to be imprisoned and fined, and those under eighteen were to be flogged in St. Mary's.[21] The curriculum in universities and schools appears to have been strongly influenced by an ascetic view of life and the education of scholars included little if any physical education except at Merchant Taylors. The Headmaster of that school from 1560–1586, Richard Mulcaster, was perhaps the most enlightened schoolmaster of his day. It is Commenius who is commonly given credit for pioneer work in the use of the vernacular, in teaching first those subjects which give scope for activity, and in teaching examples before rules, yet these doctrines had been formulated and expounded half a century earlier by Mulcaster. The tragedy is that his two books on education, *Positions* published in 1581 and *Elementarie* in 1582, soon went out of print and remained out of print for 300 years. *Positions* was first reprinted in 1888 and *Elementarie* did not reappear until 1925. In *Positions* twenty-five out of the total of forty-five chapters were devoted to physical education and in this field the neglect of his writings was particularly unfortunate.

Mulcaster was inevitably influenced by the Courtier conception of physical education and eagerly subscribed to the view that the mind and body, being partners, must not be

76

severed in training, but he departed somewhat from the Courtier tradition in making a definite attempt to relate physical education to school life rather than to the life of the court. The argument that children would look after their own exercise was answered in no uncertain terms. 'Neither is it enough to say that children will be stirring always themselves and that therefore they need not any so great care for exercising their bodies. For if by causing them learn so and sitting still in schools we did not force them from ingenerate heate, and natural stirring to an unnatural stillness, then their own stirring without restraint might seem to serve their turn without more ado. Wherefore as stillness has her direction by order in schools, so must stirring be directed by well appointed exercise.'[21] Physical education therefore must be ordered to a definite purpose and counteract the effects of school life and it was not to consist of merely playing games at random.

Like Sir Thomas Elyot, Richard Mulcaster was interested in the classification of physical activities. He outlined three main classifications. The first was purely administrative and activities were divided into those that were suitable for indoor performance such as dancing, wrestling and fencing as well as laughing and weeping (how these latter activities were initiated Mulcaster did not say), and those that needed to be done outdoors such as shooting, swimming, ball play and hunting. The second classification was according to social purpose. Activities were either athletic, or martial, or physical, that is medical. In Mulcaster's view too much attention had been paid to athletic exercises indulged in as pastimes and like Galen he deplored over specialization in such activities. Martial exercises were designed to produce strength and stamina for the rigours of campaigning. Physical or medical activities had a threefold purpose; to confirm a person's natural gifts, to produce skill that had not been bestowed by nature and to enable a person to recover what had been lost by illness or neglect, that is 'rehabilitation'. It was in physical or medical exercise that Mulcaster was primarily interested and his third classification concerned this sphere of education only. He classified exercises as exercises for muscles and joints, exercises for the circulation and exercises for respiration. He then gave examples of the effects of specific exercises. Dancing would produce warmth and streng-

77

then the lower limbs and would help to prevent numbness and palsies. Riding was 'healthful for hips and stomach, thickeneth loose shanks, and stayeth loose bellies.' Loud speaking was valuable in exercising the vocal cords and opening the lungs.

Much of Mulcaster's applied physiology was primitive not to say inaccurate, but in one particular at least he anticipated modern theories. After defining exercise as 'a vehement and voluntary stirring of the body, which altereth the breathing, whose end is to maintain health and bring the body to a very good habit', he then stated that it should begin with gentle or 'preparative' exercise, go on to gymnastics and end with post-parative exercise 'to reduce the body by gentle degrees to the same quietness in constitution wherein it was before it was so moved'. The same doctrine, put forward by Swedish medical gymnasts some 400 years later, came to be known in the world of physical education as 'The Swedish Curve'.

Mulcaster's interest in physiology did not lead him to think that the teacher should abdicate in favour of the doctor. He stated, in fact, that there was a vast field of human welfare which was not covered by priest or doctor and which should be covered by the educationist. He was equally insistent that the same person should be concerned with physical as with academic education. In this idea, as in so much else, Mulcaster was ahead of his age. His views were not accepted by schools and colleges and the close of the century witnessed a growing rift in England between the education of gentlemen, strongly influenced by the courtier tradition, and the education of scholars influenced by a monastic tradition and finding no place for physical education.

REFERENCES

1. P. P. Vergerius, *De Ingenuis Moribus*, 1404. Trans. W. H. Woodward in *Vittorino da Feltre and other Humanist Educators*. Cambridge 1897.
2. Noel Denholm Young, 'The Tournament in the Thirteenth Century' in *Studies in Medieval History*. p. 249. Ed. R. W. Hunt, W. A. Pantin and R. W. Southern. Oxford 1948.

78

3. Gervase Mathew, 'Ideals of Knighthood in Late Fourteenth Century England' in *Studies in Medieval History*. pp. 358–360. Ed. R. W. Hunt, W. A. Pantin and R. W. Southern. Oxford 1948.

4. A. W. Reed, 'Chivalry and the Idea of a Gentleman' in *Chivalry*, Chap. IX. Ed. E. Prestage. London 1928.

5. J. Burckhardt, *The Civilization of the Renaissance in Italy*. London 1945.

6. Giovanni di Bardi, *Discorso sopra 'l Giuoco del Calcio Fiorentino*. 1688.

   v. W. Heywood, *Palio and Ponte*, p. 165. London 1904.

7. W. H. Woodward, *Education during the Renaissance*, p. 36. Cambridge 1906.

8. P. P. Vergerius, 'De Ingenius Moribus', quoted in *Vittorino da Feltre and other Humanist Educators*, by W. H. Woodward. Cambridge, 1897.

9. Aeneas Sylvius, *De Liberorum Educatione*, W. H. Woodward, *op. cit.*

10. Mercenary troops had been used in Italy long before the Renaissance, but it was not until the fourteenth century and later that they came to predominate in warfare. v. Charles Oman, *A History of the Art of War in the Middle Ages*, Vol. II, p. 291. London 1924.

11. B. Castiglione, *The Courtier*. Trans. Sir T. Hoby, 1561. Everyman Edition 1944, p. 37.

12. P. P. Vergerius, *De Ingenuis Moribus*. W. H. Woodward, *op. cit.*

13. W. H. Woodward, *Education during the Renaissance*, p. 37.

14. Matteo Palmieri, *Della Vita Civile, c. 1435*, v. W. H. Woodward, *Education during the Renaissance*, p. 247.

15. Dr. Edgar F. Cyriax, *Bibliographia Gymnastica Medica*. London 1909.

16. R. Weiss, *Humanism in England*, p. 11. Oxford 1941.

17. Andrew Boorde, *A Compendious Regyment or Dyetary of Health*, 1542, and Sir John Salusbury, *Certain Necessary Observations for Health*, 1603.

18. Albert Hyma, *The Youth of Erasmus*, Michigan, p. 178.

19. Erasmus, *De Pueris Instituendis*, 503 B.

20. Sir T. Elyot, *The Governour*, first published 1531. Book I, Chaps. 16–22, 26, 27.

21. Richard Mulcaster, *Positions*, Chap. 4.

79

Renaissance Italy and Tudor England

See also

Einstein, L. *The Italian Renaissance in England.* New York 1902.

Funck-Brentano, F. *The Renaissance.* Trans. F. C. Fletcher. London 1936.

Leonard, F.E. and Afleck, G.B. *A Guide to the History of Physical Education,* 3rd Edition, Chap. VIII. London 1947.

Mercurialis, H. *De Arte Gymnastica.*

Van Dalen, D. B., Mitchell, E.D. and Bennett, B.L. *A World History of Physical Education.* New York 1953.

Woodward, W. H. *Vittorino da Feltre and other Humanist Educators.* Cambridge 1897.

Woodward, W. H. *Erasmus concerning Education.* Cambridge 1904.

80

V

Therapeutic Exercise in Scandinavia

P. C. McINTOSH

∽∽∾∾∾∾∾∾∾∾∾∾∾∾∾∾∾∾∾

T HE Scandinavian countries were the nurseries of therapeutic gymnastics. Denmark and Sweden in particular
were the countries where the pioneer work was done to
nurture this conception of physical education during the nineteenth century. Neither Finland nor Norway had an independent existence at the beginning of the century. Finland belonged to Sweden until 1809 when the country was lost to
Russia, and Norway was at first under Danish rule and then,
in 1814, was detached from Denmark and linked to Sweden. It
was not until 1905 that Norway had a completely separate
political existence. The contributions which Finland and Norway have made to physical education have not been insignifi-
cant in recent times, but for the sake of compactness this study
is confined to physical education in Denmark and Sweden
where the most significant developments took place.

One factor which has been present throughout the period
under review, that is the whole of the nineteenth and the first
half of the twentieth century, and which has played a big part
in shaping the physical education of Denmark and Sweden has
been the geographical situation of the two countries. Copenhagen lies on a latitude approximately that of Edinburgh, and
the latitude of Stockholm is the same as that of the Orkney
Islands. The summer climate of the two Scandinavian countries
is not dissimilar from that of much of the United Kingdom, but
during the winter the mean temperature of the coldest month

81

in Britain is 40°F., while that of Denmark is 31.5°F., and that of Sweden is 28°F.[1] Games and sports which are pursued out of doors throughout the winter in Britain can be played only in the spring, summer and autumn in Scandinavia. The English football season is a winter season and finishes in April when the Swedish season is just beginning. Climate has favoured the growth of football and organized games at English Public Schools, and climate has favoured the development of a gymnastic form of physical education in Denmark and Sweden.

The development of physical education in Denmark and Sweden at the end of the eighteenth and the beginning of the nineteenth centuries was also affected by political and social conditions. In the eighteenth century Denmark and Sweden had gone through stages of development not unlike those of other European countries. Towns had grown in size and the way of life of the towns-people had undergone some urbanization. This was not perhaps so marked in Sweden as in some other countries. In 1800 Swedish town dwellers numbered only 9.77% and Danish town dwellers 21% of the total populations and for the year 1870 the figures were 12.95% and 25%.[2] Nevertheless, in both countries there had been a commercial revolution and the development of a capitalist economy. The turn of the century saw a steady growth of the power and influence of the middle class as distinct from the authoritarian upper class on the one hand and the rural population on the other. At the same time the attention paid to the vernacular languages was a symptom of increasing national self-consciousness.

The period 1789–1815 was one of turmoil for most of Europe. While Scandinavia did not escape the Napoleonic Wars, nothing comparable to the French Revolution took place there. The reasons are complex but one at least is worth noting: the peasants, although often exploited by the landowners, yet had the right of access to the King who was often sympathetic and welcomed them as a check upon the power of the nobility. It has been estimated that in Denmark the power of the monarch was as great in 1815 as in 1789. In Sweden the political situation developed differently. Gustav III, who seized power in 1789, governed through the four Estates. His successor Gustav IV exercised more power and less sense and did not call a meeting

82

of the Riksdag in any year between 1800 and 1809. Moreover, he conducted a disastrous war against Russia in 1808–9 in which Sweden lost the whole of Finland and came near to being invaded herself. In 1809 there was a bloodless revolution. Gustav IV was deposed. His uncle Charles was made Regent and a new constitution was drafted restoring much of the political machinery that the King had tried to overthrow. In an effort to rehabilitate the country both internally and in the international field, the Riksdag invited one of Napoleon's marshals, Count Bernadotte, to be Crown Prince and to succeed the heirless regent. It was during this political upheaval and amid the uncertain events of the Napoleonic wars that enthusiasm for physical education began to take hold of Scandinavians, and it was directly encouraged to do so by royalty. In Denmark, King Frederick VI who, as Crown Prince, had attended a private gymnastic establishment run by Franz Nachtegall, in 1804 established a national 'Military Gymnastic Institute' and appointed Nachtegall to be its Director. In Sweden, ten years later, Count Bernadotte, the Crown Prince, actively supported the proposal of P. H. Ling to open a Central Gymnastic Institute. The powerful influence of the monarchy was thus directly associated with the early development of physical education in both Denmark and Sweden.

When Nachtegall started a gymnastic club in Copenhagen in January 1799 and later in the same year opened his own private outdoor gymnasium, this was not a bolt from the blue, even if the gymnasium was the first institution of modern times to be devoted exclusively to physical education. Pestalozzi in Switzerland had made use of gymnastics in the education of children and in Germany the philanthropist schools had been vigorously developing gymnastics. The prototype for these schools had been founded at Dessau in 1774 by Basedow and had been named by him the 'Philanthropinum'. It had included organized physical activities in its curriculum from its earliest days. At a similar school at Schnepfenthal founded in 1784 Guts Muths worked out a programme of physical education which was to gain a high reputation throughout Europe and even further afield. His contribution to physical education is considered in more detail in Chapter 6. Here it is only necessary to point out that his book *Gymnastik für die Jugend*, published in

83

1793, appeared in translation in many countries and that the date of the Danish translation was 1799, the year that Nachtegall opened his gymnastic institute in Copenhagen. Moreover at this same time Nachtegall held a part-time teaching appointment in a Danish school which had been opened in 1795 by the Court Chaplain, Christiani, to carry out the educational theories of Basedow. At first Nachtegall's gymnasium had 5 pupils; by the end of 1799 it boasted 25 and by 1803–4 the number had risen to 150.

The gymnastic movement in Copenhagen, then, owed much to developments in physical education which had already taken place elsewhere in Europe. Nor was the gymnastic movement itself an isolated phenomenon but it was part of a wider culture which originated outside Scandinavia and found fertile ground for growth in Copenhagen.

J. H. E. Bernstorff, who was foreign minister to Frederick V and Charles VII, had welcomed to Copenhagen a large colony of foreign scholars, artists and teachers and that city became the cultural centre of Northern Europe. As the eighteenth century wore on the Age of Reason gradually gave place to Romanticism. Kant's *Critique of Pure Reason*, which was popular in Denmark in the 1790's, provided the intellectual basis for a new movement which was by no means confined to philosophy. In 1803 the Norwegian born Henrik Steffens gave a course of lectures in Copenhagen outlining the new ideology of the romantics. These lectures had a profound effect upon the audience and not least upon a young Danish poet Adam Oehlenschläger. Shortly afterwards Oehlenschläger wrote the first of his poems in the new style, *Guldhornene*, a patriotic flight of fancy upon two viking drinking horns that had been stolen from the museum.

Patriotism was not merely a literary figure. The Napoleonic wars and in particular the attack on the Danish fleet in Copenhagen harbour by British ships under Admirals Parker and Nelson in 1801 brought home to the people the mortal physical danger in which Denmark stood. The gymnastics of Nachtegall were seen as a practical outlet for the new patriotic feeling and as an immediate contribution to national defence. In 1804 the King appointed Nachtegall as professor of gymnastics at the university, and when, in August of the same year, a Military

84

Gymnastic Institute was set up by royal decree, Nachtegall was made its first Director.

The years 1789–1814 saw important work done by the Danish Great School Commission. A plan for a national system of rural schools (folkeskoler) was prepared by 1799 and elementary education was finally made compulsory both in the capital and in the provinces by a royal decree of July 29th 1814. In the school code of that year gymnastics were made a compulsory subject in elementary schools. An ordinance of 1809 had already stated that instruction in gymnastics should be provided in secondary schools (laerde skoler) whenever possible. In 1808 the Military Gymnastic Institute was opened to civilians and an attempt was made to provide teachers for teachers' colleges and elementary schools. This course ceased to run after 1814 but ten of the students trained there were sent to posts in teachers' colleges (seminarier), and gymnastics became a required subject in those colleges in 1818. In 1821, Nachtegall became Director of Gymnastics with supervision of civil and military gymnastics throughout Denmark.

Unfortunately the impoverishment of Denmark after the Napoleonic wars meant that many of the plans of the Great School Commission were imperfectly realized and the decrees on education were not fully implemented, but after 1826 physical education again went forward. In that year a circular was sent out to all school authorities to urge them to find a place for gymnastics. Two years later a Teachers' Course in Gymnastics (Normalskole for Gymnastik) was opened in connection with the Military Gymnastic Institute. There civil and military instructors and teachers in schools could come, and under supervision, teach classes of children. In 1828 also the King approved for use in elementary schools the 'Manual for Gymnastics' which had been prepared by a committee of five including Nachtegall. In 1839 Nachtegall was responsible for the institution of a course in gymnastics for women teachers (Normalskole for Kvindegymnastik). Nachtegall retired from the Military Gymnastic Institute in 1842 and died in 1847. He had not been a great innovator of gymnastics and in practice he had been content to follow where GutsMuth had led. His great contribution was the organization of physical education on a nationwide scale.

85

Nachtegall's successor at the Military Gymnastic Institute was Captain Niels Georg la Cour who also became Director of Gymnastics. Under him gymnastics became more and more restricted to Military training, and from 1859 the gymnastic staff in the teachers' colleges were non-commissioned officers, 'loaned' for a term of three years. Even within the army gymnastics came to be looked upon as disciplinary, a form of punishment rather than a road to fitness. Upon La Cour's retirement in 1870 the post of Director of Gymnastics was abolished. A new post of Inspector of Gymnastics was created but the army still exercised its unimaginative control over gymnastics in schools and the next impetus to physical education in Denmark came from quite a different quarter.

In Sweden, as in Denmark, physical education developed rapidly during the early years of the nineteenth century. This development was the result of forces and influences similar to those which worked upon physical education in Denmark, but in Sweden physical education after 1814 was dominated by one man, Pehr Henrik Ling. There were two reasons for this: Ling's own contributions to the theory and practice of physical education were original and they were far reaching because they were so appropriate to the needs of the age. The more important reason, however, was that Ling was not only, in fact not primarily, a specialist in physical education but a leader of the Romantic Movement. He was a national figure quite apart from his pre-eminence in physical education. To state that Ling was a pioneer and that he, personally, shaped the pattern of physical education in Sweden, is not to deny that he was the child of his age or that he was subject to all the cultural, political and economic forces at work in Europe when he was reaching maturity. Nevertheless the relationship of physical education to the structure of society and the pattern of culture in Sweden can hardly be studied otherwise than in close association with the life and work of P. H. Ling.

Ling was born in November 1776 and was therefore 12 when the French Revolution broke out and was 32 when the Swedish *coup d'état* took place in 1809. His early manhood was spent in that period of ferment when the middle classes began to set their mark upon the economy, the politics and the culture of Sweden, and when romanticism began to flower. He was strongly in-

86

fluenced by the Romantic Movement and, in his late twenties and early thirties became one of its leaders.

Our knowledge of Ling's early life is incomplete and one of the few incidents which have been recorded is his expulsion from school in 1792 for throwing a log through the headmaster's window. He had a headache at the time. However, that may be, it is now recognized that there were two formative periods in his life, the first from 1795–1799 which he spent in Stockholm and Uppsala, and the second from 1799 to 1804 when he was in Copenhagen. Whether Ling derived his inspiration from Danish or Swedish sources has been a matter for some dispute. Signe Prytz, a Danish scholar, maintained that Ling was influenced above all by Nachtegall's gymnastics during his stay in Copenhagen.[3] A Swedish scholar, Albert Wiberg, has now produced evidence to show that both physical education and romanticism in the form of Gothicism were already gaining ground in Sweden before the end of the century, that is, before Ling went to Denmark.[4] It is almost certain that Ling was familiar with these developments. 'Gothicism' was initiated at least as early as 1772 and in the 1790's was a recognized cult. At the same time there was an awakening of interest in sport and physical education. In 1789 a number of articles on physical education appeared in the press. In 1794 Fischerström delivered his famous address to the Swedish Academy of Sciences on the need for the physical education of the people. This was followed by more articles in the press and in 1796 a swimming association was formed in Uppsala. This interest in physical education was maintained while Ling was in Denmark. In 1802 G. A. Silverstolpe presented to the Chancellor in Stockholm his memorandum on the need for encouraging gymnastics and in 1803, Halldin endowed an academic post for physical education at Uppsala. Wiberg has also now shown that swimming, horse riding, fencing and vaulting, the four sports which commanded Ling's enthusiasm, were being practised in Sweden more and more during his boyhood. Indeed Lund University possessed a wooden vaulting horse as early as 1761. It seems probable that the increasing interest in physical education and in Gothicism at the end of the eighteenth century were both manifestations of the growth of national self consciousness among the middle class and the intellectuals in Sweden. A

G 87

letter which Ling wrote to his father-in-law in 1797 complaining of the foppishness of Stockholm society suggests that he was already in sympathy with the idea of a vigorous regeneration of Swedish life before he went to Copenhagen.

Ling's interest in physical education and romanticism probably provided the motive for his visit to Copenhagen. He certainly attended Nachtegall's gymnasium and he took instruction in fencing from two French émigrés. Beuernier and de Montrichard. It is possible, as Wiberg says, that in gymnastics Ling found little new in Nachtegall's work. Probably he was already familiar with GutsMuths' books and also with C. J. Tissot's book on Medical Gymnastics.[5] Tissot had recommended, among other remedies, horse riding and this was in fact the activity which Ling had taken up for an ailment in his chest. Nachtegall subsequently referred to Ling as an ungrateful pupil and this suggests that Ling was not deeply stimulated and felt that he owed little to Nachtegall's work. The really important influence on Ling in Copehhagen was not so much gymnastics as the intellectual contact which he made with the leaders of the Romantic Movement. The lectures of Henrik Steffens and the poems of Oehlenschläger fanned the spark of Gothicism and kindled in him the desire to popularize Nordic mythology. During this period Ling composed short poems in French, German and Danish, and also wrote *Eylif the Goth*, showing his desire to revive the vigour of the ancient Noresemen in his own generation.[6]

In 1804 Ling left Copenhagen because he could no longer afford to stay there. By the end he was living in destitution. He applied to the University of Lund to be allowed to give language lessons, and then the illness and subsequent death of the eighty-year-old fencing master gave him his opening to develop physical education. At first, in April 1805, Ling was appointed merely to give fencing lessons, but he soon won the 'marked approval' of the university and began to introduce swimming, climbing, wrestling, balance exercises and others of Guts Muths gymnastic activities. He also secured permission to intall gymnastic apparatus in his fencing hall.

It was during Ling's stay in Lund between 1804 and 1812 that he developed his exercises without apparatus, his 'free standing' exercises, which came to form the core of the 'Ling

88

system'. He studied anatomy and physiology from 1806 and attended dissections. At the same time he experimented with new movements and apparatus. About 1808 he added to the apparatus gymnastics of Guts Muths a number of free movements and this was the genesis of 'free standing' exercises. The similarity of some of Ling's exercises to those in Pestalozzi's *Elementargymnastik* of 1807 suggests that Ling may have been influenced by the work of the man who was perhaps the best known teacher in Europe. Nevertheless the free movements of Ling's system which were designed to correct or prevent bad posture and to cure faults of bodily development, together with his stretching exercises, lunging exercises, and exercises with a partner to provide support and resistance, were original and far-reaching contributions to physical education.

The ultimate purpose behind these developments of physical education was to revive the ancient vigour of the North as described in the sagas. Ling had a vision of a new youth to be worthy of its Nordic ancestors and it was the same vision that inspired his literary work. While at Lund he formed a close friendship with the poet Esaias Tegner and in 1811 he was one of a group, with the poet E. G. Geijer, which formed the Gothic Association (Götiska Förbundet). [7] Ling's own poems were never highly successful although his play *Agne*, a tragedy in five acts, written in 1812, was ultimately produced on the stage in Stockholm a year after the author's death. His best-known poem was *Gylfe* which dealt with the loss of Finland in 1809 and showed his intense patriotism. In 1814 Ling used *Iduna*, the periodical of the Gothic Association, to give an account of his system of gymnastics. Gothicism and physical education were both of them part and parcel of Ling's patriotic view of life.

While exploring new avenues of physical education at Lund, Ling did not neglect his old interests and his reputation as a fencing master grew steadily. In 1813 he applied successfully for the post of fencing master in the Royal Military Academy at Karlberg just outside Stockholm. In the same year on February 1st he submitted to the '1812 Committee of Education' a proposal for founding a central training school for gymnastics. This move was not in line with Ling's previous intentions, for, in a letter to Werlauff dated 6th January 1805 Ling wrote that he was not going to found any gymnastic institute. Wiberg says

89

that Ling at that time thought that the training of teachers in gymnastics ought to be undertaken by the universities.[8] What then caused Ling to change his mind?

In the first place Ling was rebuffed by the university chancellor at Stockholm. To him he had applied for support in training gymnastic teachers and had received the reply, 'We have plenty of tight-rope walkers and acrobats without burdening the budget with their keep.' Secondly the unsuccessful war against Russia, and the loss of Finland in 1809 had a profound effect upon Ling as upon his countrymen. It may well have influenced him to abandon the universities for the support of the army and the government in an independent institution which might be expected to have quick results in the physical regeneration of the army and the nation. When Ling went to the 'Committee of Education' he gave the secretary a letter of introduction from Esaias Tegner, whose *War Song of the Militia of Scania*, written in 1808, had brought him nationwide fame. The government, the King and the Crown Prince (Count Bernadotte) were persuaded of the close connection between the work of the proposed new institute and national defence. Finally Ling must have been aware of the success and popularity of Nachtegall's Gymnastic Institute in Copenhagen where in 1808 the courses were extended to cater for civilian as well as military students. In 1814 Ling's new school was opened and some time later the King, on the recommendation of the Committee, gave it the title of Royal Central Institute of Gymnastics (Kongl. Gymnastiska Centralinstitutet), a title much prized by generations of students and teachers at the Institute, and greatly respected throughout Sweden.

Even before Ling submitted his memorandum to the Committee of Education the government had been encouraging physical education in schools. As early as 1779 Johan Murberg had included a clause on physical education in his projected regulations for schools, and in the 1790's many teachers from Sweden had travelled in Europe and came back enthusiastic about the work of GutsMuths. At Linköping a definite attempt was made to incorporate gymnastics in the school programme. By 1807 this experiment was considered to have been successful enough for the government to draft the following regulation: 'Since we regard opportunities for good physical training of youth just as

90

important for health as for developing the abilities of the body giving it strength and vigour, it is our will that, as it is already decreed at Linköping school (Lärowerk), there shall be at every place of learning (Lärostad) a department of physical training where the students, under teachers, can climb, leap, vault and swim. There shall be appropriate apparatus and this physical training shall be useful but not dangerous.'[9]

This interest in school gymnastics had been fostered at Linköping by Bishop Linblöm and was quite independent of Ling. When the G.C.I. was opened in 1814 comparatively little attention was paid to the physical education of school children. Ling himself, in *The General Basis of Gymnastics*, published in 1840, a year after his death, classified exercises into four groups, educational, aesthetic, military and medical, and it was to the latter two groups that he devoted his attention. The titles of the three books which he wrote, *Suggestions on the Value and Necessity of Gymnastics for the Military in General* (1820), *Regulations for Gymnastics* (1836), and *Instructing the Military in Gymnastics and Bayonet Fencing* (1838), indicate the trend of his work. Moreover the seven advantages which Ling claimed for his free standing exercises show that his thought was influenced by military needs perhaps more than by the needs of the schools. The advantages which he claimed were (1) that more can exercise at one time under a teacher, (2) that such movements can be made in a great variety of places, e.g. on the march, in barracks, in quarters, in a schoolroom, or in a school yard, (3) that the trouble and expense of keeping apparatus in repair are eliminated, (4) that the fact that the entire squad or class must make the exercises at the same moment promotes strength and agility and rapid attainment of bodily control, (5) that the execution of gymnastics at the word of command reinforces the effect of strict military drill, (6) that free movements are more easily adaptable to the bodily peculiarities of individuals, (7) that they are better than apparatus gymnastics for overcoming awkwardness and stiffness.

About the year 1815 Ling began to develop medical gymnastics for the relief and cure of physical disabilities. He had been interested in the therapeutic value of exercises for many years. He had read Tissot's work on the subject and had himself taken up horse riding in his youth for a 'chest complaint'.

A post-mortem examination showed that he had suffered from tuberculosis.[10] His therapeutic exercises were divided into three groups, active, passive and resisted movements, He devoted much of his time to this side of his work which became known as the 'movement cure', and it was probably in this form that the 'Ling system' first became widely known abroad. Ling himself supervised the movement cure in the summer at Ramlosa and other 'spas', and the first disciples of Ling in England were a few medical men who began to use his movements in the 1840's.

Ling tried hard to secure the co-operation of the medical profession. 'The renaissance of gymnastics' he wrote 'will soon disappear if doctors and gymnasts do not seek to come nearer to it scientifically', yet his 'medical gymnastics' were not accepted without fierce opposition from the more conservative physicians, and he complained bitterly towards the end of his life at lack of recognition. Nevertheless he was awarded the title of Professor in 1825 and became a member of the Swedish Association of Doctors in 1831 and a member of the very select Swedish Academy in 1835. This latter distinction, however, was a reward not for physical education but for a work on the mythology and legendary history of the Scandinavians which was published in its final form in 1833.

Ling's concern that science should be applied to physical education was one of the most important and lasting features of his work. Most of his published work on physical education is of little but academic interest to-day. Ling himself built up his practice empirically, proceeding by experience and observation of the effects of his exercises, but he did also study anatomy and physiology in order to apply medical knowledge as far as he was able. He insisted that medicine and physical education must be allies and that teachers of physical education must have theoretical knowledge as well as practical ability. 'Gymnastics', he wrote, 'should always include theory and practice. The gymnast who lacks the one or the other must always labour at a disadvantage for he does not know when or how he should use a particular movement.' This principle survived as the basis of therapeutic gymnastics after the movements, exercises and positions of Swedish gymnastics had changed out of all recognition.

92

The acceptance of Ling's system of physical education in Sweden was in part due to his own personality and way of life. A poet and a dramatist, he was also a student of anatomy and physiology, and saw the value of applying the findings of science to education. At the same time he commanded respect in the army as an expert fencer and he was an accomplished gymnast. He thus demonstrated in his own life that physical education was part of the education of a cultured and respected leader of society. All this, however, might not have been enough to ensure that his work survived him, had not his system of simple artificial movements without apparatus brought physical education within reach of the people at large. This popularization of physical education was not accidental but was consciously striven for and was formulated into a social policy. 'At a gymnastic establishment based on true principles, wealth as well as poverty, lowliness as well as greatness, are levelled; equality for the public good ought to prevail there.'[11] Ling's social thinking was thus in line with the peasants' struggle for education during the nineteenth century, and his system of exercises could be easily used in the many schools which parishes were required to establish under the law of 1842 creating a national elementary school system.

It was Ling's son Hjalmar (1820-1886) who was responsible for developing school gymnastics. His father had used some simple 'tables of movement' but Hjalmar arranged and systematized his father's work and, so that every part of the body from head to foot might be exercised in a single lesson, he devised the 'gymnastic day's order'. From his graded series of exercises, the 'day's order' could be made up of movements and positions appropriate to the age and ability of the class. Hjalmar Ling also invented apparatus for children so that large numbers might use it in a single lesson. Having completed his studies at the Institute in 1842, he was appointed to the staff in the following year and rose to be head teacher there. When the courses were re-organized in 1864 he was placed in charge of the section on school gymnastics.

Pehr Henrik Ling's greatest contribution to physical education was in the sphere of therapeutic exercise, but his own conception of physical education was not restricted to such exercise. Gymnastics for Ling embraced games and sports, many of

93

which he himself pursued, as well as the artificial movements which he devised. After his death, however, in 1839 it was just this restricted view of gymnastics which gained ground in Sweden and physical education settled down into a formal dull and rigid routine. Wheelright, travelling in Sweden in 1860, reported that although gymnastics was taught in schools it was not practised later; nor any cricket, rowing, football or boxing.[12] Even skating and ski-ing were not practised, at least by the town dwellers, until after 1863 when the first skating tournament was held in Oslo.

A number of factors operated to make physical education take this narrow road. The hard winters and few hours of daylight favoured a form of physical education which could best be done indoors and needed no daylight. Again, gymnastics and free standing exercises provided an easy solution to the problem of educating the ever increasing number of children that the rapid growth of the population entailed. Furthermore, in spite of the population growth, urban development in Sweden did not reach a stage where team games and other organized sports could evolve as part of the pattern of recreation of the middle class until the end of the century. Towns were small and crowded, hours of work for a great many people were long and family life was closely knit. All these facts militated against the evolution of organized sport which might have provided an alternative form of physical education as it did for the middle class in English Public Schools.

Perhaps the most important factor which led to the formal gymnastic tradition was the nature of the Gymnastic Institute which Ling set up. The royal statutes laid down that all who gave instruction at the Institute must be graduates of its courses, and the Institute had a monopoly of ideas on physical education. The founder and his written work were held in great respect both within the Institute and outside and a strong family connection persisted after Ling died.

Ling's immediate successor as Director was L. G. Branting who first came to Ling as a patient for treatment by medical gymnastics. He returned to the institute as a student and then as a teacher. He worked under Ling for more than twenty years and there grew up a friendship between the two men which was more like a family relationship than a professional partnership.

94

Anatomy was taught by Dr. J. P. Liedbeck who married Ling's daughter Jetta in 1833. C. A. Georgii who joined the staff as a young army officer in 1829 subsequently married the daughter of Liedbeck and Jetta Ling. P. H. Ling's son Hjalmar became a teacher at the Institute shortly after his father's death and his sister Hildur also joined the staff in 1848. This close connection between the Institute and the Ling family had certain advantages. Ling's ideas were developed and applied by people who had been bred and brought up with them and continuity was preserved. Branting brought medical gymnastics to a high level of efficiency and worked out a terminology for gymnastics which persisted well into the twentieth century. Hjalmar Ling developed school gymnastics, and Hildur Ling devoted some of her time to the physical training of schoolgirls. A disadvantage was that the paterfamilias was held in such great respect that gymnastic practice became stereotyped along the lines which he was thought to have laid down and progress was excessively timid. In the country at large gymnastics were not practiced after leaving school before 1867 and then they developed into a poor copy of the competitive gymnastics of Turnen and became the province of the expert. By 1900 the movement could only boast of 500 voluntary gymnasts. Within the elementary schools (Folkskolor) in Stockholm at the end of the century all children had formal gymnastic lessons daily and the older boys had military gymnastics and weapon training in the spring and autumn. Secondary schools were more generously equipped with gymnastic apparatus. Here too military gymnastics formed an important part of the curriculum and in 1900 all the specialist teachers of physical education in Stockholm and their assistants were officers in the army. At the G.C.I. the military bias was also strong.

After Branting retired in 1862 there followed a succession of army officers in the Directorship and it was not until 1946 that a civilian, Dr. Hohwü Christensen was appointed to the position. Fencing too, the physical activity at which Ling excelled, occupied a large part of the courses for students at the Institute. Even as late as 1940 amid the growing popularity of a large number of games and sports among school children and throughout Sweden, students at the G.C.I. were doing eight to ten hours of fencing a week, so strong were the traditions of P. H. Ling.

95

In Denmark a new impetus was given to physical education in the middle of the nineteenth century by two adult organizations, the Folk High Schools and the Rifle Clubs. The idea of a Folk High School was first published by N. F. S. Grundtvig (1783–1872) in 1832 in his introduction to *Scandinavian Mythology*. Himself a cousin of Henrik Steffens who influenced Ling so profoundly, Grundtvig became a leader of the romantic movement in Denmark and pinned his faith upon adult education. The first folk high school was opened in 1844 for the Danish peasant population of Northern Schleswig. National literature and history were an essential part of the curriculum. No examinations or diplomas were to be given, and the education was not to be narrow, vocational training, but the residential life for several months, the study of the Danish language and folklore were to give to ordinary people a sense of personal dignity and civic and national responsibility. The site of the first folk high school at Rodding on Denmark's frontier with Prussia was itself significant. The country had been governed for many years by German officials and upper class culture was predominantly German, so that the building of a folk high school there was an essay in Danish nationalism.

The Rifle Clubs (Skyttforeninger) were brought into being after an article by Valdemar Mønster had appeared in the Danish press in 1861. In this article he advocated the formation of voluntary clubs, like those within the English National Rifle Association, so that men liable to military service might fit themselves to defend their country. War, indeed, was not far off. In 1864 Prussia and Austria attacked Denmark for whom the war went ill. Schleswig Holstein and Lauenburg were lost to her and there was a period of deep depression throughout the country.

The depression was short-lived. A patriotic fervour for national regeneration took its place and this provided the stimulus for physical education. The folk high schools in particular responded to the slogan 'What has been lost without must be won within.' In 1862–3 there were but 505 pupils at the high schools, but by 1872–3 there were 3091.[13] At the same time an agrarian revolution took place. Measures for the freehold ownership of farm land were carried through and there was a fundamental change in the national farming economy

96

P. C. McIntosh

from arable to dairy farming and the rearing of livestock. Co-operative marketing of produce together with measures of social welfare such as health insurance and old age pensions were instituted before the end of the century. The folk high schools catered mainly for the agricultural population and introduced gymnastics first as a means of national regeneration and secondly to assist agricultural workers with their normal occupation. At first gymnastics on the German model with a strong military bias were used, but gradually they were replaced by a modification of the Swedish system, and a new attitude was defined by the principal of Vallekilde High School when he inaugurated the new gymnasium. He said, 'These gymnastic exercises are not at all designed as a form of training for a military or any other special purpose; nor are they intended merely to develop strength and agility in the human body; they aim at the improvement of the whole person. They will become a link in human education and training.'[14] The folk high schools were from the start motivated by high ideals in physical education. They led the break away from a narrow military drill, and because they trained teachers of gymnastics for the local Youth Unions their influence was very widespread in rural areas.

The gymnastics of the Rifle Clubs was naturally more military in character, but as the clubs were glad to avail themselves of leaders trained at Vallekilde and other high schools their programme broadened. The clubs did a great deal to popularize gymnastics by holding gymnastic displays in conjunction with their shooting competitions. In 1878 the Svendborg county rifle club arranged a gymnastic festival in which 1,100 gymnasts from 16 towns and 110 parishes took part. At first exercises were done in the open air and the programme was thereby limited, but in 1871 the first club gymnasium (Øvelseshus) was built and by 1897 club members had provided nearly 300 gymnasia which were being used by some 10,000 young people.

The regeneration of gymnastics in Denmark during the latter part of the nineteenth century was a rural movement and it took place among the adults and not in the schools. It was in fact resisted by those teaching in schools who were for the most part army officers. When the Folk High Schools began to adopt Ling's system in preference to the gymnastics of GutsMuths and

97

Nachtegall the conflict became acute. The Ministry for Church and School Affairs appointed a commission of three to recommend improvements in school gymnastics and to make plans for an institution to train men and women teachers of gymnastics. The commission consisted of an army officer Lieutenant-Colonel Amsink, a physician Alex Hertel, and Professor K. Kroman. They first visited the Central Institute in Stockholm and then went to Berlin to examine German gymnastics. Their report, published in 1888, included among its recommendations a suggestion that the commission should be expanded to prepare a Handbook of Gymnastics. When the new manual was published in the next year it followed the general principles of Ling's gymnastics and adopted nearly all the Swedish exercises, together with some that were in current use in Denmark. From that year onwards physical education in Denmark moved swiftly out of the army's hands, and became more and more like the therapeutic gymnastics of Ling.

In 1897 it was decided to set up a one-year's course in gymnastics to be taken by students who had done the State Teachers' Course (Statens etaarige Laerar Kursus). The new course was put under the direction of K. A. Knudsen, who had completed his two-year course at the Swedish Central Institute in 1891, had taught at Ryslinga People's High School from 1891 to 1895, and had been a strong advicate of Ling's Gymnastics. The army thus began to lose its hold over teaching posts in schools and training colleges. It maintained its grip upon the post of State Inspector of Gymnastics for some years, but on the death of Lieutenant-Colonel Ramsing in 1904, the post was given to K. A. Knudsen who was the first non-military man to hold it. Then, in 1909, the University of Copenhagen appointed Johannes Lindhard to be Docent in anatomy, physiology and the theory of gymnastics, and allowed students to take gymnastics as one of their minor subjects leading to a degree. Two years later a States Gymnastic Institute was set up to house the one-years' teacher's course and to accommodate the courses for university students.

In 1906 two visitors from Britain, Mrs. Scharlieb and Miss Ravenhill noticed and reported on the most significant difference between Denmark and Sweden in their attitude to the training of teachers of physical education.[15] In Stockholm Professor

98

Törngren organized the training of specialist teachers which lasted two years, but Herr Knudsen in Copenhagen maintained that teachers of physical education must be full and equal members of school staffs if the subject was to be given its due place in the curriculum. He therefore organized a one-year course in physical education primarily for elementary school teachers and consisting almost entirely of educational. gymnastics. This difference was of more than local interest seeing that by 1906 the training of women specialist teachers in Britain was already following the Swedish model. The training of men specialists which developed later and more slowly was similar in principle to the Danish system. These developments are discussed in more detail in Chapter 8.

It has been stated earlier that by the end of the nineteenth century Swedish gymnastics was dull and rigid in form and that by 1900 'Elite Gymnastics' could only boast 500 gymnasts. But already forces were at work which were to alter the character of gymnastics in both Denmark and Sweden and which also acted upon the general pattern of physical education in those countries. The first of these forces was the pioneer work done by women gymnasts. Courses for women at the G.C.I. were started in 1862. Elin Falk (1872–1942) and Elli Björksten (1870–1947) were both trained there, the latter after first training in German gymnastics at Helsingfors. Elin Falk developed school gymnastics for little children and made the first break with the rigid positions which had been the straight-jacket of Swedish work hitherto. Her three-volume work *Dagövningar Gymnastik för Stockholms Folkskolor* was published in 1915 and 1916. Elli Björksten gave gymnastics a more feminine form, made the movements more plastic and added an imaginative content to women's work. Her book, *Principles of Gymnastics for Women and Girls*, was published in 1918 and was widely used both in Scandinavia and England. The break with the past was courageous. A fellow student at the Central Gymnastic Institute wrote, 'No one who was not of that time can imagine how greatly the fear of spoiling Ling's creation prevented all development and killed all initiative for independent work.'[16] After this initial impetus women's work continued to go its own way. Agnete Bertram and Ann Krogh made further progress in Denmark. J. G. Thulin at Sydsvenska Gymnastic Institutet in Lund

99

developed work for little children and for women, and published extensive works on men's gymnastics. By mid-century Maja Carlquist with her girls from the Sofia club and Ernst Idla leading his group of Estonian girls had not only shown that gymnastics was capable of a specifically feminine interpretation and expression; they had also shown in public displays that women's gymnastics could be as impressive and spectacular as any work that men could exhibit.

The second force which challenged the existing gymnastic regime was the popular appeal which games and sports began to make at the end of the nineteenth century. The growth of team games and many modern sports and their organization under national governing bodies was associated with urban development and with the rise of the middle class to privilege and power during the nineteenth century. By the 1860's in Britain, Public School and university men were already refining and organizing many games and sports, and these same games were the recognized form of physical education in the Public Schools. The impact of games and sports was felt somewhat later in Denmark and Sweden but here too they were closely associated with urban development. In Denmark this association was very noticeable. It is true that cricket had been introduced by British engineers in the 1860's who were engaged on the construction of the railway from Roskilde to Copenhagen, and that thereafter open-air games were played in Danish boarding schools, but games and sports were not widely used in physical education until the Copenhagen Playground Association was established in 1891 to bring them within reach of elementary school children. In 1896 Wilhelm Bardenfleth, Minister of Church and School Affairs sent out a circular to all school authorities urging the introduction and regular use of games in the public schools. A few months later the Riksdag voted funds for three years to make the circular effective, and its expenditure was entrusted to a 'National Committee for Promoting Games among School Children' which was formally set up on 11th April 1897.

The association of games and sports with urban development was further attested in 1911 when the Copenhagen Sports Park (Københavns Idraetspark) was opened. About 22 acres were secured from the municipal authority to provide a swimming

100

bath, shooting galleries, exercise halls, indoor tennis courts, athletic stadium, hockey grounds and football pitches. By 1950 subsidiary grounds which had been opened in the suburbs covered about 300 acres.

At about the time of Bardenfleth's circular on school games in 1896, the Danish Idraets-Forbund was set up. This was to be a co-ordinating body for many different branches of sport which could draw up common rules for the conduct of amateur sport. As time went on the Idraets-Forbund performed many other tasks of common interest to the different sports federated to it. The word 'idraet' is an old Nordic word indicating activity which requires perseverance, strength and skill, and its use in this context identified the new developments in games and sports with the feelings of Nordic patriotism which had been such a powerful stumulus to physical education in Scandinavia during the previous century. The number of clubs and members of clubs affiliated to the federation grew steadily, particularly during the 1930's and by 1953 the D.I.F. claimed 4,242 clubs with 442,184 active members of whom 143,635 were children under fourteen years old. By far the most popular sport was football with 149,549 active members. Next in popularity came gymnastics with 41,243 members, then handball with 38,614 members.[17] In assessing the comparative popularity of gymnastics with other sports it must be remembered that many active gymnasts in folk high schools and clubs might not have been members of an affiliated gymnastic club, and many clubs concerned with summer sports, such as rowing, were running an intensive and popular gymnastic programme for their members during the winter months.

Indeed, one effect of the growing popularity of games and sports in Denmark was to stimulate further developments and a new approach to gymnastics in physical education. The most spectacular developments were made by Niels Bukh at his Gymnastic Folk High School at Ollerup during the 1920's. Bukh abandoned the 'held' positions of Ling's gymnastics, and in his so-called 'primary gymnastics' he emphasized continuity of movement, rhythmic exercise, and intensive stretching to seek elasticity, flexibility and freedom. In his 'apparatus' gymnastics he dispensed with much of the Swedish apparatus and used only wall bars, vaulting boxes and agility mattresses. The

101

teams of folk high school pupils which he took to many countries in Europe and America to give demonstrations created a profound impression and stirred up much controversy. By no means all of Bukh's innovations were accepted in Denmark, but his influence was marked throughout the country particularly in the use of rhythmic and linked exercises.

In Sweden the impact of games and sports on physical education was similar in many respects to that in Denmark. Pioneer work in the development of games in Sweden was done by Colonel Victor G. Balck who became known as the father of Swedish sport. In the 1870's he became keen to make Swedish gymnastics better known in other countries. He therefore took squads of Swedish gymnasts to Turnfeste at Brussels in 1877 and 1880 and in Paris in 1889 and 1900. During his journeying abroad in 1880 he visited England and was so impressed with the games and sports which he saw there, that he determined to foster them in Sweden. In the following year he founded the 'Sporting Times' (Tidning för Idrott) and through his influence sport began to gain a foothold first on military training grounds, and then in the country at large. As in Denmark, the need was felt for a central organization to co-ordinate amateur sport and on 31st May 1903 the Swedish Sports Federation (Sveriges Riksidrottsforbund) was set up. The word 'idrott' was again used, as in Denmark, to connote a Nordic ideal of skilled activity. The Federation grew at first but experienced some retardation from 1910 until after the first world war. From 1930 the increase of clubs and of club members was very rapid. In 1953, fifty years after its foundation, the Federation had 9,634 clubs and 810,002 members affiliated to it. Football was the most popular sport and 3,024 clubs were affiliated. Next came skiing with 2,006 clubs, then track and field athletics with 1,843 clubs and fourth was gymnastics with 1,667 clubs. A special association for school sport (Skolidrottsförbundet) registered 2,705 clubs.[18] Among the facilities which the Federation helped to provide two stood out. The athletes' Policlinic in Stockholm provided every club member with opportunities for health examination and advice, and promoted the study of scientific and medical problems in sport. The Sports Institute at Bosön, just outside Stockholm, provided the residential facilities for different sports organizations to run courses for leaders and for active athletes. 102

The growth of sports in Sweden stimulated a renaissance of gymnastics. On the one hand many sportsmen who were denied their recreation in the winter months were keen to use gymnastics as alternative training. On the other hand the gymnastic leaders, faced by the growing popularity of other physical recreations, were forced to think out afresh the fundamentals of their own profession. A freer kind of gymnastics, sports gymnastics (Idrott gymnastik), was evolved and the first steps were taken to apply gymnastics to the special needs of specific groups. Reinforced by its association with the Sports Federation, by monetary grants and by propaganda campaigns, gymnastics in its applied forms gained ground steadily in the twentieth century. 'Sport for all' was followed by 'gymnastics for all.' Gymnastics for shop assistants and typists, gymnastics for business men, gymnastics in the home, gymnastics for the middle-aged all showed a rising number of participants.

The Swedish Gymnastics Association was founded in 1904. By 1918 there were 8,000 members and by 1936 there were 138,000 and Housewives' Gymnastics, which mustered an initial 17 in 1942, claimed 30,000 participants in 1945.

The Sports Institute at Boson was built to cater for sports other than gymnastics and the Gymnastic Association inaugurated its own gymnastic folk high school at Lillsved on the Stockholm Archipelago in 1937. The courses there were designed not to train competitive gymnasts or sports teachers, but to take members of youth clubs, give them experience of gymnastics, and return them as trained but unpaid leaders of gymnastics to their clubs up and down the country. The movement towards 'gymnastics for all' in the 1930's became part of a folk health and hygiene movement. Propaganda for gymnastics was associated with propaganda for personal cleanliness, the building of vapour baths, a balanced diet and healthy living. The influence of these developments outside the schools had some effect upon the work within. Gymnastics became less formal and less rigid; skiing trips with cheap travel and accommodation were arranged; the government permitted a number of 'outdoor days' which schools could use when and how they liked; in many schools a summer programme of sports and athletics was arranged. Nevertheless in 1949 the physical education of schoolchildren was still dominated by gymnastics.

H   103

The rapid and varied development of the physical education of both adults and schoolchildren in Scandinavia during the first half of the twentieth century was in part due to progressive social legislation and the liberal policies of the governments, but there were other factors bearing more directly upon physical education. The central federations of sports clubs in Denmark and Sweden have been described already. Their contribution to education was enhanced by the provision of incentives and facilities. In both countries a Sports Badge was instituted (Idraets maerk in Denmark and Idrottsmärk in Sweden) and in Sweden by 1952 badges, bronze, silver and gold had been won by 194,500 men and 37,000 women. The provision of facilities by the Federations became more generous after they were granted a percentage of the takings from nationalized football pools. In Sweden the first time that a sum of any significance was placed at the disposal of the sports movement was in 1908 when the Central Association for the Promotion of Sport was granted permission to hold a lottery. In 1931 the lottery funds were handed over to the Sports Federation and in 1934 the Government controlled Tipstjänst Company began to operate football pools. Each year thereafter the government allocated a percentage of the takings to the Federation for the provision of facilities for games and sports and for other purposes such as participation in the Olympic Games. By 1948 more than £11,000,000 had been made available in this way.[19] It was in 1948 that Denmark passed her own Pool-Betting Act which enabled Danish physical recreation to benefit in a similar way.

Similarities in the development of physical education in Denmark and Sweden are obvious. Many features of this development would have rejoiced the heart of P. H. Ling. He himself had not had a rigidly gymnastic outlook; he would have welcomed the impact of games and sports upon physical education; he would have welcomed the attempts to popularize gymnastics and to apply them to the specific needs of different groups within the community; above all perhaps he would have welcomed the physiological research that was started by Professor Lindhard at the Central Gymnastic Institute in Copenhagen and was thereafter pursued in Stockholm as well. There were, however, differences of development in the two countries, and one of the most noticeable was the more rigid adherence of

104

Sweden to the gymnastic tradition which centred around the memory of P. H. Ling. In 1941 the Central Gymnastic Institute in Copenhagen changed its name to The High School for Physical Activities (Danmarks Højskole for Legemsøvelser) to indicate that its object was to train teachers in all the different categories of physical exercise used in the schools. The term 'Højskole' was used to bring the title into line with the titles of other institutions of higher education in Denmark, such as the 'tekniske Højskole' and the 'pharmaceutiske Højskole'. The facilities included two gymnasia, a swimming bath with a learners' pool, and a large sports hall with a sand pit and equipment for athletic training indoors. By contrast, when the Central Gymnastic Institute was rebuilt on a new site near the Olympic Stadium in Stockholm in 1944 the buildings erected consisted of laboratories, daytime accommodation for students and staff, and four fully equipped gymnasia. Games and sports were not neglected in the curriculum of students at the Institute, but most of the training in those activities was done elsewhere. A swimming bath and other facilities were included on the plans but had not been erected by 1950. The four gymnasia, however, were in constant use both by students in the Institute and by outside organizations, so strong was the gymnastic tradition which P. H. Ling had fostered.

In both countries, whatever differences of approach there were, and whatever the general pattern of physical recreation was, gymnastics, after a hundred and fifty years of development, continued to be the basis of physical education. They had started as a form of military training and of therapy, they had grown to be a means of systematic development and then became a robust and vigorous activity in their own right. In both countries gymnastics developed hand in hand with other features of life, in particular, a regard for adult education, and high standards of hygiene in home and school and in daily life. The close connection between gymnastics and health was one of the main ideals of early pioneers and was a striking feature of subsequent developments. Finally, in both countries, the growing popularity of alternatives to gymnastics as means of physical education and recreation in the form of games and sports resulted not in the decline of gymnastics but in their regeneration.

105

REFERENCES

1. S. F. Markham, *Climate and the Energy of Nations.* Oxford 1947.
2. B. J. Hovde, *The Scandinavian Countries 1720–1860,* p. 209. New York 1948.
3. S. Prytz, *P. H. Ling og hans gymnastikpedagogiske Indsats.* Copenhagen 1941.
4. A. Wiberg, *Gymnastikhistoriska Studier.* Vaxjo 1942.
5. C. J. Tissot, *Gymnastique Medicinale et Chirurgicale.* Paris 1780.
6. This poem, written during the period under review, was not published until 1814.
7. B. J. Hovde, *op. cit.,* p. 456.
8. A. Wiberg, *op. cit.,* p. 113.
9. A. Wiberg, *op. cit.,* p. 10.
10. A. Svahn, 'Pehr Henrik Ling—His Life and Work', *Journal of Physical Education,* Vol. XLI, No. 122, March 1949.
11. C. A. Westerblad, *Ling, the Founder of Swedish Gymnastics.* Stockholm 1909 (English translation: London 1909, p. 39.)
12. B. J. Hovde, *op. cit.,* p. 765.
13. H. Begtrup, H. Lund and P. Manniche, *The Folk High Schools of Denmark and the Development of a Farming Community,* p. 133. Oxford 1929.
14. H. Begtrup, *et. al., op. cit.,* pp. 64–65.
15. M. Scharlieb and A. Ravenhill, 'Physical Training in Stockholm and Copenhagen' in *Nineteenth Century.* December 1906.
16. E. Björksten, *Principles of Gymnastics for Women & Girls.* Helsingfors 1918. (English translation 1937. Part I, p. vi.)
17. *Dansk Idraets-Forbund Aarbog* 1953, p. 107.
18. *Sveriges Riksidrottsforbund Overtyrelses Berättelse,* 1952–3, pp. 6–7.
19. *The Official F.A. Yearbook 1950–51,* p. 6.

See also:—

Hansen, E. *Danmarks Højskole for Legemsøvelse.* Copenhagen 1947.
Hansen, E. *Sports in Denmark,* Copenhagen 1956.
Hedley, G. W. and Murray, G. W. *Physical Education in Denmark and Sweden.* London, H.M.S.O., 1935.
Holmström, A. *Swedish Gymnastics To-day.* Stockholm 1949.
Leonard, F. E. and Affleck, G. B. *A Guide to the History of Physical Education.* Springfield Edition 1947. Chaps. 15–18.
Swedish Sports Federation. *Sweden, A Land of Sports.* Stockholm 1949.
Van Dalen, D. B., Mitchell, E. D. and Bennett, B. L. *A World History of Physical Education,* Chaps. 15, 16. New York 1953.

106

VI

Prussia, Politics and Physical Education

J. G. DIXON

∞∞∞∞∞∞∞∞∞

1. BEFORE 1700

ALL the communities which this book discusses engaged frequently in war, and the arts of homicide influenced to some extent their systems of physical education. The warrior-aristocrat and the mercenary require to master a variety of physical skills, and have ample time in which to do so. But until recently only small minorities in any community have had much leisure to practise unproductive arts of peace. Despite this handicap creative impulses too have always been at work, and have redeemed the history of physical education. However laborious the life of the masses, their young have always found some time for physical recreation; and whenever a leisured minority has been free to reflect upon human destiny it has tended to evolve an ideal in which physical as well as mental qualities were important. The interplay of creative and destructive influences is seen clearly in the history of physical education in Germany.

Two thousand years ago the ancestors of the present-day Germans were a group of warlike tribes pressing on the Rhine-Danube frontier of the Roman Empire. Plutarch [1] relates that the first glimpse of these tall warriors so disconcerted Marius' legionaries that he had to avoid battle until they were used to the sight of the new foe. Fifty years later Caesar reported, 'Their whole life consists of war and hunting.'[2] They practised from earliest youth throwing, jumping, riding, swimming,

107

and fencing. They had picked troops of runners who loped into battle with the cavalry, grasping in one hand the horses' manes.

Tacitus praised their morals, whose object was to preserve racial vigour. Both youths and maidens were virtuous, and did not mate until they reached full maturity. 'The man at the height of his powers pairs with a healthy woman, and the children testify to the bodily strength of their parents.'[3] But though chaste, they were not prudish, and bathed naked in the cold streams.

Were they really like this? Perhaps; but it should be remembered that Tacitus was a sophisticated Roman seeking in a primitive race the virtue which he felt that the urban Roman stock had lost. What is important is that from such sources Germans have in recent times formed an ideal picture of their origins which has influenced them deeply.

Physical prowess is the hallmark of the warrior-heroes of all the German myths and sagas. In the Nibelungenlied Brunhilde's suitors have to compete with the doughty maiden in stone-throwing, spear-throwing, and ditch-jumping. Siegfried alone is able to overcome her. It is worth noting that many German women's names are fighting names. The roots 'hild', 'wig', and 'gund' all refer to battle.

During the migrations every man and almost every woman was a fighter. When a feudal system arose, physical prowess became the prerogative of the knight, and the peasant's lot was hard labour. Yet the overburdened peasantry kept alive an immemorial tradition of games and pastimes. Above all they loved dancing; and they danced far into the summer night with an abandon which would make twentieth century bebop enthusiasts look tame.

Medieval Christianity despised the flesh, and physical education had no place in the curriculum of the monastery schools. Knightly schooling, on the other hand, was based upon the seven accomplishments of the 'Ritterspiegel'—riding, swimming, shooting, climbing, jousting, fencing, and courtly manners. From the thirteenth to the fifteenth centuries the growth of towns led to the emergence of a prosperous middle-class, which emulated the aristocracy in manners and accomplishments. This extended the social area of physical education.

The Renaissance brought an intellectual liberation which

108

included a more respectful attitude towards the human body. In England and Western Europe this liberation went hand in hand with a great increase in wealth and power, but in Germany it was accompanied by a dramatic decline. The opening of ocean trade-routes led to the decay of the Hanseatic League. The German middle class and aristocracy were alike impoverished. Germany became a power-vacuum, and suffered the protracted horror of the Thirty Years War (1618-1648). Its cities were laid waste, and its population reduced by a third.

This may explain why the enlightened attitude of German humanists such as Camerarius towards physical education had scarcely any practical consequences. The churches, which controlled popular education in the sixteenth to eighteenth centuries, were strongly hostile to physical education. Warning tracts about the folly of various games and pastimes were written. The wickedness of bathing was a theme of recurrent comminations.

In the seventeenth century German culture was largely imitation-French. The German princes built little Versailles and moulded their behaviour on the French ideal of the 'galant homme'. This necessitated a modicum of skill in riding, dancing, and fencing, which they acquired in 'Ritterakademien'. The cultured middle-classes visited the universities. Seeking to emulate the aristocracy, they took from them the French 'point d'honneur', and started the vicious fashion of sabre-duelling which has persisted until to-day.

These stilted and snobbish forms of physical education were barren and dead even at that time. But in France the current of humanist thought was flowing strongly, and in the following century German educationists drew from it the inspiration for a great movement of educational reform. It included a new and creative approach to physical education.

2. BASEDOW AND THE PHILANTHROPINE SCHOOLS

During the eighteenth century the German middle-class gradually began to regain a little of the strength and confidence which it had lost in the sixteenth and seventeenth centuries. The influence of French humanism spread widely. Above all stood Rousseau's *Emile ou de l'education*. There emerged, too, the

109

educational movement of the Philanthropists, whose leader was Johann Bernhardt Basedow (1724–90).

Basedow was a highly unconventional person, at once cynical and idealistic, with a burning zeal for human advancement.

In the fourth volume of his massive *Elementarwerk* he dealt with physical education. He emphasized the importance of handwork and manual activities, and continued 'So away with you vowel-books, Donatuses, pot-bellied grammars, phrase-books, expounding, analysing, imitating, varying, memorizing, reciting, being beaten!' and 'Welcome physical education, many-faceted experience, healthy commonsense, youthful delight, exercise in manners without superfluous moralizing, love of God without hypocrisy!'[4]

In 1774 he founded in Dessau the 'Philanthropinum': Its avowed aim was to develop 'a healthy and well-exercised mind and a pure conscience in a healthy and well-exercised body'. But his temperament was too fiery and uncontrolled for him to be a tolerable colleague, and he laid down the leadership of the school four years later. His assistants Campe, von Wolke, and Neuendorf carried on the school until 1793, and were successful pioneers of his ideas. They sought to replace the arduous intellectual grind of the 'Gymnasium', with its endless Latin and Greek studies, by the effortless and joyful acquisition of knowledge through activity. In fact it is here that 'activity methods' and 'learning by doing' originated. Lessons were alternated with gymnastics, games, and excursions.

The two gymnastic teachers in Dessau were Simon and Du-Toit. Simon worked out a first syllabus of exercises subdivided into age-groups; Du-Toit extended it. Peter Villaume, another gymnastic teacher who spent a short time at Dessau, later wrote the first thorough treatise on this new aspect of education. It appeared in a ten-volume *General Review of the Entire School-and Educational-System* by Campe, Trapp, and Stuve. It was entitled, 'On the Cultivation of the Body with a View to the Perfection and Happiness of Men, or on Physical Education in Particular.' This book later had a considerable influence upon GutsMuths.

Basedow was temperamentally incapable of team-work, yet his genius drew a highly-gifted group of young teachers to Dessau and provided them with an inspiration which lasted throughout their lives. One of these was Salzmann (1744–1811). In 1784 he founded his own school in Schnepfenthal, at the foot of the Thuringian forest; he avowedly took Dessau as his pattern. His biographer says, 'Since he knew the high value of bodily health for mental happiness, his first care was devoted to the bodily hygiene of his pupils. The healthy situation of Schnepfenthal, the light and cheerful living-rooms, class-rooms, and bedrooms, the good water, and the simple and nourishing food, in themselves contributed to this end, but there were in addition special features. These included early rising and going early to bed, pauses of ten minutes between lessons when the pupils romped in the open, and much other open-air activity— on the average three hours a day—such as gardening, bathing, swimming, snowball fighting, sledging and skating, school-outings, and above all an hour of gymnastic exercises daily.'[5]

In 1786 Salzmann offered a post on his staff to a visiting tutor. The tutor, who was GutsMuths, accepted. He remained at Schnepfenthal for the rest of his working life. In and through him the powerful creative impulse of the eighteenth century in the field of physical education came to full fruition.

3. *GUTSMUTHS*

Johann Christoph GutsMuths (1759–1839) was the only son of a dyer. As a child he enjoyed much affection, having several sisters and an adoring mother. He was studious and well behaved. Before he joined Salzmann's staff he had been tutor to the two sons of the widowed Frau Ritter. He was devoted to her and continued as tutor to her boys even when she was unable to pay him a salary. Industry, loyalty and affection were salient qualities in his character.

At Schnepfenthal he soon revealed himself as a teacher of genius and a skilful propagandist. His principal subject was at first geography, but a year after his arrival he took over gymnastics also. He inherited a good deal of both theoretical and practical experience. Basedow and Villaume had written books about physical education. Salzmann was able to pass on to GutsMuths the practical knowledge which had been acquired by Du-Toit and other teachers at Dessau and Schnepfenthal. By sensitive observation of his charges, and continuous creative

111

experiment, GutsMuths built upon this foundation the most complete system of physical training for schoolchildren which the world had till then seen.

The first of his fundamental writings appeared seven years after he had begun to teach at Schnepfenthal. It was called *Gymnastik für die Jugend*. Its motto was an implicit attack upon the attitude of the Churches:'You teach religion and civic sense, but for bodily health you don't care twopence!' Part I of the book is mainly concerned to amplify this statement. He asserts that orthodox educational methods neglect the body and practise an excessive 'refinement' which leads to debility. But body and mind interact intimately and continuously upon one another. Education must therefore seek to promote harmony between them. Part II opens with the sentence, 'Gymnastics is work in the garb of youthful joy.' He recognizes three main types of physical education—gymnastics, manual work, and games. He subdivides gymnastic exercises into eight types— jumping, running, throwing, wrestling, climbing, balancing, lifting, and dancing or drilling. Part III deals with bathing, swimming, reading aloud, exercises to promote presence of mind, and exercises for the senses. Finally he gives hints on method, arranges the exercises according to the parts of the body affected, and in the second edition adds a defence of physical education for girls.

His second main work is the *Spielbuch*, which describes many games which he had observed in Germany, or collected from foreign books. He classifies them into Lively and Quiet Games. He deals at length with the nature of play, and concludes that it is a special recreative form of the impulse to action. It is morally neutral, depending entirely upon the nature of the emotions aroused, and upon the degree to which skill rather than chance determines the outcome. For a child it is the only natural form of activity, work being an unnatural employment for a child. Games are a microcosm of human life. In them the child is rubbed smooth like a pebble in the stream, and made fit for social life. It acts without the inhibitions which affect it in adult company, and reveals qualities which at other times are hidden. Games are thus a fruitful field of observation for an educator, and a means whereby he can win the hearts of children. But they do have their dangers, in that by excessive

112

Swedish gymnastics being performed by the Sophia girls' team led by Madame Carlquist in 1947.

Keystone Press Agency

[*face page 112*

"The leap in length, with and without a pole"—
an illustration from *Gymnastik für die Jugend* by
Guts Muths—published in 1793.

[*face page 113*

addiction to them a child may so exhaust itself as to be incapable of mental activity. It is the function of the teacher to avoid such excesses. 'Games are flower-chains with which one binds youth to oneself; therefore I give them rather into the hands of the teacher than of the children themselves.'[6]

His third important book is *Ein Kleines Lehrbuch der Schwimmkunst zum Selbstunterricht*. It gives practical advice on land-drill, habituation to water, practice in shallow water, and in deep water with appropriate support. 'Swimming,' he says, 'must become a main feature of education. Hitherto drowning has been fashionable, because swimming is unfashionable.'[7]

GutsMuths continued to teach gymnastics at Schnepfenthal up to the age of seventy-six. In his later years his fame was rather overshadowed by that of Jahn, who took this new form of education, re-labelled it 'Turnen', and made it the instrument of a national movement with profound political and social implications. But though Jahn plucked the fruit, it was GutsMuths who ripened it. His books were translated into many languages, and had a widespread influence abroad.

4. JAHN

Johann Friedrich Christoph Ludwig Jahn (1778–1852), a clergyman's son, was born in Lanz bei Lenzen, a village in the corner of Prussia close to the boundaries with Hanover and Mecklenburg. At school his rebellious character brought him into continual clashes with his schoolmates and teachers. When Jahn left school his father wanted him to become a clergyman, but he himself wished to study law. After an unhappy year at home a compromise was reached whereby he was to study theology at Halle but had permission to study other subjects in addition.

From 1796 until 1810 Jahn's career was a chequered one. He gave up serious study after two years and, until 1803, endeavoured to reform student life which was at that time dominated by the Students' Corps (Verbindungen). To this end he founded a new secret student order, the Unitisten. In 1803 the university authorities terminated his career as a student and Jahn went to live as a house tutor to Baron von Lefort in Mecklenburg. While he was there, he tried out various physical

113

activities with his pupils. He then fought in the Prussian army against Napoleon's armies, and he spent several years wandering round Germany trying to obtain employment and whipping up opposition to the French occupation.

In 1810 he published his *Deutsches Volkstum*, which may be translated as 'The German Way of Life'. It was a vigorous assertion of the superiority of everything German over everything foreign. It had an immediate success, and Jahn became a public figure. To understand this it is necessary to remember that during the seventeenth and the first half of the eighteenth centuries educated Germans had felt a deep sense of cultural inferiority to France. Manners were modelled on the French court, and literature was French pastiche. In the second half of the eighteenth century a growing admiration for things English marked the beginning of a break-away from this tutelage. Then, in the last two decades of the century, came the Romantic Movement; there was a splendid flowering of the arts, and a robust insistence upon Germany's separate cultural individuality.

But the Napoleonic Wars showed that this independence had no political basis. In 1806 most of the western states of Germany were organized in the Confederation of the Rhine under Napoleonic hegemony. In the same year Prussia declared war on France, and within three weeks was decisively defeated at Jena. These events inflicted a severe set-back upon Germany's nascent pride, or at least upon the pride of Prussia.

Seven years later the Prussian army had its revenge at the Battle of Leipzig. Doubtless the chief credit for this reversal of fortune belongs to Scharnhorst and Gneisenau, who had secretly reorganized the army, and introduced a system of short-term training which enabled them to put 300,000 troops into the field. But during the same period the journalist-philosopher Fichte had initiated a 'movement of national regeneration' in which Jahn played an important part. It is at least arguable that the propaganda of Fichte and Jahn strengthened the morale of Prussia's army of short-term conscripts.

The immediate personal benefit of the book to Jahn was the prospect of a teaching post in a college in Königsberg. For this, however, he required to pass an examination. The Minister of Education, Humboldt, recommended Jahn to the examining body in very favourable terms, but the result of the examination was disastrous. Jahn was found to be deficient in philosophic sense and clarity of conception, and weak in Latin, Greek, and Ancient History. His knowledge of Modern History, although extensive, was said by the examiners to be disorganized and subjective. As a teacher he was incapable of presenting his subject-matter in a consecutive form and maintaining due proportion. With the younger children these defects led to inattention and noisiness.

This critique of Turnvater Jahn on the threshold of his career is significant. He was neither the first nor the last of the German prophets to wield great influence on men's minds despite (or because of) striking mental limitations.

Turned down in Königsberg, he obtained a post at the Plamann Education Institute in Berlin. Here too, as in Mecklenburg, he began to take his pupils into the country out of school hours, and to devise games and exercises. In 1811 he opened the first 'Turnplatz', or open-air gymnasium, in the Hasenheide. The political objective, to make youth strong and resolute for the forthcoming struggle to throw off the French yoke, was already clearly formulated.

Two years later the opportunity for revolt arose with the defeat of Napoleon's army in Russia. Jahn hastened to join the Lützow Free-Corps, and played a leading part in the enrolment of volunteers. He left the rapidly-growing gymnastic movement in the hands of his assistant Eiselen. As an enroller of volunteers he was highly successful; as an officer less so. He clashed continually with the Junker regulars who were his superior officers, and at one crisis asked to be released from his commission. The Free-Corps did not play any significant part in the Battle of Leipzig, but on the rare occasions when it arrived in the right place at the right time Jahn fought with distinction.

He had become an influential public figure with astonishing rapidity. He took part in the negotiations at Versailles and at Vienna, and did not hesitate to express his opinions in his rough and aggressive way in the presence of Prussian Ministers of State. He returned to Berlin full of confidence, and determined to use his gymnastic movement to advance the cause of a united and constitutional Germany.

Meanwhile, under Eiselen's loyal care the 'Turnbewegung'

115

had spread all over Germany, and the number of clubs multiplied each year. It was a system of physical education whose content was at first borrowed largely from GutsMuths. But whereas GutsMuths thought in terms of the schoolboy and schoolgirl, Jahn envisaged the physical education of the entire able-bodied population, without distinction of class.

He took as his starting-point Fichte's plan for national education, in which physical education had an important, but by no means dominant place. Using this as his *point d'appui* Jahn launched his movement with the immediate aim of the physical and moral strengthening of German youth for the liberation of the Fatherland. He stated this aim without equivocation. 'Only when all men of military age have become capable, through physical education, of bearing arms, have become ready for combat through weapon-training, prompt to strike through new kinds of war-games and constant alertness, and battle-keen through love of the Fatherland—only then can a people be called militarily prepared.'[8]

But he was far from being a mere militarist. Above and beyond the immediate military aim he wished to use 'Turnen' as an instrument for the regeneration of German youth. 'Indispensable is education to true manhood, to rational thought, compassionate feeling, and self-reliant action. Only the harmonious development of the whole man can give protection against any and every form of physical and mental crippling and distortion.'[9] But the individual attains fulfilment only through strenuous participation in social tasks. Liberation from the 'French yoke' was for Jahn the first step towards the creation of a united Germany, free from feudal class distinctions and with a liberal constitution.

Accordingly there were no distinctions of rank or age on the 'Turnplatz'. All addressed one another familiarly as 'Du'—a revolutionary innovation in a country of such stiff manners. This egalitarianism was reinforced by the simple uniform of linen jacket and trousers. Respect was due exclusively to ability. The 'Turnlehrer' was often an artisan with little formal education. He won his position by superiority in physical strength and skill, and in qualities of character. He was expected to set an example of clean and temperate living. 'Frisch, frei, fröhlich, fromm' (alert, free, cheerful, devout), was the motto of the

116

movement).[10] The last adjective was a disavowal of atheistic or subversive tendencies, probably made necessary by the known radicalism of Jahn and other leading Turner.

The military objective led to a greater emphasis on weapon-training and scouting games than in GutsMuths gymnastics. But their importance should not be over-estimated. The scouting games were a means of occupying large numbers of youngsters for whom room could not be found on the over-crowded 'Turnplatz'. Jahn's big technical innovations were the introduction of the horizontal and parallel bars. He derived the former from observing how his pupils delighted to swing on the branches of trees; the latter was essentially an extension of the pommels of the horse. In five years of excited experiment he and his assistants worked out an elaborate system of spectacular exercises on these two pieces of apparatus.

Jahn also enriched the German vocabulary, not only with technical words—'Turnsprache'—but with others expressing the ideals of the movement. 'Volkstum' is the most famous of these.

In its political campaign the 'Turnbewegung' linked up closely with the 'Burschenschaften' in the Universities—the new students' movement which had grown from Jahn's 'Unitisten'. Jahn and Eiselen's book *Die deutsche Turnkunst* appeared in 1816, and was as successful as his *Deutsches Volkstum*. Chancellor Hardenberg conferred a pension of 500 dollars, later raised to 1,000, upon him, and he appeared to be going from strength to strength. But he had made powerful enemies.

The King of Prussia had been very willing to pose as the liberator of Germany in order to rally popular support for the struggle against France. He and his ministers had therefore given the radical Jahn temporarily a free rein. He had served their turn well, and they were willing to reward him suitably. But now they found him at the head of a mass movement whose aims alarmed them considerably.

In 1817 Jahn announced that he was going to give a series of twenty-one public lectures on his book *Deutsches Volkstum*. All tickets were speedily sold out. In these lectures he lashed the Prussian state with all the force of his reckless tongue. He did not hesitate to mention ministers and officials by name, including Von Kamptz, the chief of police. He received repeated

117

official warnings, but carried the series of lectures doggedly through to the end.

In October of the same year the Burschenschaften held a celebration on the Wartburg, in the course of which they burned a mass of 'un-German' literature, including some of Von Kamptz' regulations. The following year saw a bitter public argument about the gymnastic movement in Breslau. It ended in the gymnasia in Breslau and Liegnitz being closed down. In the spring of 1819, when Jahn wished to re-open the Hasenheide 'Turnplatz' after the usual winter interval, he was forbidden by the police. Shortly afterwards a student named Sand, who belonged to the 'Burschenschaft', murdered the dramatist Kotzebue. Kotzebue's plays were bad enough to make the deed understandable on aesthetic grounds, but the actual motive was political. He was a bitter pamphleteer against the 'Turnbewegung', and was thought to be a police hireling.

Von Kamptz seized upon this heaven-sent occasion. He closed down all the 'Turnvereine' in Prussia, and arrested Jahn in the small hours, as he was watching by the bed of his dying child. He was accused (after long delay) of complicity in the murder, and of heading a subversive movement.

He spent six years either in prison or under strict surveillance before he was able to establish his innocence and regain freedom. Even then he was required not to live in a town where there was a university or higher school, upon pain of forfeiting his pension. The prolonged struggle against an unscrupulous and despotic state had broken his spirit. He withdrew from public life, and devoted himself to a history of the Thirty Years War, which he was never able to finish. (This might not have surprised his Königsberg examiners.)

The King of Prussia died in 1840. His successor was more liberal. He freed Jahn from all restraint, and raised the ban on the gymnastic movement. Jahn was able to enjoy a sunny old age as the revered patriarch of the 'Turner'. But the political crisis of 1848 showed that he was little more than a figure-head. The movement had left him behind. The socialist ideas of the younger generation of 'Turner' shocked him profoundly, and he withdrew again from the active counsels of the movement. He died in 1852.

His impact on history is thus confined, in effect, to the years

118

1811–1819. In this short time he created a movement on a broad social basis, using physical education as a means for the attainment of constitutional reform.

5. *THE BAN ON 'TURNEN' (1820–1842)*

Although it is customary to speak of a ban on 'Turnen' (Turnsperre) during this period, the truth is that in some states with a tradition of independence, such as the Hansa cities Hamburg and Lübeck, a ban was never imposed, while in others such as Württemberg and Bavaria it was lifted soon after it was imposed. Prussia maintained the ban during the whole period, but even there 'Turnen' persisted in various undercover forms.

Germans attach much importance to words. In any country one may give a dog a bad name and hang it, but in Germany one may sometimes save a dog from hanging by changing its bad name for a harmless one. Jahn's henchman Eiselen was aware of this, and opened in Berlin in 1825 a 'Fencing and Vaulting Salon'. The activities which he carried on there were indistinguishable from those which he had previously carried on under the name of 'Turnen'. But the label was different, and the authorities did not intervene. They were not so blind as might be thought. Their anger had been directed against Jahn the demagogue. Eiselen the technician they rightly held to be innocuous to them. He founded a similar institution for girls in 1832, and another for men in 1836. The following year he abandoned even the verbal disguise, and boldly published an illustrated brochure entitled 'Turntafeln' depicting all the exercises which he used.

The attitude of the doctors to physical education had changed radically since the namby-pamby days of the mid-eighteenth century, and Eiselen's efforts received powerful support from influential doctors. One of them, Doctor Lorinser, published a pamphlet 'In defence of schools' (1836). He argued that schoolboys, especially in higher schools, studied too many subjects for too many hours per week, and bore an excessive burden of homework. He claimed that as a result many of them suffered a decline in both physical and mental vitality. Many pens were broken in the 'Lorinser School-dispute' which followed this

I   119

publication, but the effect was beneficial. Next year the Prussian authorities gave permission for the introduction of physical exercises into higher schools, and three years later (1840) advanced from permission to recommendation. Thus the period of the ban actually witnessed an important step forward towards school physical education.

Pioneers were at work in other states. Klumpp (1790–1868) campaigned in Württemberg for school physical education. He also brought forward the idea of a system of 'Turnfeste' (Gymnastic festivals) building up from local to national level, which was later to bear notable fruit. In Saxony, Werner (1794–1866) paid special attention to physical education for girls, and developed a theory of modest and graceful movement—'Amoena' —which earned him some rough critical buffets from his colleagues. He was a life-long friend of Eiselen, and in their correspondence his other leading idea—that of 'Turnen' as an instrument for the spiritual unification of the German people— finds frequent expression. One passage in which he speaks of this is of interest. 'Uniformity of education' he says, 'must produce a uniformity of outlook, so that . . . the entire nation is fused to a single whole. Only then will the German people have a collective will, a collective strength, and a true national feeling.'[11] This kind of mysticism has always been an important element in the Turnbewegung, and its dangers are obvious enough to-day.

The poet-king Ludwig of Bavaria was a believer in educational reform, and expressed his enthusiasm for physical education and his contempt for the over-intellectual regime of the higher schools (Gymnasien) in flowing hexameters.

What! They call them 'gymnasiums' to-day, the places
Where Youth sits bound to a desk, while its body decays?
The name once meant a place where the body was strengthened.
The Greeks were people of deeds, we only of words.[12]

He revoked the 'Turnsperre' in the year following his accession (1826), and called upon one of Jahn's earliest disciples, Massmann (1797–1874) to supervise physical education. Massmann built an open Turnplatz in Munich on the lines of the Hasenheide, which was used by all the schools in the city. His conception of Turnen was out-door and romantic. He wished to

120

carry on the banner of Jahn. The task of the Turnlehrer, he believed, was to fire youth with the ideals of physical fitness, patriotism, and freedom. Despite his success in Bavaria, he longed to return to Berlin and continue Jahn's work in the place where it had begun. In 1841 the Prussian Cabinet asked his advice about the re-introduction of Turnen. He submitted a memorandum entirely in Jahn's spirit, envisaging the rebirth of a mass movement embracing all ages and classes.

The Cabinet, however, had taken the precaution of asking the advice of another gymnast, Spiess, whose ideas were totally opposed to those of Massmann. Spiess was a schoolmaster's son, who possessed in a high degree the pedagogic passion for systematizing human activity. He was by no means benighted— he had taught for eleven years in Pestalozzi's Burgdorf—but his approach to Turnen was entirely academic. Massmann wanted to use Turnen as a revolutionary weapon. Spiess merely wanted to absorb it into the school curriculum. His memorandum proposed that the subject-matter of Turnen be arranged according to school-classes and stages of development. There should be periodic examinations to determine promotion from one class to another. Colleges of physical education (Turnlehrerbildung-sanstalten) should be founded to produce properly-qualified teachers. An official syllabus and a team of inspectors would provide the necessary supervision and guidance. Naturally Spiess's memorandum appealed strongly to the authorities, while Massmann's inspired their deep misgivings. The introduction of physical education into Prussian schools followed substantially the lines which Spiess had laid down.

6. REVOLUTION AND REACTION (1842–1860)

As soon as the ban on 'Turnen' was lifted the movement began to spread again with astonishing speed and vigour. More 'Turnvereine' were founded in the 1840's than in any other decade. There were two reasons for this. The first was that most Germans were now convinced of the importance of physical education both as a means of maintaining health and as a form of pre-military schooling. (Relations with France were again strained in the early '40's and patriotism spurred many young Germans into the 'Turnvereine'.) The second was the rapid advance of democratic ideas. All over Europe the newly-created proletariat was sullen and restive. In England the Chartists were active, and in France socialist ideas were spreading widely. In countries such as Germany, whose structure was still feudal, the discontent of the proletariat was shared by many elements of the middle classes. This was the decade which culminated in the publication of the 'Communist Manifesto', and in revolutionary outbreaks all over the continent.

The 'Turnvereine' of the '40's were true to the Jahn tradition in that they were dedicated to the struggle for a strong, united, and free Germany. But many of them went a long way beyond Jahn in the radicalism of their outlook, and sometimes frightened the venerable 'Turnvater'. It was precisely this radicalism which was responsible for the swift increase in the numbers of clubs and in the size of their membership. Two examples may be noted. The Karlsruhe club, founded in 1847, already had 457 members in 1848 and 550 in 1849. Heilbronn was founded in 1845 and had 240 members in 1847. The membership of the clubs represented a fair cross-section of the middle and working classes. Apothecaries, bakers, clerks, doctors, firemen, shopkeepers, schoolmasters, labourers, carpenters, masons, representatives of all the professions, crafts, and trades figure in a typical list—that of the Dresden club in 1849.

One symptom of growing radicalism was the struggle over the 'fourth F', i.e. the adjective 'fromm' (devout) in the motto of the movement, 'Frisch, frei, fröhlich, fromm'. In the early '40's it was still customary to begin festivals with a divine service, and to use the Pauline saying, 'The body is the temple of the Holy Ghost'. But already in 1846 a gymnast published an essay suggesting that the adjective 'fromm' was obsolete and totally out of keeping with the contemporary spirit of the movement.[13] There followed a fierce argument, in which Jahn intervened with an equivocal defence of the adjective on the grounds that its original root-meaning was 'voran' (forward). This defence was in fact a complete abandonment of the accepted meaning of the word. The following year the Frankfort Festival broke up in disorder because it could not agree as to whether or no the sentence 'God has granted you long life' should be inserted in a message of congratulation to Jahn on his seventieth birthday.

These anti-clerical and democratic tendencies were strongest in the south of Germany. In the Prussian north the police-regime was too severe for such outspokenness to be possible. Even in the comparatively liberal states of the south and west the authorities took alarm, and ordered the dissolution of a number of clubs. However, the clubs usually reformed after a short while under a new name and carried on much as before.

There were indeed some leaders such as Georgii and Lion who urged that the introduction of party-politics into the movement could lead only to schism and disaster, but for the most part their voices went unheard.

The spirit of equality and of comradeship in the movement expressed itself in various outward forms. The familiar 'Du' became the universal form of address in the south, though some clubs in the north still hesitated. The greeting 'Gut heil!' was generally adopted, after a comic argument in which one of the suggestions put forward was 'GutsMuths!' The black, red, and gold colours (already associated with the Burschenschaft and the struggle for German unity in Jahn's prime) were proudly flaunted on banner and sash. A universal membership-card ('Turnpass') was devised, which would admit the holder to clubs anywhere in Germany. The gymnastic costume of belted jacket and trousers of yellow-grey linen was worn not only at club-evenings but at dances and outdoor excursions. The fashion prevailed of growing the hair long, cultivating a moustache and pointed beard, and wearing a soft black hat with a cock's feather. The general effect was reminiscent of Buffalo Bill, and certainly very dashing.

These were outward signs. Inwardly the 'Turner' must be characterized by a free and resolute spirit, and a simple and natural mode of life. The various gymnastic magazines of this period carried many condemnations of all forms of self-indulgence. Spirits, tobacco, and coffee were frequently singled out for attack. Clearly the 'Turner' looked upon themselves as an elite, a kind of Samurai, and their intellectual leaders wished them to impose upon themselves the discipline appropriate to the role.

The vitality of the movement was shown by its eager proselitization. Gymnastic festivals grew year by year more numerous and more ambitious until in 1844 Ravenstein proposed an

123

all-German festival. Political conditions made the proposal impracticable at the time, but the idea took root, and was never abandoned. Eventually, when Germany was united in 1870, it became a regular annual event.

The gymnastic festivals and other activities, in which clubs from larger or smaller areas participated jointly, made regional associations desirable, and these quickly sprang up. They were called 'Turnerbünde' (gymnastic associations). Inevitably the aspiration grew to amalgamate them all into a nation-wide association. This was in keeping with the political ideal of a united Germany which the movement had at heart. During 1847 there was much discussion in the gymnastic periodicals about the form of such an association, and particularly about the formulation of its aims in the statutes. Then in the spring of 1848 the Hanau club, which was one of the most vigorous and most resolutely radical in the south of Germany, issued an invitation to all other clubs to send delegates to a conference to discuss the question. Jahn attended the conference, and was its titular president, but the real leader was the moderate liberal Georgii. After long discussion it was decided to found a 'Deutscher Turnerbund'. The crucial point was Section 2 of the statutes, which declared the general aims of the 'Bund'. The radical elements wanted an outright statement that the movement sought to realize in Germany a government and social institutions based on the principles of liberty, equality, and fraternity. The more cautious elements wanted to avoid trouble with the authorities. Georgii eventually steered a compromise through. The paragraph read, 'The aim of the Gymnastic Association is to work for the unity of the German people, to increase the sense of brotherhood and the physical and spiritual strength of the people.'[14] Hanau was appointed the headquarters of the Bund.

Unfortunately Georgii's diplomatic finesse satisfied neither the right nor the left wing of the movement. The left held to their original views, while the right wanted all reference to political aims to be omitted. It should be said that many of the so-called 'right' were in fact entirely in agreement with these aims, but held it unwise to declare them in the statutes. The Hanau leaders thought it best to call a new conference expressly for the purpose of discussing Section 2. At the conference argument

124

centred round a proposal to include in the paragraph a reference to the desirability of a democratic German republic. Most of the southern clubs were in favour; the northern clubs, standing in the shadow of the Prussian police, were against. In the voting the proposal was defeated by 91 votes to 81. Those who had voted in favour thereupon withdrew and founded a 'Demokratischer Turnerbund'. The following year there was an attempt to reunite the two associations at a conference at Eisenach. A 'General German Gymnastic Association' (Allgemeiner Deutscher Turnerbund) was founded with a statute which it was hoped would please everybody. It merely made confusion worse confounded, for the clubs were now split into four groups:

1. Those who adhered to the original 'Deutscher Turnerbund.'
2. Those who adhered to the 'Demokratischer Turnerbund'.
3. Those who joined the new 'Allgemeiner Turnerbund'.
4. Those who would have nothing to do with any of them.

This typically German tragi-comedy reflected faithfully the political disunity of the country. For the declaration of a French Republic in February 1848 touched off a revolutionary movement all over Germany, in which gymnasts played a leading part. As a result a National Assembly met at Frankfurt in May with the task of drawing up an All-German constitution. After 9 months of acrimonious debate it produced a draft which the Emperor of Prussia and most of the Princes immediately rejected. We have space only to relate the sequel in Baden, where the people determined to implement the draft by force. Prussia and other big states reacted at once and invaded Baden. The Provisional Government in Baden sent out messengers appealing for help, and one of them came to Hanau. The Hanau Turnverein at once sent a company of 300 armed gymnasts to Baden. It grew *en route* to 600. For four weeks this unpractised and poorly-armed band held out against the finest army in Europe. But the issue could not be in doubt. About 240 succeeded in reaching the Swiss frontier. Most of the remainder were killed in action, or shot as rebels after capture. Of those who crossed into Switzerland many emigrated to U.S.A. and became pioneers of the gymnastic movement there. Those who think of the German people as lacking in civil courage should bear in mind the story of the Hanau volunteers.

125

The collapse of the movement for a united, free, and democratic Germany had a disastrous effect upon the gymnastic clubs. Many were dissolved as the princes recovered their shaken confidence. But even in those which remained it seemed that the heart had gone out of them. The 1850's are a period of stagnation and decline for the gymnastic movement.

7. *SPIESS v. JAHN (1860-1880)*

In 1859 a threat from France once again brought renewed life to the flagging 'Turnbewegung'. Napoleon had conducted a successful campaign against the Austrian Empire in Italy, and now claimed France's natural Rhine-boundary. The various German states were as usual at odds with one another, and patriotic bosoms were full of care. There was a rush of new members to the 'Turnvereine', and the veteran Georgii summoned them all to a conference. It took the form of the first all-German Gymnastic and Youth Festival (Coburg 1860), and marks the actual foundation of the 'Deutsche Turnerschaft'— although the formal act took place eight years later.

In the same year (1860) a keen dispute took place on a point which, for a change, was primarily physical rather than political. Gymnastic training in the Prussian army was under the direction of an officer named Hugo Rothstein who had become acquainted with the Ling system in Sweden. Besides his army post he was also director of the Zentralturnanstalt (College of Physical Education) in Berlin. In both capacities he used his considerable talents as expositor and propagandist to spread the Ling system and to deride German Turnen as planless and physiologically unsound. He banished horizontal and parallel bars from his gymnasia, and put beam and box in their place. His two assistants in the Zentralturnanstalt were pupils of Eiselen, and protested vigorously. He dismissed them. The great 'Barrenstreit' then broke out, which lasted two years, until the Prussian Deputation for Medical Affairs formally pronounced in favour of the national apparatus. Rothstein's methods nontheless continued to be used in the Prussian army up to 1914.

Although the 'Turnbewegung' never recovered the radical audacity which it had in the '40's, its spirit was still decidedly liberal. The 'Turner' all detested compulsory military service.

126

J. G. Dixon

They were patriotic and anxious to serve their country, but as volunteers, not as conscripts. Moreover they could not tolerate the class distinction in the army, which was contrary to the spirit of their own movement. Their sense of pan-German unity made them strongly opposed to the Prussian-Austrian War of 1866, but they were enthusiastic or uncritical about the campaign against Denmark in 1864 and about the Franco-Prussian War of 1870–1.

The movement never tied itself to a political party or committed itself to any programme more specific than the attainment of a free and united Fatherland. Nonetheless the conservative parties looked upon it with suspicion, whereas the progressive parties supported and encouraged it. Naturally the 'Turner' reciprocated these attitudes, and at the Leipzig Turntag in 1863 the second greatest number of votes for the Committee of Seven was obtained by the radical Parliamentary deputy Virchow.

The Prussian Ministry made every effort to ensure that 'Turnen' in its schools was taught according to the methods of Spiess, and not Jahn. Spiess laid great emphasis upon 'Ordnungsübungen' (order exercises), which were consciously designed to promote a habit of automatic obedience. According to a reported conversation, 'He was decidedly opposed to Jahn's "Turnen", which he considered would help the Democrats. He expected a great deal from his "Ordnungsübungen", believing that by this subjection of all to a single will a sense of order would be fostered which would later prevent any revolt or rebellion against established authority.'[15] Spiess's 'Turnen' was in the most literal and exact sense 'reactionary', where Jahn's was liberal and progressive.

Despite the efforts of the authorities Jahn's methods were so strongly established that they continued in these decades to be used not only in clubs but also in many schools. But the effect of the ban had been to drive 'Turnen' indoors, and thus greatly restrict the range of its activities. The new gymnasia, built with public assistance and intended largely for school use, were all indoors. Spiess' system was convenient for the routine-minded teacher, and it steadily gained ground.

127

8. SPORT v. 'TURNEN' (1880–1914)

This period witnessed an unprecedented increase in the numbers of Germans participating in physical education. The Deutsche Turnerschaft alone grew from 170,315 members in 1880 to 1,263, 573 in 1914—and increase of 750%. At the same time many other associations engaged in various forms of physical education had come into being. There were the Workers' Gymnastic Association (Arbeiterturnerbund), the gymnastic sections of religious youth associations, associations for every branch of sport and for scouting and rambling. Neuendorff estimates their total membership at about 1.25 million.[16] Added to the 1.25 million in the Turnerschaft this gives a total of two and a half millions who were organized in associations for some form of physical recreation—an almost twenty-fold increase on 1880. Moreover a multitude of people engaged in physical recreation without belonging to a club. They swam or rowed in summer, and skated or ski-ed in winter. Statistics therefore scarcely indicate the full scope of the revolution in popular habits which had taken place.

In contrast to the 'Turnbewegung' the sports movement in Germany was completely spontaneous. It had no leaders of any consequence, at least up to the turn of the century, no political ideals, and no explicit philosophy. It was a natural reaction to new conditions of life. It also contrasted with 'Turnen' in being a foreign importation, not an original native product. The main games and pastimes, such as football, athletics, tennis, rowing, water-polo and competitive swimming, boxing, wrestling, and mountaineering, were all borrowed from England. Very often English consular and diplomatic representatives, business men, or students resident in Germany, personally introduced their favourite sports in the locality where they happened to be staying, and were leading members of German sports clubs. English sporting expressions were taken over wholesale. Cries of 'Foul' and 'Offside' echoed across German meadows. In Berlin the fashion went so far that notices of forthcoming sports-contests were printed in English.

Commercial interests were quick to cash in on the fashion, and to foster it. Exhibitions were held in Berlin (1882) and other

128

Facilities for physical education and recreation at a State University (Minnesota) in the U.S.A. They include the stadium, two field houses, football practice pitches, tennis courts, baseball diamond and fields for other activities.

Aerial Photograph by Dick Palen of Edina, Minneapolis

[*face page 128*

Cricket, a traditional feature of physical education in English Public Schools.

Picture Post Library

[*face page 129*

cities showing the equipment for every kind of sport from horse-racing to billiards. The newspapers too were quick to see the possibility of improving their circulation by sports-reporting. Headlines such as 'Vienna Cannot Withstand Berlin Assault' soon became a feature of back pages.

These developments roused the fierce opposition of leading 'Turner' and of others anxious to preserve the purity of the German tradition. They denounced sport as un-German, a symptom of Anglo-Saxon superficiality and materialism, a product of the land without music or metaphysics. They inveighed against its ruthless pursuit of the record, its domination by number and measure, and its fostering of egotism by the public praise (and sometimes rewards) granted to outstanding achievement. They decried its lack of higher ideals. They thought it deplorable that Germans should engage in physical activity as an end in itself, without reference to any lofty goal such as Freedom or The Fatherland.

The fact remained that sport offered large numbers of Germans physical and mental satisfactions which they could not find in orthodox 'Turnen'. Education authorities were systematically fostering the Spiess system in schools and in the Prussian Physical Training College (Turnlehrerbildungsanstalt) in Berlin. Schoolteachers who had been trained in this way were permeating the clubs, so that here too the Spiess system was gaining the upper hand. The wrestling, scouting games, rambling, and other out-of-door activities which had been so important a part of Jahn's methods had virtually disappeared. 'Turnen' had become restricted to indoor gymnastics of a highly formal and elaborate kind. The new generation wanted fresh air and play. They ignored the critics and continued to stream into the sports clubs.

As an indication of the scope of this development it may be worth while to give the principal sports associations with the dates of their formation. They are the German Rowing Association (1883), the German Cycling Association (1884), the German Swimming Association (1887), the German Skating Association (1888), the Reich Association for Athletics (1891), the German Fencing Association (1897), the German Sport-Authority for Light-Athletics (1898), the German Football Association (1900), the German Lawn-Tennis Association

129

(1902), and the German Ski-ing Association (1904). In addition there were four Rambling Associations.

The foundation of the International Olympic Committee in Paris in 1894 at the instigation of Baron de Coubertin gave a further stimulus to public interest in sport. At the same time it intensified and embittered the Turnen *v.* Sport argument. Coubertin intended the revived Olympic Games to be a means of drawing the nations together in brotherly emulation. But the Turner inherited the narrow and arrogant patriotism which had been Jahn's reaction to the French occupation. They distrusted international contacts altogether. Coubertin gave grist to their mill by omitting to invite a German representative to the Paris meeting. However, two years later Germany was invited to the first Games in Athens, and although the Turner declined to participate a 'Committee for Participation in the Olympic Games was formed with Dr. Gebhardt as its Secretary. This later became the German Reich Committee for the Olympic Games. The 'Turnerschaft' continued its resolute opposition up to 1908, although teams of gymnasts took part in the face of its stern disapproval. Then, as a result of press criticism, it agreed to take part in the 1908 London games. The outcome was unfortunate. The *Entente Cordiale* was at its most cordial, and the German navy scare was at its height. The German delegation had a rather cold reception from the public, and the gymnastic team gave a brilliant performance before empty benches. The Marathon race, with the spectacular collapse of the Italian Dorando who was first man into the stadium, gave a fresh argument to the opponents of 'record-sport'. The 'Turnerschaft' again declined to participate in the 1912 Games.

It was not until the turn of the century that the sports movement discovered a spokesman of comparable stature to the leaders of the "Turnbewegung'. Carl Diem, who became General Secretary of the German Olympic Committee in 1906, speedily revealed himself as such a man. He energetically counterattacked the 'Turner' on the subject of the 1908 Games, declaring that their reception in London was the result of their own arrogant behaviour, and in numerous press articles defended sport against its detractors. He made the point that while sports facilities for youth were still so inadequate it was foolish to talk about the dangers of excess. He pressed ahead with

130

preparations for the 1912 Games, engaging an American trainer
Kraenzlein for the most promising German athletes. When
results in the 1912 Games were still disappointing from the
German point of view, the Americans being apparently un-
conquerable in track and field athletics, he went with a commission to the U.S.A. to study conditions there. On his return
he published a book, *Sport and Physical Education in America*, which
gave a vivid picture of American sporting life. He made contrasting sketches of conditions in Germany, to the disadvantage
of the latter, and concluded with a series of eleven demands.
The first three were for a sufficient provision of sports-grounds
and swimming-baths, the training of special sports-teachers, and
the introduction of sport into schools.

In 1913 the Berlin Stadium was built, in anticipation of the
1916 Games. But the following year a larger argument began
which distracted both 'Turner' and sportsmen temporarily from
their esoteric dispute, and brought developments in physical
education to a standstill for five years.

It is evident that during the period 1880–1914 the 'Turnbewegung' had stiffened and become a conservative rather than
a progressive force. The victory of the Spiess system over that
of Jahn had contributed to this change. In addition the unification of the German Reich under Bismarck had fulfilled one of
the aims for which the movement had striven, and it was now
pledged to defend this Reich. Differences on this and other
questions between conservative and radical elements led to the
hiving-off of a separate Workers Gymnastics and Sports Association in 1896, which by the turn of the century had 50,000
members. Another symptom of growing reaction was the welling
up of anti-semitism in the movement. This was the cause of a
further split in 1889, when the anti-semitic Deutscher Turnerbund also broke away from the parent 'Turnerschaft'.

The failure of the 'Turnerschaft' to keep up a rate of growth
comparable with that of the sports associations compelled its
leaders in the end to realize that they must do something more
positive than merely denounce the evils of sport. They began to
incorporate more and more games and sporting activities into
their programme, though insisting very aggressively that they
conducted them in an entirely different spirit—namely that of
true German 'Turnen', as opposed to meretricious Anglo-Saxon

131

'sport'. A reaction set in against the formal exercises on the bars. Fritz Eckhardt tried to lead the younger gymnasts back to more free and natural types of movement. Gaulhofer later developed this 'natural Turnen' much further in Austria. Thus the younger sports movements permeated and rejuvenated the 'Turn-bewegung', despite its antagonism, with the result that it regained much of the range and freedom of activities which it had originally possessed under Jahn. But with the formation of a separate working-class organization in the '90s the parent-body lost most of the progressive and freedom-loving elements which were so vital to its political health, and became the willing tool of the imperial state.

9. PARLIAMENTARY WEEK-END (1918–1933)

The German military effort from 1914–1918 was gigantic, and her subsequent collapse was the more profound. The force which had united Germany in 1870 was the Prussian army, and the Prussian-officered Reichswehr had been the main unifying force ever since. During the war the titular authority of the Kaiser was a transparent disguise for the military dictatorship of the Prussians Hindenburg and Ludendorff. The Parliamentary parties did not overthrow this dictatorship at the end of the war. It decreed its own dissolution, and thrust the reins of government contemptuously into their hands.

Democracy thus lacked prestige and authority in Germany. Real power remained with the Junkers and industrialists, who despised Parliamentary Government, and tolerated it only as a temporary necessity. The mutiny of the fleet at Kiel and the Spartacus uprising in Berlin have lent some colour to the belief that a Communist revolution threatened Germany in 1918. But the far deadlier threat came from Right-wing organizations such as the Free Corps and the National-Socialists, who had plenty of powerful backers. Post-war Germany had no political stability.

Its economy was equally unstable, being deranged and exhausted by the immense war-effort. The majority of Germans refused to accept this factual explanation of their troubles, and blamed everything on the Treaty of Versailles. A steeply-graduated scale of taxation, such as both England and Ger-

132

many have to-day, might have sufficed to bring Germany's
finances on to an even keel again. But the Government failed
to impose it. The inflation of 1923 followed; it impoverished the
middle classes, but helped industry by wiping out its debts.

One might have expected that in these circumstances most
Germans would have been too worried and depressed to bother
about sport. But the contrary was true. The moment hostilities
ceased, the pre-war efflorescence of sport resumed its course with
a redoubled impetus. Young people streamed into the gymnastic and sports clubs. The flight from the towns to the country
in leisure hours assumed greater proportions than ever before.
The 'week-end habit' ceased to be a characteristic of the wealthy
few, and spread through the entire population. Youths and
maidens wandered in the woods and mountains with rucksack
and guitar. There were rowing-boats and canoes on the lakes
and rivers. Every village seemed to have its swimming pool. In
winter the trains to the mountains bristled with skis. All over
Germany playing-fields, running-tracks and gymnasia appeared.
Forms of sport which before the war had ranked as 'Gesell-
schaftssport' (upper-class sport) such as tennis, rowing, and ski-
ing were taken over by the masses. Germany threatened to
usurp England's traditional title as the 'Land of Sport'.

There were powerful psychological causes for this renewed
popularity of sport. Germans were exhausted emotionally as
well as economically by the war. Many of the more intelligent
and sensitive among them had lost belief in the future of their
country, and indeed of Europe as a whole. Theories of the
imminent collapse of civilization were current. Spengler's
Decline of the West (*Untergang des Abendlandes*) was the most
monumental statement of this point of view. Scarred by the
past and sceptical of the future, Germans sought avidly whatever relief the present could afford. The nineteen-twenties, in
Germany even more than in England, were a pleasure-seeking
decade. The search for pleasure took some perverse forms;
Berlin night-life was notorious throughout the world. Noel
Coward's song 'Parisian Pierrot', which summed up so well the
melancholy hedonism of this era, was written after a visit to a
Berlin night-club. But the search also took some healthy and
and instinctively sound channels—including sport.

Despite the deep-seated lack of faith in democracy, the pro-

133

gressive governments of the Weimar period (1919–33) carried through a great work of social reform and amelioration. The Eight-hour Day, comprehensive measures of state insurance, the building of houses and blocks of flats for workers at reasonable rentals, and the enlightened wages policy, all gave the masses a degree of leisure and freedom which they had not possessed before. These social advances were the seed-bed which permitted sport to flourish.

Sport also received direct encouragement from the Government on a generous scale. The liberal and socialist parties had always favoured the subsidization of P.E., and now were able to make their views effective. They were spurred on by doctors in the public health service, who were alarmed by the bodily deterioration of the population in the immediate aftermath of war. Shortage of food, accentuated by the blockade, had led to a greatly increased prevalence of rickets and tuberculosis. Medical research had clearly shown the value of sunshine and fresh air in combating these diseases. There was now universal agreement on the importance of sport as a form of social hygiene.

As always, there were military considerations. Germany's invincible army was disarmed and dissolved; the Peace Treaty set a narrow limit to rearmament. Behind the enthusiasm of Reichswehr generals for fitness of youth there was a fairly blatant *arrière-pensée*.

All these predisposing factors could not have brought about such striking achievements in a few short years had it not been for the existence of the Reichsausschuss für Leibesübungen with a clearly-formulated programme of action, and a propagandist of genius in the person of Carl Diem. The broad lines of the programme had been laid down already in 1917, when Diem was summoned from the trenches to a conference to consider post-war action. At that time it seemed to the Committee that its original purpose of promoting German participation in the Olympic Games could have no post-war relevance. They therefore decided that their role must be that of diplomatic go-between to the sports associations and the government, and in Diem's words 'the conscience of the people in the matter of physical education'.[17] The measures which they decided to advocate included:

1. A sports-ground law, proposing five square metres of sports-

134

ground, and one-tenth of a square metre of gymnasium-space per head of population, and one indoor pool per 30,000.

2. A daily sports lesson in schools.

3. A gymnastic-and-sports duty for youth.[18]

None of these measures became law during the Weimar period, but their persistent and energetic advocacy exerted a strong influence upon local authorities; the standards proposed in the 'Sports-ground law' were in fact attained in many German cities. The allocation of time to P.E. in schools became more generous, and the scope of instruction was greatly widened and liberalized.

In 1921 a Gymnastic-and-Sports Badge was introduced on Diem's initiative. He took the idea from the Swedish 'Idrottsmark'. It was awarded on the basis of five tests; there was some liberty of choice, but a running and a swimming test were compulsory. There were badges for youths and women, with tests of lesser degrees of difficulty. The institution of the badge was a brilliant stroke. It appealed enormously to a trait in the national character, and was an instant success. During the Weimar period over a quarter of a million badges were awarded.

Germany built most of its sports facilities in the years 1923–30 —that is in the period between the inflation and the slump. There is an instructive contrast between the economic policies of England and Germany in these years. English policy sought to maintain the credit of sterling by living strictly within our budgetary means. German policy, encouraged by optimistic American financiers, sought to stave off unemployment by ambitious schemes of public works. The most splendid memorials of this policy are the great sports-stadia which are to be found in every major German city. Diem borrowed the idea during his visit to Chicago in 1913, but the beauty, magnificence, and social idealism of the German stadia are native and original. The Cologne Stadium, opened in 1923, was the first, except for that in Berlin, and is one of the finest. It owes its existence to the enterprise of Dr. Adenauer, who was at that time Mayor of Cologne. He bought up the Prussian fortress-belt around the city at a low price during the inflation, and converted it into a green-belt. He then persuaded the British Occupation Authority not to demolish the old forts, but to allow them to be used as sports club premises. So the green-belt is dotted all round with

K   135

playing-fields. But its chief adornment is the Stadium, which occupies two square miles of ground, is bedded in woods and parkland; and apart from the athletic stadium proper offers a wealth of facilities for almost every kind of sport. It is an enduring source of vitality to the city.

Economic catastrophe overtook both England and Germany in 1931. The parsimonious English economy weathered the storm rather better than the spendthrift German. On the other hand Germany has something to show for its bankruptcy. Our solvency was by comparison barren.

Another notable achievement of the Weimar era was the net of Youth Hostels which rapidly covered the country. There had been a vigorous 'Wandervogel' movement in Germany since the turn of the century. It sprang from an impulse deep in the German heart, which had found many charming literary expressions in the romantic movement. 'The search for the blue flower'—the theme of *Heinrich von Ofterdingen*, a novel by Novalis, [19] had become a phrase which summed up a whole world of nostalgic and irridescent dreams. The Wandervögel pursued these dreams on foot, instead of on paper. They strolled out into the laughing morning, and when dusk fell sought shelter in barn or hay loft. Jealous of their independence of parental support— and authority—they tried not to spend more than a Mark a day. They would not touch tobacco, alcohol, or other stimulants. Like the wandering evangelists of the middle-ages, they felt themselves to be heralds of a new spiritual dispensation. But as the movement grew it became apparent that it would soon encounter a practical difficulty; it was outrunning the supply of barns and hay-lofts. An idealistic but hard-headed Prussian, Richard Schirrmann, put forward in 1910 the suggestion that every town should make available a hostel where young people could put up at a nominal charge. The purists were horrified, but the practical need for such an arrangement became ever more obvious. By 1914, 83 hostels and 2,000 camping-sites had already been provided.

After the war Schirrmann's assistant Walter Münker became Secretary of the Youth-Hostels Association. He furthered its growth with great skill. He succeeded in securing the support of central and local governments, of big business and of the trade unions. By 1931 the number of hostels exceeded 2,000, and in

136

that year there were more than 4,000,000 visitors. Many hostels were schools converted for the space of the summer holidays, but others were fine buildings in lovely situations. Thousands of young foreigners stayed in Youth-Hostels on their first visit to Germany. They glimpsed gentle and appealing aspects of its traditions. The present writer recalls sitting in the courtyard of a hostel by Lake Constance on a summer evening in 1929 and listening to a boy and girl entertain the sunburned young company with guitar and mandolin. All the bitterness of later years cannot efface the charm of such impressions.

Two developments of the 'twenties which were of importance for the training of P.E. specialists were the foundation of the Deutsche Hochschule für Leibesübungen in Berlin, and of institutes for physical education in the universities. Diem proposed the setting-up of the Deutsche Hochschule in a memorandum in 1919, and such was his impetus that a year later it was formally opened. An eminent surgeon, August Bier, was Rector, but Diem was the effective leader from the outset. The school was situated in the Berlin Stadium, where the facilities for P.E. were already good. In the next few years they were greatly improved by the building of the Sport-Forum, with magnificent indoor and outdoor swimming-pools, gymnasia, research laboratories, administrative and residential accommodation. (Many British servicemen have made acquaintance with these amenities since the war).

The Hochschule provided a four-year course with a marked scientific trend, and exacting demands in the way of personal achievement. It existed to some extent in rivalry with the Landesturnanstalt in Spandau, which alone had official recognition from the Prussian Ministry of Education. The head of the Spandau school was Neuendorff, a veteran Turner and Wandervogel, a traditionalist and a man with little sympathy for sport. There is no doubt that the technical lead which Germany obtained in sports coaching in the 'thirties was largely due to the Berlin Hochschule, which in addition to turning out its élite of four-year specialists provided hundreds of short-term courses for club-leaders and teachers, and had a flourishing research department.

The institutes of physical education in the universities came into being as a result of student-agitation. They provided

137

recreative facilities for students in general, and opportunity for those who wished to take physical education as a major degree subject. They were rather alien to the intellectual tradition of German university education, and even to-day have scarcely been fully assimilated.

The Workers' Sports Association was an important cultural factor in the 'twenties. Before the war it had been handicapped by severe restrictions imposed by the Imperial and Prussian governments, which heartily detested it. Now, not only freed from its shackles but actively encouraged, it grew mightily. Disdaining all co-operation with 'bourgeois' organizations it organized its own competitions, and even its own Workers' Olympiad (Frankfort, 1925). It had an excellent training-school at Leipzig, and enjoyed the fervent support of more than 600,000 workers.

Although Germany never had a feminist movement comparable with that of England, post-war Germany saw a greatly increased participation of women in life outside the home. In England women had set up their own schools and sports clubs; our women's colleges of physical education and women's hockey clubs are examples of this tendency. In Germany women succeeded in infiltrating the men's institutions and organizations. The Turnerschaft and all the sports-associations, save those for exclusively male sports such as boxing and football, admitted women on equal terms with men. The institutes of physical education of the universities and the Deutsche Hochschule were co-educational. On hundreds of running tracks sturdy nordic girls sped, baton in hand; they flashed from the towers of open-air pools, and flew between slalom-sticks on the white mountains. They slept innocently among men in the 'kameradschaft' of the Alpine huts. They walked naked on the beaches of Westerland and the Kurische Nehrung. The radical changes in dress, manner, and general bearing which resulted from this new freedom roused the grave misgivings of the Churches. The Catholic bishops met in solemn conference at Fulda to discuss women's participation in sport. They passed a series of resolutions forbidding the wearing of form-revealing dress, exercise in public, participation in displays, mixed bathing, and mixed rambling.[21] They do not appear to have been very effective.

138

The 'twenties saw the beginning of that remorseless pursuit of the world-record which has continued ever since. It led to a rationalization of training and movement comparable to that achieved in industry through time-and-motion studies. The level of sporting skill rose greatly in consequence, but there were many people who felt that this streamlined sport was no longer providing a release from the pressure of daily life. They felt it was just another form of Nietzschean over-emphasis of the will, at the expense of the more artistic and intuitive faculties of the soul. So argued the leaders of the rhythmic-gymnastic schools which acquired a large following in these years. These schools varied greatly in their origins and their approach to the subject. Bess Mensendieck's aims were hygienic and physiological. Laban was a professional dancer. The Loheland community looked upon rhythmic-gymnastics as a ritual of their collective life. But all shared a common dislike of sport and orthodox 'Turnen'. Bode, the most articulate and intellectually gifted, derived his ideas from the philosophers Klages and Palagyi, and his art from Dalcroze. Following Klages he held that the conscious mind was the tyrant of life. The modern age was enslaved by the rational intellect, and therefore doomed. He designed his rhythmic-gymnastics to be the basis of a new healing education which would restore the balance of the conscious and unconscious minds. He called his system 'Ausdrucksgymnastik'—literally 'Expression-gymnastics'. His aim was to express the invisible wing-beat of the soul spontaneously in visible movement.[22]

His technique of relaxation, and his theory that all movement must be of the whole body, and must originate at the centre and flow to the extremities, have been fruitful outside his own school. But the schools of rhythmic-gymnastics pitched their claims a little high, and their shrill squabbles sometimes reduced them to absurdity. Their following was almost exclusively among women.

The system of 'natürliches Turnen' which Gaulhofer and Margarete Streicher developed in Austria had a great influence upon gymnastics in schools. They too distrusted both sport and orthodox 'Turnen'; sport they considered to lay an excessive emphasis upon measurable achievement, and 'Turnen' they dismissed as acrobatics. Their point of departure was study of

139

children's own movement-impulses and spontaneous play. (This technique is as old as GutsMuths, and from time to time has been re-discovered.) In the first five years of school life they confined themselves to encouraging the free development of the child's urge to movement. Thereafter they introduced exercises for correction of defects and maintenance of good posture which were taken from Bode's rhythmic gymnastics. They also included swimming, walking, and traditional folk-games in their programme. They used gymnastic apparatus as obstacles which the child could overcome in its own way. Although Gaulhofer and Streicher's methods never superseded orthodox 'Turnen' in Germany they exerted a beneficial liberalizing influence. [23]

In physical education, as in politics and the arts, Germany of the Weimar Republic seethed with ideas and movements. There were some eccentricities and exaggerations, but they were the eddies of a vast creative effort, which has left a rich and living inheritance. The Republic came nearer to providing adequate physical education facilities for all its citizens than any other large country had done hitherto. It did so in the aftermath of war and defeat, and under the ever-present threat of economic collapse and political upheaval. This was no mean achievement.

In the autumn of 1929 a Wall Street crash signalled the onset of world economic crisis. The flow of American money which had sustained Germany since 1924 began to dry up. Many short-term loans, which private enterprise and local government had rashly been using for long-term purposes, were re-called. Germany faced the dreaded collapse. In the following year France withdrew its troops from the Rhineland. The two props of German democracy—American money and French arms—were removed, and Brüning, who had taken office to deal with the crisis, began to rule by decree. This event really marks the end of the Weimar Republic, but its simulacrum lingered on through various shifts of decree-government for another three years. Then the Roman Catholic von Papen engineered an alliance of Junkers, industrialists, and Reichswehr generals, which resulted in the appointment of Hitler as Chancellor. The same interests which had installed democracy in 1918, nominated in 1933 its executioner.

140

J. G. Dixon

10. *RUNNING THE MASTER RACE (1933–9)*

Hitler was a masterly mob-orator, who knew how to appeal to every popular German prejudice. The Party programme promised all things to all men, and was a thoroughly opportunist document. Hitler did not hesitate to secure the support of large numbers of workers by his attacks on capitalism while secretly drawing a subsidy from the German Coal Trust as a result of promises to rearm, and to destroy the Trade Unions. Paragraph 24 of the Party programme promised religious liberty. The Roman Catholic Church, which hastened to conclude a Concordat with the Third Reich, discovered too late the value of Nazi promises. It might be inferred that Hitler and the Party leaders were merely careerists, with no sustaining convictions. Such an inference would be wrong. Behind the lies and contradictions of their demagogy lay a coherent, if crude, philosophy. Its sources are to be found in Nietzsche's worship of power and cult of the superman, together with the racial mysticism of Gobineau and Houston Chamberlain. Hitler's *Mein Kampf* and Rosenberg's *Myth of the Twentieth Century* are the most important statements of its tenets, which may be summarized as follows:

1. History consists of a struggle between the 'higher' and the 'lower' races.

2. The Aryan-Nordic race is the 'highest', and the Jewish the 'lowest'.

3. Efforts to soften or avert this struggle by propagating a gospel of universal love or ideas of freedom, brotherhood, and equality, are symptoms of racial degeneracy. The struggle must be carried through relentlessly to its conclusion.

4. Germany, though not quite racially pure, is the most powerful expression of the Aryan-Nordic racial will. Its destiny is to unite the Aryan race and thereby to dominate the world.

As a first step towards the fulfilment of this destiny it was necessary to effect total mobilization of Germany's energies and resources, and put the country on a war-footing. To this end Goering introduced the Four-Year Plan. Its main features were economic, but it also proposed to revolutionize education, and give physical education the foremost place in its scale of educational values.

141

Given this educational outlook, it is perhaps not surprising that Hitler should have been successful in harnessing the enthusiasm and idealism of thousands of physical education teachers and coaches. No doubt many of them understood and approved his ultimate aims, but many more simply rejoiced naïvely in the unparalleled professional opportunities which opened before them.

It is a common misconception in England, which the Nazis sedulously fostered, that they were responsible for building Germany's magnificent sports-facilities. This is untrue. They took the credit for the achievements of the Weimar Republic. The Third Reich concentrated on building barracks and motor-roads. It could afford to do so, since the running-tracks and gymnasia were there already. But it made notable changes in legislation, administration, and organization.

In July 1933 Hitler appointed S.A. Group Leader von Tschammer und Osten 'Reichssportsführer'. Tschammer dissolved all left-wing sports associations, and confiscated their property. He put the others under a common roof-organization, the Reichsbund für Leibesübungen. For purposes of Party administration Hitler divided Germany into 'Gaue', and each 'Gau' had its 'Gausportführer'. The sports organizations thus lost their independence, and were geared in to the party apparatus.

Tschammer worked in close association with Baldur von Schirach, the Youth Leader. Von Schirach dissolved the left-wing youth organizations, and incorporated the others in the Hitler Youth, which has sole responsibility for out-of-school education of young people. Up to the age of fourteen this occurred in the junior department, the Deutsches Jungvolk, and from fourteen to eighteen in the Hitler Youth itself. It was based on a strenuous programme of outdoor physical education in which boxing, wrestling, ground-agility, shooting and scouting games were the main ingredients. The Youth Leaders also advised their charges as to which sports clubs to join. Each boy had an 'Achievement Book' recording his progress. The girls were similarly organized in the 'Bund Deutscher Mädel'.

Physical training was an important part of the duty of all members of Party formations. The S.A. had their own Sports Badge and Reich Sports Contests; the latter were the peak of a

142

massive pyramid of contests at all formation levels. They invented their own ball game, called Fight-ball (Kampfball). It resembled the 'bloody murthering pastime' against which Philip Stubbes had inveighed in strong terms.[24] They also had severe battle courses (Kampfbahnen) with high walls, palisades, moats, hillocks, grenade-throwing, pistol-shooting, and a sprint in a gas-mask to round things off.

Conscript service in the Reichsarbeitsdienst (Labour Service) was introduced in 1934, and military conscription a year later (in defiance of the Versailles Treaty). In both these services the conscript underwent a form of physical training designed to promote toughness and foster an aggressive spirit.

When he eventually returned to civilian life he found that the German Labour Front was taking a paternal interest in the physical welfare of the workers in his factory or business. The Strength Through Joy organization in fact did valuable social work, in a totalitarian way, through the provision of recreative facilities and cheap holidays.

Hitler's *Mein Kampf* shows in some passages an admiration for the English Public-School. He contrasted the intellectualism of the German 'Gymnasium' unfavourably with the English Public School's emphasis upon character-training. He appointed Wilhelm Rust as Minister of Education, and Rust announced that in future education was to mean physical education, first, foremost, and all the time.[25] He created a Department K (Körpererziehung) in the Ministry, and also attached advisers on P.E. to all the school departments. There was a hierarchy of advisers at different levels of local government.

This was no mere empire-building, for the Party soon revealed its determination to revolutionize the spirit of school education. Rust introduced a Third Period of P.T. in 1935. It was intended to be devoted to team games and contest-sports, and great quantities of equipment were distributed to schools to enable this use to be made of it. Two years later, after nationwide research, he issued a Directive on Physical Education. It decreed a daily P.E. period—the goal for which Diem had campaigned in vain throughout the Weimar era. Moreover there was to be no flinging of the whole school together for mass P.T. Classes were to be taught separately, and not more than one at a time in one place of exercise. The Directive laid down norms

143

of achievement in five departments of physical education—athletics, gymnastics, swimming, games, and boxing. The School Report carried a separate note on performance in each of these departments, followed by a personality-assessment.

The German higher schools ('Gymnasien') had an educational tradition of long standing, and proved rather intractable to the crusading zeal of the Nazis. Hitler therefore went on to create his own schools, the 'Napolas' (Nationalpolitischeerziehungsanstalten). They were designed to train an élite of young leaders. Here again Hitler drew his inspiration partly from the English Public Schools. The Napolas were usually situated by lake or sea, and were equipped with superb facilities for every kind of physical activity. Physical and political education were the two main subjects in their curriculum. They were highly selective, and their pupils were excellent physical specimens. There were Napolas for girls, too. Together with the 'Ordensburgen', in which selected adult members of the S.S. received further indoctrination, they constituted an educational apparatus for producing a ruling caste for a 'helot' state. (Eugen Kogon's book, *The S.S. State* makes this clear.) A final logical consequence of this objective was the founding of human stud-farms, in which eugenically-approved members of the S.S. and the Frauenschaft mated to produce the supermen of the future.

In October 1934 a 'Hochschulsportordnung' (Directive on University Sport) appeared. It made physical education compulsory for students in their first three semesters, and extended the provision of opportunities for voluntary activities in later semesters. It laid down the principle that physical education teachers in higher schools must be university-trained, and must graduate in two academic subjects as well as P.E.

Carl Diem must have watched all these developments with mixed feelings. He deserved more credit than any other man for the achievements of the Weimar Republic in physical education, and might reasonably have expected that the Third Reich would afford him even greater scope. Instead, he saw many of the most ambitious proposals in his post-war programmes taken over and carried out, while he personally was thrust into the background and Party figures such as Tschammer stole the limelight. Diem had two defects from the Nazi point of view. He was not a Party man, and he did not share its racial theories.

144

His fame was associated with the Weimar Republic, and he moved in patrician rather than Party circles. He was friendly with eminent Jewish patrons of sport such as Lewald, the President of the Olympic Committee. More seriously, he had married one of his most talented women students at the Deutsche Hochschule, Lieselotte Diem (later to become a pioneer of small children's physical education), who was of partly Jewish extraction. Diem was relieved of his post as Pro-Rector of the Deutsche Hochschule, which was renamed the Reichsakademie für Leibesübungen, and adopted a new policy in which the emphasis was upon the mass-production of an army of coaches through fortnightly courses. His unique talents and experience made it essential to retain him as Secretary of the Olympic Committee in view of the approaching Berlin Games in 1936. Whatever may be felt about the spirit of these Games, the supreme competence of their organization, which was due in large measure to Diem, can hardly be called into question. After the Games he was dropped from the office of Secretary also. He retained only a somewhat tenuous post as Secretary of the International Olympic Committee, which was not in the gift of the German Government.

The Third Reich furthered physical education on a mighty scale. But the ends for which it strove were perverse, and all its means bore the mark of this perversity. The most unattractive features of physical education in the historical periods with which this chapter deals had been due to its association with a ruling caste bent on war abroad and oppression at home. Its noblest achievements had been due to men inspired by ideals of human freedom and brotherhood. Basedow and GutsMuths were such men. So were many of the 'Turner' of the eighteen-forties. But bitter experience had led many Germans to believe that these ideals were ineffective, and that force was the only reality in human affairs. The 'Land of Philosophers' now set out deliberately to produce a generation of young barbarians. The ceaseless inculcation in the Hitler Youth and the S.A. of gangster qualities of toughness and aggression contrasted shamefully with the universal philanthropism which had animated Dessau and Schnepfenthal. The role of physical education in the Third Reich might seem to discredit the subject for ever.

But a movement with the tremendous driving-force of

145

National-Socialism must correspond, however faultily, with deep social needs. The Nazis' lack of scruples enabled them to see some truths which were hidden from minds more virtuous and more conventional, while their ruthless energy enabled them to execute speedily constructive plans which a freer but more complacent country might have shelved for years or not conceived at all. The institutions of the Third Reich all have a quality of demented prophecy about them. Through them one can see the future as in a glass darkly. Even the pathetic boast of the 'Reich of a Thousand Years' was not utterly empty. For though the aims of the enlightened states of the future will be totally opposed to those of Nazi Germany, their care for their citizens will certainly be equally comprehensive; and in providing the conditions in which humanity may attain full stature physical education, far from being discredited by past misuse, must play a part as vital as that which the Nazis assigned to it in their conspiracy to enslave the world.

REFERENCES

1. Plutarch, *Marius*, Chap. 16.

2. Caesar, *De Bello Gallico* VI, 21.

3. Tacitus, *Germania*, 20.

4. R. Strempel, *Von der deutschen Aufklärung bis auf GutsMuths, Quellen zur Geschichte der körperlichen Erziehung.* Weidemann 1934.

5. E. Ackermann, *Salzmanns Lebensbeschreibung*, 2nd Edition. Langenscheidt 1897.

6. *Quellenbücher der Leibesübungen*, Schwarze & Limpert, 9 vols., Limpert, Dresden. Vol. 1, *Die Gymnastik von GutsMuths.* 1793.

7. GutsMuths, *Kleines Lehrbuch der Schwimmkunst.* Weimar 1798. 2nd Edition 1833.

8. *Quellenbücher der Leibesübungen*, Vol. IV, Jahn *Das deutsche Volkstum.*

9. *Ibid.*

10. *Quellenbücher der Leibesübungen*, Vol. III, Jahn-Eiselen *Die deutsche Turnkunst.*

146

J. G. Dixon

11. G. Rasmus, Dr. *Adolf Werner in seinem Wirken auf dem Felde der Gymnastik.* Dessau 1848.
12. Saurbier & Stahr, *Geschichte der Leibesübungen*, p.163. Voigtländer. Leipzig 1939.
13. 'Vom Rhein', in the *Turnzeitung*, (1846, p. 187.)
14. Neuendorff, *Geschichte der neueren deutschen Leibesübungen*, Vol. 3, p. 450.
15. Neuendorff, *ibid*, Vol. III, pp. 202–220.
16. Neuendorff, *ibid*, Vol. IV.
17. *Ibid.*, Vol. IV, p. 587.
18. *Ibid.*, Vol. IV, pp. 591–593.
19. Novalis, *Heinrich van Ofterdingen*, Schriften, 1802, ed. Tieck.
20. *Ibid.*, Vol. IV, p. 596.
21. *Ibid.*, Vol. IV, pp. 651–652.
22. Bode, *Rhythmus und Körperkultur.*
23. Gaulhofer-Streicher, *Grundzüge des österreichischen Schulturnens.* Vienna 1922. Also Gaulhofer-Streicher, *Das neue Schulturnen. Kleine Pädägogische Texte*, Booklet 8, Julius Beltz, Langensalza.
24. Philip Stubbes, *Anatomie of Abuses.*
25. G. Zeimer, *Education for Death; the Making of the Nazi.* 1942.

See also

Bogeng, E., *Geschichte des Sports aller Völker und Zeiten.* Leipzig 1926.

Wassmannsdorff, K. *Kurzer Überblick über die Entwicklung des deutschen Schulturnens von GutsMuths bis auf die neueste Zeit.* (Neue Jahrbücher der Turnkunst, 1855.)

Euler, C. *Geschichte des Turnunterrichtes*, 3rd Edition by Carl Rossow. Gotha 1907. (Vol. V in Kehr's *Geschichte der Methodik des deutschen Volksschulunterrichtes.*)

Diem, C. *Theorie der Gymnastik.* Berlin 1930.

Wassmannsdorff, K. *Die Leibesübungen in den Philanthropinen.* Heidelberg 1870.

Rossow, C. *Italienische und deutsche Humanisten und ihre Stellung zu den Leibesüngen.* Leipzig 1903.

Euler, C. *Enzyklopädisches Handbuch des gesamten Turnwesens und der verwandten Gebiete.* 3 vols. Vienna and Leipzig 1894–1896.

Neuendorff, E. *Die deutschen Leibesübungen, grosses Handbuch für Turnen, Spiel und Sport.* Berlin and Leipzig 1927.

Mehl, E. *Grundriss des deutschen Turnens.* Vienna 1930.

Altrock, H. *Kleine Sportkunde.* Leipzig 1928.

147

Prussia, Politics and Physical Education

Cotta, C. *Die Frühlingszeit des deutschen Volksturnens.* Leipzig 1913. Voigtländers Quellenbücher, Vol. 53.

Deutsche Turnzeitung, published in Leipzig since 1856.

Jahrbuch der Leibesübungen. Berlin 1924–32. Edited by Carl Diem.

Politische Leibeserziehung, Limpert, Berlin. Issued by the N.-S. Lehrerbund (National-Socialist Teachers' Association) 1933–1939.

148

VII

Physical Education in
The United States of America

A. D. MUNROW

∽∽∽∽∽∽∽∽∽∽∽∽∽∽∽∽∽

AMERICAN parents wishing to obtain the best conditions for physical education for their children might well be tempted to move to California. The temperate Californian climate makes physical activity possible, out-of-doors, all the year round. Some of the best teachers are attracted there by the relatively high salary scales; State law requires that five hours a week of physical education be provided. In other states conditions vary considerably. In Iowa, in the Middle West, for example, winter temperatures below zero seriously curtail physical activities in the smaller schools or, in the larger schools, necessitate expensive indoor facilities: in the summer, extreme heat makes much physical activity difficult. Teachers are not so well paid; State law requires only one weekly hour of physical education. Yet one might go further than Iowa and fare worse in some respects. For example, in 1946 the average salaries for teachers in some Californian cities were $2705, in comparable cities in Iowa they were $2153 and in South Carolina only $1650.[1] Local districts as well as states vary in facilities. Much financial support for education in America comes from taxes on local property. Yet it was possible some years back to find adjacent districts in which the same tax rate yielded for each child more than twenty times as much in the one district as in the other.[2] Physical facilities are affected not only by economic factors; in some areas German apparatus abounds, in some it is

149

absent; in some areas facilities for coloured children are markedly less than for white. A boy playing basket ball for his high-school may find himself front page news in the local press, while his sister finds no competing high-school team which she can enter.

Historical, economic, geographical and racial factors all contribute to produce a physical education of remarkable diversity, yet characteristically American. We must try to examine the factors which make for diversity as well as those which unify and characterize American physical education.

There were already three distinctive attitudes towards Education within the thirteen original states of the Confederacy.[3] In the north, the New England States were settled originally by communities of religious dissenters, mostly of middle-class origin. They were for the most part narrow, intolerant and tyrannical, with a fixed belief in their own rightness.[4] These New England Puritans respected education for both civil and religious reasons. It has been pointed out[5] that these New England colonies were really little church states. Early in their history came laws affecting education; indeed, by 1642, a law of Massachusetts directed the official of each town to ascertain if parents and masters were attending to their educational duties. Five years later, a further law of Massachusetts was more specific and required all towns of fifty householders to appoint a teacher of reading and writing and towns of one hundred householders to provide a Latin Grammar School.

Not all writers on the subject discern in these laws the origins of state education in America.[6] But the New England States were always early, and often first, in the field with educational developments. It was a Massachusetts law in 1827 which first required townships to provide high school education (though individual town high-schools were known earlier and private high-schools or academies earlier still) and in 1837 Massachusetts appointed Horace Mann the first secretary of a State Board of Education. It is true that public education in America is now entirely secular while the early Puritan settlements were dominated by a religious outlook. But the very uniformity of the early townships (until 1691 no person could vote in Massachusetts who was not a member of the church) implied an identity of opinion and organization on religious and secular matters

150

and there was thus a secular organization of education withou
any suggestion that the church was losing power. In the Nev
England States, too, there soon emerged a flourishing commer
cialism co-existing with poor, mixed farming. Life began t
centre round many small towns and the germ of later urba
development was present.

In the middle group of the original states there was no sucl
early uniformity and from them has come no such characteristi
legacy of educational design. Early education there was—but i
was linked to a variety of churches—Quakers, Lutherans an
Catholics were all strongly represented and parochial school
were scattered through the community. The schools were privat
schools and their fortunes waxed and waned. When state con
trol was finally established, there was less general opposition t
it in principle than to the payment of taxes to support it. In th
area of these middle colonies the early academy, modelled o
the English Latin grammar school also received support, espec
ially from Benjamin Franklin and his liberal and scientific friends

In the southern states, during the colonial period, there was
markedly contrasting background. A scattered population, witl
the exception of the one considerable town of Charleston, woul
have made any organized education difficult. Added to this wa
the existence of a small, rich and very often cultured, aristo
cracy whose children had tutors or were sent to private board
ing schools, quite often in England. For the rest of the popula
tion there was little provision; this, when it existed, took th
form of the so-called pauper school. It was in these souther
states that the subsequent struggle for control was often greates
and with least to show for it when the fight was over.

Replacing articles of the Confederacy of the thirteen origina
states, came the Constitution of the United States of Americ
governing both the original states and those which came sub
sequently into being. That constitution did not specificall
assign to the Federal government any control over educatio
and thus, by the Jeffersonian interpretation of the constitution
education was state-controlled.

Autonomy at state level and the pattern of differences eve
among the early colonial states indicate clearly the possibilitie
for diversity in the American educational scene. In fact, contro
at state level was relatively slow in evolving and even to-da

L   151

the control at state level is variable and characterized by much less permanent official organization than it is in England. The State Superintendent of Schools (or Commissioner of Education—there are a variety of titles) is usually a political appointment. In roughly three-quarters of the states he is elected by popular vote, in some others he is an appointee of the State Governor, and in relatively few is he appointed by the State Board of Education.

Local district, town or township or, in some cases, county boards were, therefore, the first unit to be in effective control of local education. The changing nature of state supervision and the relatively few permanent state officials have contributed to the retention of power at the district level, to which must be added a third factor, the local responsibility to find a comparatively large proportion of the funds. In about three-quarters of the states less than a third of the funds for education come from state sources and in only two or three does more than half originate from the state. Local taxes are the major source of the remainder. In the great majority of cases this local tax is levied on the value of property and there are very great disparities in the monetary yield of taxes in various districts.

The individual school principal is usually able to procure books and other material through direct purchase and in a general way to administer his school funds. Often he attempts to secure local funds for specific projects by parent, pupil and alumni subscriptions or by other means and this, as we shall see, affects the practice of High School Athletics (in some degree).

But it has already been noted that, in spite of the variations within American education, it is nevertheless very characteristic in growth and shape. Many factors in the history and development of the American people have contributed to its evolution.

Since the classical contest between Hamilton and Jefferson over the establishment of a national bank, the 'doctrine of implied powers' has been the basis for much of the encroachment of Federal power over the sovereign rights of the states.* The

* The changing relationship of the "States" to "The United States" is too fundamental a topic to be completely ignored in an historical treatment of American Education. It is also too complex to be dealt with in a few paragraphs or a footnote. James Truslow Adams gives a good account of the issues involved and of the general growth of Federal power in "The Epic of America" Chapters IV and IX and in "America's Tragedy" Chapters I and II.

152

Supreme Court, by its interpretation of constitutional powers, has been able to uphold or curb both Federal and State legislation. In the field of education, the pattern of development has been mainly one in which there has been prompting, encouragement and financial aid at Federal level but no direct interference. In one particular area—that of Vocational Education —the Federal government initiated developments (through the Smith-Hughes Act of 1917) and still retains control and direction of certain specific aspects.[7]

The Morrill Act of 1862 attempted to stimulate interest in instruction in the mechanical and agricultural arts. For those states willing to set up such colleges, a grant of public land was made and Congress made further grants to colleges instituted or benefited by the original Morrill Act. Eighteen states added the land grant to their existing state universities and combined the two institutions, three of the older states gave the grant to private institutions already established within the state; the remainder established separate agricultural and mechanical colleges, the so-called land-grant colleges.

These are but two examples of many in which Federal money has paid the piper and to some extent called the educational tune. There were notable extensions of this principle during the slump and the Roosevelt administration.

For one brief year, in 1867, there was a Federal Department of Education but it was replaced in 1868 by the Office of Education in the Department of the Interior. During the Hoover administration, a National Committee recommended the re-establishment of a Department of Education but its recommendation was never implemented. The Division of Vocational Education is a part of the Office of Education.

The action of the Supreme Court may be illustrated by two examples. In 1816 the legislature of New Hampshire tried to take over Dartmouth College, a private college (actually the last of the nine colleges founded during colonial times) and make it a state university. But the Supreme Court ruled otherwise, a decision which subsequently gave something of an impetus to the establishment of other private schools and colleges, for, with the final separation of School and Church, all instruction at state schools became secular and a great many of the private schools and even universities in America owe their origin to

153

sectarian religious backing. In 1923 the State of Oregon attempted to make attendance at public schools compulsory, but again the Federal courts declared the amendment null and void.

Correspondingly important decisions have been taken by the state courts. In 1872 in the city of Kalamazoo in Michigan, the right of the state to levy taxes for high school education was challenged and a ruling given in the State's favour. In 1926 the right of a State Commissioner of Education to direct a school district to raise sufficient funds by local tax to provide for the transportation of children to school, was upheld.

Apart from the specific enactment by which the Federal Government has exerted educational influence, the Office of Education has performed an extremely useful function in publishing reports of investigations and generally giving wide publicity to varieties of practice and varieties of standards in a number of aspects of education. In particular its biennial surveys of education collect and publish data from all the states over a wide range of education matters. As one reads the biennial surveys, one is aware of an almost steady tendency—a process of levelling-up. The gap between the lowest standards in salaries, in school attendance, in high-school enrolment (the lowest standards being usually in the southern states) and the highest standards (usually in the eastern states, California and certain mid-western states) tends to close. This is probably connected with the publication of the biennial survey statistics, but not just a simple result of it. One has to add the more imponderable factor of local pride or local boost.

A strong and sometimes fierce spirit of local patriotism is a feature of America which many writers have noticed and tried to account for.

United we stick, divided we're stuck.
United we boost, divided we bust.[8]

one local slogan tersely puts it. One outstanding club woman in the same locality addressing a group of children says, 'You must have community spirit. You must think that there is no finer town in the whole United States than this. There is no finer school than yours, no finer parents than yours, no finer opportunities anywhere than you have right here. People talk of California where there is sunshine all the year round, but I've

154

lived in California, and give me Middle Western rains! I tell you there's no lovelier place on God's footstool than this old state of ours.'[9]

Very often the urge to local boost is combined with the urge to overstatement, which Brogan [10] describes as a surviving habit of the days when man-power and immigrants were needed, both by American in general and by each new frontier town in particular.

To this feeling of local pride, one must add yet another factor, a very real enthusiasm for education. The early legislation in the Puritan states has already been noted. Under the Land Ordinances of 1785 and 1787, the states which ceded territory to Congress laid down conditions for its subseqeunt disposal. In those conditions were certain stipulations for land in each township to be sold for the benefit of public education. In the 1830's the Lyceum movement grew up in which voluntary societies of citizens agitated for the extension of the common schools, and arranged lectures of general educational interest. The lecturing movement itself has become a characteristic feature of some parts of America, especially the west and south. Womenfolk in the nineteenth century married to men perpetually on the move, saw in education a means of securing their men in one place during the years when the family was growing up. Foreign immigrants saw in it the means of social acceptance for their next generation [11] and, if the German immigrants were in some degree an exception to this rule, they nevertheless, as we shall see, embraced the idea of education as a means of preserving their own culture.[12]

This enthusiasm has reflected the spirit of a nation confident 'that the answers to the present, lie not in the past, but in the future' and it has itself been reflected in the unequalled provision for education which America offers. From the staggering range of statistics about American education, it is difficult to select the most striking: perhaps that 73 per cent of Americans between sixteen and seventeen years of age are in school; or perhaps again a total student population in American institutions of higher learning greater than in comparable institutions in all the rest of the world together (1937); or possibly that in the period 1890–1920, while the national population increased 68 per cent, the high school enrolments increased 986 per cent.[13]

155

With or without the aid of statistics, the growth of higher education in America and the physical facilities available for it are remarkably impressive. In education, as in so many ways, America has drawn from Europe but has also turned its back on Europe. It may have been inspired by the German Volksschule in shaping its early elementary school curriculum,[14] but in secondary and higher education the conscious decision has grown to eschew both the intellectual and the class distinction of the European Gymnasium and the English Grammar School. The following might be the opening paragraph of almost any book on American education which seeks to describe or justify the nature of high-school or college education. 'The structure of the school system in the United States is determined in large measure by the ideal of equality of opportunity through education. Ours is a one-track school system.'[15] The American high-school then (and to some extent the American College) is free and open to all regardless of income, almost regardless of race (America appears to be tackling the last hurdles in this problem at the present time), and regardless of intellectual equipment. Nor within the schools is there a streaming or multiple track system. It is, as one American writer puts it, 'a system whose programme seems to the European to be an audacious experiment in democracy and to entertain an extremely optimistic view of the original nature of man.'[16]

Because the high-school has become non-selective, both at the bottom and at the top (i.e. at the college entrance level) there has grown up no nation-wide or state-wide public examination system, nor any rigid demarcation line between elementary and secondary education on the one hand or secondary and college education on the other.

The earliest pattern was one of eight years of elementary school from 6–14 years, followed—if at all—by four years of high-school and, for a minority training for a profession, by four years or more at the university. The school section of this pattern was known as the 8–4 plan. It has been replaced in large measure by the 6–3–3 plan, in which six years of elementary school are followed by three of Junior High School and three of Senior High School. But these are merely common patterns set round by a host of others, some of them including two years of Junior College in the general educational scheme.

156

This lack of uniformity of school courses and comparative absence of syllabuses and university entrance examinations, led to some overlapping or, more often, gaps in college student education. In 1893, to effect some articulation between various types of course, a committee of ten was set up, chaired by President Eliot of Harvard. This committee stated as a principle that subjects studied for the same length of time were educationally equal. This principle was destined to have profound effect on American university and high school education. Six years later it was adopted by The Committee on College Entrance Requirements. The Carnegie Foundation for the Advancement of Teaching defined a unit of learning as a subject studied throughout an academic year for five periods each week.

So has grown up the system of defining college entrance requirements in terms of units and even of defining university courses of study in terms of units. The so-called elective system has enabled students to group together unrelated subjects or even parts of subjects to form a 'course'. The elective system operates even at high-school level enabling youths and girls to choose certain parts of their courses. At Middletown [17] the high school pupil can group his studies round twelve different courses varying from a college preparatory course, through shorthand and applied electricity courses to home economics. Each of these involves a number of prescribed courses to which electives may be added. The 16 yearly courses are selected from a total of 102. McConnell [18] cites the case of a school offering 128 different work units. A student might remain for thirty-two years without duplicating his courses.

It is easy to see that the multiple course offerings and elective subjects have presented at least a partial answer to the problem raised by a form of secondary education which has no streaming and which brings together students of vastly differing native intelligence. It can also be appreciated that physical education can more easily find a place in the sun in schools where the academic pace is slowed, where there is little competitive entry to college and where many who remain to seventeen or eighteen are not in any degree academically inclined.

We must soon turn to a closer examination of physical education itself, but not without a final glance at the variegated and

157

somewhat bewildering pattern of American high-school and college education.

However high-school education measures on an academic yardstick, it must be respected as a great socializing influence and the value of that influence is not easily overestimated in a country comparatively lacking in traditions, and where, until the turn of the century foreign languages were spoken in the homes of many American-born children. What the home has lacked, the school has provided, in teaching new generations to become Americans. The shared experiences of school life have helped to bridge many racial and economic gaps.

There has been a re-thinking and re-assessment of the content and purposes of education, led by John Dewey (19, 20) which has attracted interest and had effects beyond the borders of the United States of America. By the general public, however, says Lynd [21], 'Education, appears to be desired frequently not for its specific content but as a symbol—by the working classes as an open sesame that will mysteriously admit their children to a world closed to them, and by the buisness class as a heavily sanctioned aid in getting on further economically or socially in the world.'

In a perplexing and rapidly changing world, it is difficult to assess the worth of American high-school education. Assessed by academic standards alone it will certainly rank lower than European and British 'high schools'; equally certainly it will not then have been fairly assessed. Perhaps no one assessment is fair or even practicable of an educational system which includes 'algebra' and 'physics', as well as 'cosmetology' (or the science of cosmetics) and 'cultivation of appearance, dress and personality.'[22] At university level academic standards should apply. Severe criticism of the system emanates from America itself.[23]

We have indicated that physical education in the American school flowed into the partial vacuum caused by the sudden expansion of high-school and college education. But the volume of physical education is a result of positive as well as of negative pressure. Physical attributes have been important and esteemed in America; they are part of the frontier tradition. Physical courage and dogged perseverance were the necessary qualities in a frontiersman—other qualities were often more of a hind-

158

rance than a help.[24] Prominent men in early American history, men like Benjamin Franklin and Thomas Jefferson, not only recommended physical activity as a part of educational training but even held views as to the nature of the most suitable activities.[25] One finds mention of physical education—as well as of athletics—in general university histories,[26] and, before the turn of the century, a university president's annual report discussing the relative merits of athletics and systematic physical exercise.[27] It has been the development of high-pressure competitive athletics (using the word athletics in its American sense, as a generic term for all competitive sports) that has greatly complicated the task of assessing American social attitudes to physical education. On the one hand there has developed an interest, even glamour, involving almost the whole of a local community [28, 29], and on the other, the distrust and opposition of sincere and thinking educationists to the misuse of the educational medium for wholly inappropriate ends.

Whatever the fundamental causes, there can be little doubt that, on balance, physical education in America has made considerable impact on the consciousness of the general educator and is often well integrated into the general educational scheme at secondary and at college level. If, for example, one compares English and American publications on the principles and practice of education one finds those emanating from England are exceptional if they make more than a passing reference to physical education and it is not unusual to find this aspect of education completely ignored. In American publications, on the other hand, it is common to find the physical implications of education discussed [30] and even whole chapters devoted to it.[31]

During its growth, American physical education has drawn mainly from four sources, from the gymnastic systems of Germany and Sweden, from the games-playing 'system' of the English public schools and universities, and from the particular contributions and developments of its own people. Wherever it has borrowed, it has also characteristically shaped and modified. The legacies from Germany, Sweden and Great Britain differ considerably in extent and in the degree to which they have survived 'pure' or modified. Each will now be considered in turn.

159

Germans are and always have been the largest group of non-English speaking immigrants in America. But their great period of influx was the half-century from 1840–1890, more than 70 per cent of their total numbers arriving in that period. During the '50's and the '60's Germans constituted about 30 per cent of the total immigrants. The period 1848–66 has been distinguished [32] as the second of three periods of German immigration and it was during this period that the importation and establishment of Turnen in America was effected. There had, it is true, been an attempt at establishing German gymnastics in 1826–30 but it had been short-lived. This second wave of German immigration contained many men of unusual type, certainly not frontiersmen in the usual sense. Many were intellectuals, professional men, teachers, lawyers and doctors. A great many came with their families,[33] a number settled in towns. Those who farmed tended to settle on established farms rather than in new frontier land. The intellectuals turned farmers were often referred to contemptuously as Latin-Farmers and the main group of settlers of this period as the 'Greens'. They in turn nicknamed the earlier settlers the 'Grays' (Gray—having the connotation 'old fossil' in German). Particularly outstanding from the point of view of physical education among the members of the second period of German settlers were 'The Forty-Eighters'. These men became political exiles after the abortive revolutions in Germany in 1848. Via Switzerland, Holland, England and other countries, some after periods in prison, they left Europe. They were, by the nature of things many of them gifted speakers who had been politically active. They were idealists, often radical in their views and often with powers of leadership. A good number of them found their way by their subsequent work in America into the *Dictionary of American Biography* [34]. From these Forty-eighters came men who had previously been members of the Burschenschaften or the Turnvereine, suppressed through the Karlsbad decrees, and re-instated in 1842. Their practice of Turnen was associated with their whole way of life including their political and cultural activities which have been discussed in Chapter V. Thus it was that, shortly after the arrival of the first Forty-eighters in America, the first Turnverein was established in Cincinnati in November of 1848;[35] others followed rapidly,

160

twenty-two Turnvereine being in existence in the North by 1852. The individual societies or Turnvereine rapidly formed an association (1850) known first as the Sozialistischer Turnerbund (1851).

It must be pointed out that Beck and Follen, who had started the first two groups in America practising German gymnastics, at Round Hill School 1825 and at Harvard in 1826 respectively, were similar men to the forty-eighters. Both had been Turners in Germany. They too were political exiles, after the Kotzebue murder of 1819. The essential difference between the early attempt to start German gymnastics and the later, conspicuously successful one, was that the second attempt was made, not with English-speaking Americans, but with Germans.

In terms of the effect on the development of physcal education, it need not concern us whether German-America resulted from a conscious attempt to retain social and cultural islands of 'Deutschtum' within America or not.[36, 37] Certainly many Germans did congregate geographically and politically. The barrier of language must have contributed as well as the Nativism of the Know-Nothing Party.[38] The anti-prohibitionism of many, and the free-thinking Sabbath-breaking of some and the anti-slavery of most, caused them to fit badly into the general party alignments politically. Thus it was that German-gymnastics, or Turnen, flourished within the areas where the 'hyphenated' German-Americans lived. By 1861, the first attempt was made to set up a Normal School to supply teachers for the Turnerbund, which, by the time of the Civil War had grown to embrace some 10,000 members.

The practice of gymnastics by the Turners flourished in that isolation and, indeed, because of it. But political activity is not possible in isolation and, however much some forty-eighters may have manoeuvered to establish and maintain a German bloc at some stages,[39] there were certain issues, notably that of slavery, on which the Germans had to declare themselves. This political aspect of the Turnerbund arose as early as 1855 and a policy declaration strongly in favour of abolitionism caused the secession of four of the southern Turnvereine from the Bund.[40] But the attempt to rally the southern Germans to a separate association failed and six other Turnvereine located in southern states remained faithful to the north.

161

It is possible that the German vote was decisive for Lincoln and certain that he himself entertained great regard for the services of some of the able German political leaders, notably Carl Schurz. Certain it is, too, that the Turners enlisted in great numbers and fought with loyalty and distinction in the Civil War. Hawgood speaks of the Germans suffering from arrested development after the war.[41] The forty-eighters had not yet acquired party alignment and allegiances and many were by express statement not prepared to support policies or persons simply on a party ticket. In the untimely death of Lincoln, some of them lost a link with American politics which they had come to trust and respect.

In spite of the continuance of the language and other social barriers for a great length of time (there were still twenty-nine German newspapers published in Texas in 1904), the history of German gymnastics after the Civil War is one of growth and subsequently of steady assimilation into the American pattern. Turners were offering gymnastic teacher-training before any other group or organization in America; similarly they were offering school programmes and in many states causing schools to be equipped with German apparatus. The aim of the Turners was more and more towards an educational contribution to the whole country.[42] The normal college demanded that its graduates give instruction in the English language. The Sozialistischer Turnerbund became the Nordamerikanischer Turnerbund in 1865 and in 1919 the American Gymnastic Union. When the American-born population formed the American Association for the Advancement of Physical Education, representative Turners were invited to the second annual meeting; subsequently reciprocal visits by other American physical educators took place. One might say that the final act of complete assimilation took place as late as 1941 when the Normal College of The American Gymnastic Union was taken over by the State University of Indiana.

The assimilation of Turnen into the American system has been a two-way process. Turnen has spread out of the purely German-American groups through the agency of the high-schools and universities, the Y.M.C.A.'s and through other European minority groups (e.g. Swiss, Czech, Norwegian). At the same time, many Turnvereine gymnasia have added the

162

characteristic American gymnasium apparatus—the basket-ball backboard. The apparatus gymnastics has a wide following, the national championships of the American Athletic Union attracting entries from east to west coast and from north to south.[43] Apart from the actual survival of apparatus gymnastics as a sport and the technical contribution to the present-day programme, the Turners in many respects blazed a trail. Because of the 'hyphenation' their impact on the rest of America was not, in the early days, so great as it might perhaps have been but, on the other hand, without the early nurture of Turnen in its own soil, it would hardly have survived transplantation.

By contrast to the Germans, Swedish immigration was small and did not reach appreciable proportions until the 1860's. During that decade the whole Scandinavian group constituted 7·6 per cent of the total immigration figures. By the decade 1890–1900 it was 8·5 per cent of the total. Back in Sweden gymnastics had by this time a well established place in the educational system (see Chapter VI) but it was mainly a formal school training and not the focus of political activity, though its contribution as a form of social activity should not be entirely neglected. Nor, with a land famine in Sweden as one motivating cause, were the immigrants in any way a homogeneous group, politically or intellectually. In consequence there was no natural flourishing of Swedish gymnastics through Swedish immigrants. As a therapeutic exercise system, the 'Swedish Movement Cure' had attracted limited attention in America by 1860.[44] As a form of physical education, its introduction is due to two Swedes, Hartvig Nissen who came to Washington in 1883, and Baron Nils Posse who arrived in Boston two years later. In its manner of introduction into the schools, it owes its origins to another characteristically American factor—private benefaction.

James Truslow Adams comments that visitors to America early observed that money-making was apparently enjoyed as an activity for its own sake. The money once made was often lavishly spent or given away readily.[45] Certainly the educational endowments and other benefactions of philanthropic Americans are a byword in many countries. Mrs. Mary Hemenway, a prominent and wealthy Boston citizen was such a person.

163

Her son had already, in 1879, given the Hemenway Gymnasium to Harvard. She had already stimulated some domestic training for girls in the Boston schools by the simple procedure of paying for the training of the necessary teachers. Now she did the same for Swedish Educational Gymnastics, having been convinced of its value by Nils Posse. Experimentally in 1889 one hundred teachers were trained for one year at Mrs. Hemenway's expense. Subsequently, in 1890, the Boston Normal School of Gymnastics was formed to provide training based on the Swedish system.

Swedish gymnastics made more headway with women and girls than with men and secured more hold in the New England area than in the other Eastern or Central States. It never did secure as much official support as the German system. The emergence of the Dewey philosophy of education, caused a move away from formal systems and directed programmes, towards individual programmes and education for leisure-time recreation. This worked even less in favour of Swedish gymnastics, which had little core of intrinsically interesting activity, than of German gymnastics, from which the apparatus gymnastics was rescued as an individual participation sport.

It is interesting to note that during the period when Swedish gymnastics attracted most attention in American circles, a number of the most prominent men in physical education were medically qualified. Dr. A. Hitchcock, Dr. D. A. Sargent and Dr. E. M. Hartwell are typical examples. Hartwell personally identified himself with the Swedish system when he became principal of the Boston Normal Gymnastics School. Sargent, who in 1879 had taken charge of physical education at Harvard in the new Hemenway gymnasium, certainly had considerable interest in form-giving exercises and he tried to cull the best from both the German and Swedish systems while developing and modifying a great deal of apparatus himself. With his weight and pulley systems he appears to have anticipated some of the developments of strengthening work usually credited with more recent origin. Recent writers [46] tend to discount the idea of Sargent developing a system. Perhaps this is true in the sense that Sargent's work was always progressive and developing and never practised as a disciplined routine. But in terms of contribution to and advancement of the subject, one

164

must give great credit to Sargent as the pioneer in much work which is typically American, especially that of tests and measurements in physical education.

It is sometimes difficult to determine who evolved a 'system'. Earlier than Sargent and at about the time that the Swedish Movement Cure attracted attention in America, a Dr. Dio Lewis also attracted much attention and started a Normal School to train teachers in his new system. There is some question of the extent to which his system was original, and the qualities of his work were dependant in no small measure on his own classes and lectures, on which he brought to bear his considerable histrionic powers. His system was relatively short-lived, his Normal School opened in 1861 and he ceased to teach in 1868. But it is noteworthy that this was the first instance of a normal school in physical education for English-speaking Americans. It is also noteworthy that it was established in Boston, and indicates that there was a potential interest in callisthenic training some twenty years before the arrival of Swedish gymnastics into the American scene. Further accounts of the interesting career of Dio Lewis's may be read elsewhere. [47, 48]

In appointing Dr. Hitchcock to the physical education department at Amherst in 1861 with full faculty and professorial status, that college did something quite remarkable. Eighteen years were to elapse before any other university followed suit and then Dr. Sargent was appointed to Harvard. Sargent's ability and academic status, the coincidence of his appointment with the presidency of Eliot may well have had far-reaching effects on the status of physical education in the colleges of America. Certainly other colleges and universities rapidly followed suit and although study courses leading to degree awards in American universities developed only slowly, the connection of teacher training with universities dates back to the Harvard Summer School which became something of an institution during its long life from 1887–1932.

Before and during the period of growth of university departments of physical education, another feature of American college life was developing—inter-collegiate athletics—and this has exerted a profound effect on physical education in America. Up to 1852 such games as there were in American universities

165

were spontaneous and organized by the students themselves, and there were no intercollegiate (or, as we should call them, inter-varsity) games. In 1852 Harvard rowed against Yale and intercollegiate contests developed in the succeeding years. Harvard played Yale at baseball in 1868; a league of college teams played football from 1869 onwards, but, by 1876 the intercollegiate football association adopted the rugby rules, from which the characteristic American game has developed. During the early years, both before and after intercollegiate contests grew up, sport ran along the same haphazard, self-governing and self-maintained lines as English university sport. The games played were English in origin, even cricket being played along the eastern seaboard. But shortly after inter-collegiate competition was developed, it took on characteristics which developed rapidly.[49] Non-playing supporters attended games on an organized basis, rowdyism and hooliganism frequently resulting afterwards. Football playing became a half-time occupation, hours of practice being needed every day. During their training periods the players were entirely in the hands of the coach who might not be, and often was not, educationally a desirable person. Individuals were enticed into universities simply to play football, often without any serious attempt to be students. Betting was frequent on the games. In 1885 rough play and unpleasant incidents had reached such a pitch that the Faculty at Harvard banned football for a year.

It is difficult to account for the deterioration in playing practices which took place in this period. Some note has already been made of extreme local pride as a frequent characteristic of American behaviour. Adams has pointed out[50] that the contions of westward advance created socially accepted standards in which success became a virtue in itself. These two factors may have contributed to the behaviour of the alumni. Certainly it was the alumni (i.e. old students) of the colleges who were mainly responsible for the appointment of coaches, the enticement and subsidizing of players and the general pressure to win. Although betting took place, it is doubtful if financial gain was often the major motive in the action of the alumni. Indeed, many of them must have paid heavily for their share in the control of college teams. Newspaper publicity became an important factor later, focussing attention and stimulating excessive

166

public interest. With added public interest, gate receipts produced a steady revenue for many of the colleges. On the whole, Faculties were completely passive. With both eyes on their books, or one on gate receipts and publicity (it is usually stated that up to 1909 or thereabouts, universities were competing for students), little action was taken by university officials until the situation became intolerable. Starting with the action at Harvard, various university authorities took some steps to control athletics. By 1905, however, the situation was still deteriorating: there were serious injuries in games and dissension over the eligibility of players. Some universities banned football. Inter-university consultation brought into being the Inter-Collegiate Athletic Association (later called the National Collegiate Athletic Association).

University Faculties and the N.C.A.A. have between them tried to bring some order into the administration of inter-collegiate athletics and to stamp out the worst of the malpractices. Faculties have tackled the problems of the status of coaches and their appointment and the conduct of supporters. The N.C.A.A. has tackled the problems of professionalism and the conduct of players. Both have tackled problems of eligibility and recruiting.

Most Faculties have set up controlling committees having student, alumni and Faculty representation. In many cases, the effectiveness of such committees has depended on their constitution. In their action to regularize the status of coaches, some universities made them members of existing physical education departments,[51] others instituted such departments to accommodate them.[52]

Without doubt the situation has improved in many institutions but the Carnegie Foundation Bulletin No. 23 revealed in 1929 a great many ways in which regulations could be circumvented and instances of malpractices still being carried on.[53] The recent revelations at William and Mary College indicated that these problems are still not solved. A great deal of money is involved in the matches of the biggest universities, gate receipts of the order of a million dollars being reported in the Carnegie Bulletin.[53] Stadia seating 50,000 are not uncommon and one of 97,000 exists.

These difficulties with college athletics have had considerable

M   167

repercussions on physical education in the colleges. Departments have in some cases had to take both students and staff who had little sympathy with the educational aims of the department; sometimes these departments have been swallowed up or completely obscured by the business of 'big time' football and basketball. On the other hand, the income from athletics has, in some instances, subsidized physical education so that departments can offer remarkable facilities to the general student body. At one mid-western university, for example, a building costing $100,000 in 1928 and with an annual spending budget of $20,000 is financed in this way. The main building contains a large sports hall 275 ft. by 115 ft., 14 handball courts, 13 squash courts, a large swimming pool with seating accommodation for 2,000 spectators, an auxiliary gymnasium 90 ft. by 50 ft., special rooms for boxing, fencing, weight lifting and wrestling, and 4,000 individual lockers for students. Departments can carry large, highly specialized staffs and, for any research work on skill or training, there is within the university a standard of skill, physique and physiological performance not commonly to be met in academic circles.

The problems arising from intercollegiate sport have reflected on high-school sport. Here the identification of the community with the local teams has sometimes reached excessive proportions.[54] Occasionally the local stadium is built by a loan from local businessmen who take a substantial percentage of gate receipts to repay the loan,[55, 56] the school receiving the remainder. Usually the funds for athletics are administered by the school principal, but not always. Roughly two-thirds of schools finance interscholastic athletics mainly through the money paid by spectators.[57] Sometimes the facilities for interscholastic games may involve a school in a liability of as much as $100,000.[58] One can appreciate that in such instances the importance of winning is out of all proportion to the game itself.

Margaret Mead has pointed out that the children in America tend to occupy the limelight in the domestic scene. Brogan points out how much the foreign immigrant centres his hope on his children who, at an early age, can often speak with more knowledge and authority as Americans than their parents. The result is often an exceptional degree of self-confidence and self-possession in teen-agers. Those who are high-school athletes

168

certainly need self-possession for in the games themselves and in the local press their physical achievements often receive the attention of almost the whole local population.

The relationship between high-school and collegiate athletics gives rise to several difficult situations. There is the temptation of the university or its members to scout the schools for talent; the temptation of the boys to hawk their athletic talents to the highest-bidder—to 'shop round' as it is called.

With so much emphasis on winning, the high-school may decide it needs a coach rather than a physical educator. With star college athletes graduating in physical education, it is not difficult to confuse the one with the other.

If, in men's athletics, as in the masculine world of business, anything goes, this is markedly in contrast to women's and girls' athletics. It is sometimes maintained that women are the moral guardians of much of American conduct.[59] To a limited extent excessive competition has touched the girls at school but, in the main, the women have avoided it. In a country where co-education is the rule, this has not been easy and sometimes, in order to avoid excessive competiton, competition of any sort has been avoided. Schools, or colleges in this case, visit each other for 'Play Days' and play together informally with sides chosen informally from both schools.

For both boys and girls at both school and college, there has developed a system of intramural sport comparable with inter-house, inter-form, and inter-faculty games in England. The number of students who participate in these, varies very much in both countries and no comparison is likely to be very informative. At its best in America this intra-mural sport is very highly organized, involving full-time staff and takes in a high proportion of students. One university claims that 70 per cent of its students participate in intra-mural sport.

We have spoken of local patriotism and desire for local success. Each 'Middletown' wants its best players to represent Middletown, be they Catholics or Kluxers, Poles, Negroes or purest Mayflower stock. In sport, the inescapable factor of ability knows no racial bounds and thus it has been that in sport as nowhere else—except perhaps the arts—racial prejudices have been broken down. One writer [60] says competitive sport '. . . is the one big area of life that promises more oppor-

169

tunities for the promotion of inter-racial understanding . . . than any other single area.' Brogan [61] points out that Hitler in refusing to receive Jesse Owens after his victories in the Olympic Games at Berlin in 1936, made more of a mistake than if he had snubbed a great American scholar. One American Quaker, working in the field of race relationships,[62] acknowledged the value of sport in breaking down racial barriers, including both high-level spectacle sport and spontaneous playground games.

America has not yet solved its racial problems, but makes steady progress in that direction. Some of that progress is made by legislation. Other progress has to be made by changing the attitudes and prejudices of individual people. When Jackie Robinson played baseball in Georgia, and Levi Jackson was captain of the Yale football team, they made significant contributions to that progress.

It was really after 1900 that the colleges in America began to train teachers by producing graduates in physical education. Before that time the Turners, some private colleges, Y.M.C.A. colleges and the summer schools were the chief means. Even then, progress was slow and only fourteen courses were in existence by 1914.[63] The effect of the depression years when unemployment was wide-spread was to raise the qualification requirements for teaching including physical education teaching. Many colleges instituted four-year courses leading to bachelor's degrees. Emergency certificates were issued during and after World War II but there was a rapid return to graduate status as the normal requirement until, in 1950, over 400 colleges and universities offered a 'major' in Physical Education.

In the past, the teaching profession in America has been characterized in many states by a 'hire and fire' policy with annual re-appointment or short-term appointments. By 1935 there were five states with state-wide tenure laws and some 23 per cent of teachers with security of tenure after a probationary period.[64] In up-grading the basic qualification for certain posts, some states require teachers at present employed to have obtained the necessary extra qualification in a given period. The summer school movement makes it possible in many instances to do this. Knight stated (1934) that probably one-third of all teachers in U.S. were found to be annually in summer or

170

vacation schools and quotes a figure of 14,000 students registered in summer session at Columbia University, three-quarters of them at Teacher's College.[65] Physical Education has followed the general pattern, especially with graduate studies and a number of summer schools now offer graduate work. Masters degrees are commonly required for certain posts.

There has been trenchant criticism of some of America's graduate work from which physical education could certainly not claim to be excepted, yet, at their best, American research publications are of high quality. Works like McCloy's *Iowa Studies in Child Welfare* and A. H. Steinhaus's *Chronic Effects of Exercise* have added to knowledge and to the status of the subject.

During the nineteenth century most of the emphasis in American physical education was on health or the purely physical effects of exercise. Callisthenics in one form or another figured prominently in the programmes. By 1900, the tide of opinion was turning against callisthenics, for example in 1903, E. W. Lyttle could write, 'We might as well try to feed a boy on Charlotte Russe as to provide proper physical education from callisthenics.' By 1926 J. F. Williams [67] was using the past tense, 'Formal physical education, an imported scheme, never caught the imagination of boys and girls in America.' Its place has been taken by activity centred and individual-centred programmes, in line with the changing concept of education already outlined. An era of economic prosperity and unprecedented technological progress made facilities available through which a broad recreative programme could be developed. (Paradoxically enough, when the slump came in the 1920's and early 30's, much building continued, especially federally-sponsored public-work programmes, to absorb unemployment.)

We have already noted one instance of remarkable facilities provided by money from inter-collegiate football. But American schools and colleges often enjoy equally remarkable facilities not financed in this way. The Yale gymnasium was built from funds supplied by private benefaction. It rises nine storeys from the ground in its central tower, these floors of the central tower are relatively restricted in size being 65 ft. square and each of them is given over to some specialized activity—boxing, fencing and the like. At the fifth floor the main building spreads, housing

171

on its roof a small jogging track and an assault course (1949). From this floor downwards are facilities for swimming (two practice pools and a large exhibition pool 75 ft. by 42 ft.), squash (28 courts), handball (8 courts), rowing tanks, netted rooms for golf practice, indoor tennis courts, basket-ball courts, remedial rooms, games rooms, apparatus gymnasia and many other facilities. Nor are good facilities restricted solely to universities and by benefaction. In Jersey City six of the thirteen public elementary schools have swimming pools and all four high-schools and one special school for physically handicapped children possess their own pools. Jersey City is a densely built-up area; in the more expensive cities of the mid-west and the west, facilities are often better.

The effective use of a recreative games programme was further helped by the invention and rapid spread of two games of American origin. Basket Ball was invented by James Naismith in 1891 and Volley Ball by William Morgan in 1895. Both have become characteristic and almost invariable adjuncts of American physical education programmes.

Led by Hetherington, closely followed by Nash and Williams, an expressely stated philosophy was evolved, urging that physical education was not so much an education of the physical, as a physical means of providing educational opportunity for self-realization and self-development in a general sense. This underlying philosophy has been generally accepted, but the programmes to which this has sometimes given rise, have met with sharp criticism.[68, 69] They have been called the 'What would you like to do to-day?' programme.

Perhaps, with the emphasis on 'education', the 'physical' was sometimes neglected. Certainly there was criticism of the school programmes by some who had to assess the physical condition of the army intake in the second world war, though the profession replied vigorously.[70] Wartime programmes in colleges and universities moved towards more specific physical achievements and even included callisthenics programmes again.[71] If the swing away from formal training was a little vigorous, the move nevertheless encouraged physical educationists to cover areas in which they have since been active with conspicuous success. The development of summer camps in America during this century has been widespread and remarkable. Folk-dancing including

172

square-dancing has increased in popularity at both schools and colleges and has a considerable following in the adult population. Modern dance had grown as an educational medium in America well before World War II and was established in many schools and colleges. It grew from the theatrical form, which America pioneered through the work of Isadora Duncan, Ruth St. Denis, Ted Shawn and Martha Graham and, through them and many others, has since extensively developed.

A characteristic which has accompanied these broad American physical education programmes is readiness by many of its practitioners to experiment and innovate. Lacrosse has spread rapidly as a major game of recent years, rugby football is played in some eastern colleges, synchronized swimming to music is popular in girls and women's work.

A characteristically American physical education has emerged, its chief characteristic being its wide variety in content, standard and method. In its origins it learned from Europe, now Europe, and most of the rest of the world, learns from America; America continues to absorb and innovate, with both typical enthusiasm and energy.

REFERENCES

1. Calculations from data taken from *The Biennial Survey of Education in U.S.A.* 1945–6, Chapter III, pp. 34, 35, 44. Office of Education, Washington 1947.

2. *The Crisis in Public Education in Illinois.* The Illinois State Teachers' Association Publicity Committee, March 1921, pp. 14–15.

3. E. P. Cubberley, *Public Education in the United States*, pp. 23–26. Boston 1934.

4. J. T. Adams, *America's Tragedy*, Scribner 1934.

5. C. E. Skinner & R. E. Langfitt (Ed.), *Introduction to Modern Education*, p. 32. Boston 1937.

6. E. W. Knight, *Education in the United States*, pp. 85, 106. Boston 1934.

7. *Administration of Vocational Education*, Bulletin No. 1. Federal Security Agency, pp. viii–ix. Office of Education, 1948.

173

8. R. S. and H. M. Lynd, *Middletown*, p. 487. New York 1929.

9. *Ibid.*, p. 487.

10. D. W. Brogan, *The American Problem*, pp. 37–39. London 1944.

11. G. Gorer, *The Americans*, pp. 40–41. London 1948.

12. J. A. Hawgood, *The Tragedy of German–America*, New York 1940.

13. C. E. Skinner and R. E. Langfitt (Ed.), *Introduction to Modern Education*, p. 9. Boston 1937.

14. C. H. Judd, *The Evolution of a Democratic School System*, pp. 38–55. Boston 1918.

15. *The Structure and Administration of Education in American Democracy.* Educational Policies Commission 1938.

16. C. E. Skinner and R. E. Langfitt, *Introduction to Modern Education*, p. 31. Boston 1937.

17. R. S. and H. M. Lynd, *Middletown, op. cit.*, Chapter XIII, p. 192. New York, 1929.

18. C. E. Skinner and R. B. Langfitt (Ed.), *Introduction to Modern Education*, pp. 29–30. Boston 1937.

19 and 20. John Dewey, *The School and Society*, New York 1916.

21. R. S. and H. M. Lynd, *Middletown*. New York 1929.

22. J. E. Strachan, quoted in *New Zealand Observer*, New York 1940.

23. J. A. Flexner, *Universities—American, English, German.* Oxford 1930.

24. J. T. Adams, *Epic of America*, p. 126. London 1931.

25. Van Dalen, *World History of Physical Education*, pp. 367–381. New York, 1953.

26. E. P. Cheyney, *History of University of Pennsylvania.* Pennsylvania 1940.

27. H. D. Sheldon, *History of University of Oregon.* Oregon 1940.

28. R. S. and H. M. Lynd, *Middletown*, p. 285. New York 1929.

29. R. S. and H. M. Lynd, *Middletown in Transition*, p. 291. New York 1937.

30. G. S. Counts, *Education and American Civilization*, p. 320. New York 1952.

31. *The Challenge of Education.* The Stanford University Education Faculty. New York 1937.

32. J. A. Hawgood, *Tragedy of German-America*, pp. 21–23. New York 1940.

33. *Op. cit.*, pp. 26, 133.

174

34. A. E. Zucker (Ed.), *The Forty-Eighters*, Preface, p. viii and pp. 269–357. New York 1950.

35. E. A. Rice, *A Brief History of Physical Education*, p. 162. New York 1929.

36. J. A. Hawgood, *The Tragedy of German–America*, p. 43. New York, 1940.

37. A. E. Zucker (Ed.), *The Forty-Eighters*, pp. 76–78. New York 1950.

38. *Op. cit.*, Chapters III and V.

39. *Op. cit.*, pp. 130–138.

40. *Op. cit.*, p. 101.

41. J. A. Hawgood, *The Tragedy of German-America*, p. 253. New York 1940.

42. E. A. Rice, *Brief History of Physical Education*, p. 169. New York 1929.

43. A.A.U. Yearbook, 1949.

44. Van Dalen, *World History of Physical Education*, p. 393. New York 1953.

45. J. T. Adams, *The Epic of America*, p. 187. London 1931.

46. Van Dalen, *World History of Physical Education*, p. 408. New York, 1953.

47. E. A. Rice, *A Brief History of Physical Education*, pp. 176–180. New York, 1929.

48. F. E. Leonard and G. B. Affleck, *History of Physical Education*, Chapter XXII. London 1947.

49. *American College Athletics*, Carnegie Foundation for the Advancement of Learning, Bulletin No. 23. New York 1931.

50. J. T. Adams, *Epic of America*, p. 125. London 1931.

51. E. P. Cheyney, *History of University of Pennsylvania*, Pennsylvania, 1940.

52. H. D. Sheldon, *History of University of Oregon.* Oregon 1940.

53. *American College Athletics*, Carnegie Foundation for the Advancement of Learning, Bulletin No. 23. New York 1931.

54. R. S. and H. M. Lynd, *Middletown*, pp. 485–487. New York 1929.

55. R. S. and H. M. Lynd, *Middletown in Transition*, pp. 291–292. New York 1937.

56. *Intramural and Interscholastic Athletics.* Monograph 27, p. 86. Office of Education, Washington, 1932.

57. *Op. cit.*, p. 82.

58. *Op. cit.*, p. 87.

175

59. G. Gorer, *The Americans*, Esp. Chapters II and VI. London 1947.
60. J. S. Brown, *A Study of Collegiate and Professional Negro Athletes* (M.Sc. Thesis unpublished). George Williams College, 1949.
61. D. W. Brogan, *The American Problem*, p. 145. London 1944.
62. Ralph Rose, *Racial Problems and Education*. Lecture to the Physical Education Society, University of Birmingham, 1953.
63. E. A. Rice, *A Brief History of Physical Education*, p. 266. New York, 1929.
64. C. E. Skinner and R. E. Langfitt (Ed.), *An Introduction to Modern Education*, p. 273. Boston 1937.
65. E. W. Knight, *Education in the United States*, p. 339. Boston 1934.
66. E. W. Lyttle, *National Education Association of the United States. Annual Address and Proceedings*, pp. 823–828. 1903.
67. J. F. Williams, *Physical Education in the School*, pp. 285–294. School Review, April 1926.
68. C. H. McCloy, *Philosophical Bases of Physical Education*, pp. 75–85. New York, 1947.
69. *The Physical Educator*. Published by Phi Epsilon Kappa Fraternity. Vol. X, Nos. 2,.3 and 4. May–Dec. 1953.
70. Van Dalen, *World History of Physical Education*, p. 480. New York 1953.
71. *Physical Fitness for Students in Colleges and Universities*. U.S. Office of Education, 1943.

176

VIII

Games and Gymnastics
for two Nations in one

P. C. McINTOSH

∘∞∽∞∽∞∽∞∽∞∽∞∽∞∽∞∽

URING the nineteenth century, while systems of gymnastics were being developed into programmes of physical education in Germany and Scandinavia, English Public Schools evolved their own peculiar physical education which was no less comprehensive and just as highly organized as its continental counterparts. It took the form of games and sports and, by the end of the century, these activities occupied a higher place of honour and absorbed more time and energy in Public Schools than gymnastics ever did in Swedish or German schools. Yet games and sports were rarely thought of as physical education. It was not that the physical effects upon those that played games were negligible; the opposite was in fact true; but games were valued more highly both by boys and masters for the qualities of character that they brought out, and the courage, team spirit and sportsmanship which they demanded than for the mere physical effects which they had. Physical prowess came to be admired, on occasion some critics thought too much admired, but the real justification for the Public School system was sought in character training. In 1864 the Royal Commission on Public Schools under the chairmanship of the Earl of Clarendon expressed this view in its Report. 'The bodily training which gives health and activity to the frame is imparted at English schools, not by gymnastic exercises which are employed for that end on the continent—exercises which are undoubtedly

177

very valuable and which we should be glad to see introduced
more widely in England—but by athletic games which, whilst
they serve this purpose well, serve other purposes besides. . . the
cricket and football fields . . . are not merely places of exercise
or amusement; they help to form some of the most valuable
social qualities and manly virtues, and they hold, like the classroom and the boarding house, a distinct and important place
in Public School education.'[1]

Public School education, referred to by the Clarendon Commission was essentially a nineteenth-century development and
it coincided with the rise of the middle class to prosperity, privilege and power. At the beginning of the century there were but
seven boarding schools, Winchester, Westminster, Eton, Harrow, Charterhouse, Rugby and Shrewsbury which answered to
Sidney Smith's definition of a Public School as 'an endowed
place of education of old standing to which the sons of gentlemen
resort in considerable numbers and where they continue to
reside from eight or nine to eighteen years of age'.[2] Christ's
Hospital was certainly also an endowed place of education of
old standing and was sometimes referred to as a Public School
but it did not on the whole attract 'the sons of gentlemen'. In
addition to the boarding schools two London day schools, St.
Paul's and Merchant Taylor's, enjoyed a national reputation
as Public Schools. It was, however, the boarding school which
was the distinctive feature of middle-class education in the
nineteenth-century and it was in the boarding school that the
games system grew up.

The seven boarding schools 'of old standing' had not always
been used by the middle class or by the aristocracy for the education of their sons. Winchester, the oldest of them had been
founded in 1382 by William of Wykeham for 'pauperes et
indigentes'. Harrow, Rugby, Charterhouse and Shrewsbury had
been endowed by wealthy individuals for the education of local
boys, not for the sons of the well-to-do. For a long while the
schools served their original purpose and the aristocracy
educated their sons privately. However, during the eighteenth
century the nobility gradually adopted the practice of sending
their sons away to school so that by the beginning of the nineteenth century the Public Schools were largely patronized by
the upper classes to the exclusion of the poor. A few middle-class

178

parents had also gained entry for their sons but the schools did not furnish nearly enough places to meet the demand of the middle class for the same educational privileges which were enjoyed by their betters. Other provision for the education of the middle classes was inadequate.

Between the Public Schools for the rich and the parochial schools for the poor were a number of what were called English or commercial schools. They were, for the most part, private undertakings started to provide a livelihood for the schoolmaster and his family. Teaching in these schools was often inefficient, discipline was bad and sometimes the moral fitness of the master was questionable. At the same time the increasing wealth and manufacturing power of the country were making the demands of the middle classes for political power harder to resist and the needs for the effective education of their sons more urgent. In 1832, the year in which the first Parliamentary Reform Bill was passed, Dr. Thomas Arnold, the great Headmaster of Rugby from 1828 to 1842, wrote two letters to *The Sheffield Courant* on 'The Education of the Middle Classes'. He pointed out that the Reform Bill would at once increase and consolidate the power of the middle classes yet the education available for them was not such as to enable them to discharge their important trust.[3] Arnold did not specifically recommend that the model of Rugby School should be copied elsewhere yet it was, in the event, the Public School as Arnold reformed it that became the model for very many other schools up and down the country. The earliest middle-class schools, King's College (1829), University College School (1830), Blackheath (1830) and Liverpool College (1840), catered for local inhabitants but between 1841 and 1847 Cheltenham, Marlborough, Rossall, Brighton and Radley were all founded with the intention of drawing boys from a distance and were modelled on the older Public Schools. In 1848 Nathaniel Woodard published his *Plea for the Middle Classes* and had already founded Lancing College which was the first of 17 Woodard Schools to provide 'a good and complete education for the middle classes at such a charge as will make it available to most of them.'[4] They were strongly influenced by the older schools. Again, some existing Grammar Schools, like Uppingham and Oundle, under forceful headmasters lost their character as local schools and became pros-

179

perous boarding schools with national reputations. Most characteristic of the new middle-class schools were those which were founded and developed as capitalist ventures, at first known as 'proprietary schools'. The education in them was modelled on the older Public Schools but their financial arrangements were more like those of an industrial enterprise. Some failed but many prospered and earned acceptance as Public Schools.

By the 1860's, then, the middle classes had forced their way into the educational preserves of the Public Schools, some entering the existing foundations, others the new foundations modelled on the old. So it was that in 1869 Matthew Arnold, a son of the Headmaster of Rugby, was able to make a division in the upper classes and wrote, 'I often, therefore, when I want to distinguish clearly the aristocratic class from the Philistines proper, or middle class, name the former in my own mind, the Barbarians.'[5]

The winning of educational privilege by the Philistines coincided with the growth of organized games, particularly cricket and football. At the beginning of the century both these games were certainly being played. In 1805 Lord Byron played cricket for Harrow in the first recorded cricket match with Eton, and various games of football were being played at the different schools, but games were not highly organized; they were largely confined to the older boys and they were by no means the only form of outdoor recreations. Some of the alternative amusements involved hunting, poaching, and forms of lawlessness which made the schools notorious. Nor did games receive approval let alone encouragement from masters. Headmasters were often hostile. Dr. Keate, headmaster of Eton, forbade the proposed cricket match with Harrow in 1821 and successive headmasters of Westminster tried to prevent rowing races with Eton in 1818 and 1829. Dr. Butler, headmaster of Shrewsbury from 1798 to 1836 thought that football was 'only fit for butcher-boys'.[6] Some games in some schools were tolerated by authority but nowhere were they encouraged as positive instruments of education.

By the 1860's the position within the schools had changed in at least three important respects; in the attitude of headmasters and assistant masters, in the time spent on games and

180

P. C. McIntosh

in the degree of organization. Outside the schools middle-class and upper-class opinion was moving towards approval of a games 'cult' and the Clarendon Commission reported that it was not easy to estimate the degree to which the English people were indebted to the Public Schools for the qualities on which they prided themselves most. Among these qualities the Commission included a love of healthy sports and exercise.

The change in attitude by authority was brought into sharp relief by the dicta of two successive headmasters of Winchester. Dr. G. Moberly (1838–66), spoke of 'the idle boys, I mean the boys who play cricket', while Dr. G. Ridding (1866–84) said, 'Give me a boy who is a cricketer. I can make something of him.' Edward Thring who was appointed Headmaster of Uppingham in 1853 inaugurated his term of office by declaring a whole holiday and playing in a cricket match. Subsequently he played fives and even football with the boys, an unheard of performance by a Public School headmaster but one that was to be repeated by many another.

Games gradually absorbed more and more of the boys' leisure time until in the 1860's boys at Eton who hoped to obtain a place in the school rowing eight spent as much as four hours a day on the river and Winchester cricketers spent three hours a day in playing or practising. The Clarendon Commission reported that 'the importance which boys themselves attach to games is somewhat greater, perhaps, than might reasonably be desired, but within moderate limits it is highly useful.'[7]

The organization of games was entirely in the hands of the boys. Now, after 100 years of compulsory games, which have received the sanction of authority, it is worth noting that the system was originally devised and imposed by the boys not by the masters. The origin of compulsory games was stated unequivocally to the Clarendon Commission by Rev. H. M. Butler, Headmaster of Harrow.

'I ought perhaps to conclude what has been said on this subject by explaining that fagging and compulsory attendance at football are parts of the internal government which was, so far as we know, originally established by the boys themselves, and is now certainly administered by them alone.

'The existing system is conducted with the full knowledge and sanction of the masters and would of course be modified to any

181

extent if the headmaster saw reason to desire it. But it was not created by any master, nor does any master, except on rare occasions, interfere with its administration. Its value consists in its being in the main independent of masters, though subject to their general control.'[8]

This essential feature of games in Public Schools in mid-nineteenth century persisted and still persists in British schools, colleges and universities in the twentieth century. It makes intelligible several aspects of the English attitude to the physical education of boys. In the first place it explains why the Clarendon Commission and many leaders of thought and opinion valued games so highly. The Public Schools produced leaders in many spheres of life; in industry and politics at home, as officers in the Army at home and abroad, in commercial enterprise throughout the world, and in the administration of a large and growing colonial empire. A great part of Public School life consisted of the organization and supervision of boys by other boys. In no part of school life was self-government so highly developed as in games and sports. The 'capacity to govern others and control themselves, the aptitude to combine freedom with order'[9] were practised by the boys on each other throughout adolescence at Public Schools especially in their physical recreations.

The tradition of self-government in games explains too the attitude which was adopted to coaching and instruction. The Clarendon Commission regretted that cricket had become so elaborate an art as to need professional instruction.[10] Nevertheless professional instruction in cricket, and some other games, with the notable exception of football, became the custom at Public Schools and members of the teaching staff who had themselves shown prowess at school or university acted as 'games masters'. Still, however, boys organized their own games and in many cases made their own mistakes in selecting or coaching their teams. The persistence of this tradition meant that the coaching of games and sports did not offer sufficient scope or status as a profession to attract many men of real ability and ambition. On the other hand it prevented games and sports at schools and universities in Britain becoming dominated by their coaches as they became in the United States. Lastly, the practice of self-government in games helps to explain

182

how the system of organized games ever rose to be the accepted pattern of physical education in Public Schools.

On the continent the development of this or that system of physical education in the early nineteenth century was closely associated with the pioneering efforts of one or two individuals, Nachtegall in Denmark, Ling in Sweden, GutsMuths, Jahn and Spiess in Germany. From time to time attempts have been made to link the development of organized games in England with the work of Dr. Arnold, the great reforming headmaster of Rugby, but there is evidence to show that games were already developing in Public Schools and even gaining recognition from masters before Arnold's reforms at Rugby took effect.

Charles Wordsworth, a nephew of the poet William Wordsworth, went to Harrow in 1820 and records that cricket, racquets and football were the chief sports, that masters had begun to encourage them but had not begun to place them on a par with, or even above intellectual achievements. In preparation for a cricket match against Eton the Harrovians had a professional down from Lord's cricket ground for the season as a coach. This was probably the first instance of a coaching professional at a Public School, and not, in Wordsworth's view, a desirable institution.

Wordsworth himself, when an undergraduate at Oxford, was responsible for bringing about the first cricket match with Cambridge in 1827 and the first Oxford and Cambridge boat race in 1829. As second master at Winchester from 1835–45 Wordsworth took a keen interest in boys' games and even joined in. He persuaded the Warden to finance from College funds the draining of the Meads as a cricket field. At other schools, too, there were signs that games and sports were developing during the 1820's and even winning approval from some masters.

At Rugby there was a similar trend in favour of games during Arnold's time as headmaster, and in 1840 the school's cricket team played at Lord's for the first time. Some years before this Arnold had written of the cricket field as a place 'where no profane person may encroach'. This remark is highly significant of the place that cricket had come to occupy in the esteem of the boys.

There is scant evidence that Arnold himself directly encouraged games. It is true that he played informal games of

N   183

cricket with his own children on the school field during the holidays, that he arranged for his sons to have professional coaching and that he wrote in 1833, 'The work is full heavy just now, but the fry are learning cricket, and we play nice matches sometimes to my great refreshment.'[11] However, it seems that the activities in which Arnold was personally most interested were such individualistic sports as swimming, throwing the spear, and gymnastic exercises on the pole and 'gallows'. Indeed, by 1831 he had a 'gallows' erected at Rugby. The impetus which organized games received from the Headmaster of Rugby was an indirect one and it resulted from his reforms, some of which were quite remote from the physical activities of the boys.

In the first place he forbade certain recreations such as hare hunting, which had led to lawlessness, and he disbanded the boys' pack of hounds. Inevitably, after this, boys spent their time on those pursuits which were not banned, especially games within the school grounds. Secondly, the very nature of Arnold's moral and religious reforms entailed an encouragement of athleticism. Public Schools at the beginning of the century were as notorious for their vices and lawlessness as they were famous for their classical education. At Rugby and at Winchester, school rebellions reached such dimensions that the military had to be called out to quell them. Arnold set out in 1828 to infuse a new moral tone and a religious idealism into Rugby. He once said that what he looked for in a Christian school were first religious and moral principles; secondly, gentlemanly conduct; thirdly, intellectual ability.

To achieve his ends he resorted to expulsion and superannuation of unsuitable and unco-operative pupils, and above all things he strove to establish confidence between himself and his Sixth Form whence were appointed the Praepostors, and then to secure their co-operation in implementing his principles throughout the school. 'When I have confidence in the Sixth', he said, 'there is no post in England which I would exchange for this; but if they do not support me I must go.' Arnold accepted that essential feature of Public School education, government of boys by boys, and sought both to administer the school and to effect his reforms through his Praepostors. He staked his future at Rugby upon this and he achieved his object.

184

Because games and sports were the sphere in which self government by boys was most thorough, athleticism received an unexpected filip from Arnold's reform as did consolidation of the prefect system of school government.

Benjamin Jowett wrote in a letter to Stanley, Arnold's biographer and disciple: 'Arnold's peculiar danger was not knowing where his ideas would take other people or ought to take himself.' Frances J. Woodward has shown how four of Arnold's distinguished pupils were affected by this 'peculiar danger'.[12] The danger is also to be observed in the development of athleticism in Public Schools after Arnold's death in 1842.

Probably the school in which games in general and cricket and football in particular were first actively encouraged by a headmaster for disciplinary and then educational ends was Marlborough. This school had been founded in 1843 but neither headmaster nor staff had experience of boarding schools of the Public School type, and, after a school rebellion, a new headmaster was appointed in 1851. He was G. E. L. Cotton who had been a master at Rugby under Arnold. He soon showed himself a true disciple by announcing that he hoped to govern the school as a Public School and not a private one and that he would try to make it govern itself through its prefects.[13] He also circularized all parents soon after his appointment asking for their support in his encouragement of cricket and football as wholesome recreations and antidotes to lawlessness.[14] The particular type of football that was played at Marlborough was the Rugby game. During the 'fifties and 'sixties a number of former pupils and masters of Rugby school were appointed to headmasterships of Public Schools. They seem to have introduced not only the Rugby system of education and school government but also the Rugby variety of football. The Arnoldians began to encourage games for their educational merits as well as their disciplinary value.

The growing cult of games first found popular expression in a novel. *Tom Brown's Schooldays*, written by Thomas Hughes and published in 1857, purported to give an account of life at Rugby School in the time of Dr. Arnold. A game of football, a fight and a cricket match were each described and held up for admiration. Perhaps the passage which did as much as anything to popularize the theory of the educational value of team

185

games was a conversation between Tom Brown and one of his masters, who was in fact G. E. L. Cotton, about cricket.

‘ "Come, none of your irony, Brown," answers the master, "I'm beginning to understand the game scientifically. What a noble game it is, too!"

‘ "Isn't it? But it's more than a game. It's an institution," said Tom.

‘ "Yes," said Arthur, "the birthright of British boys old and young, as *habeas corpus* and trial by jury are of British men."

‘ "The discipline and reliance on one another which it teaches is so valuable, I think," went on the master, "it ought to be such an unselfish game. It merges the individual in the eleven; he doesn't play that he may win, but that his side may.'

‘ "That's very true," said Tom, "and that's why football and cricket, now one comes to think of it, are so much better games than fives or hare and hounds, or any others where the object is to come in first or to win for oneself, and not that one's side may win."

‘ "And then the captain of the eleven! "said the master, "what a post is his in our school-world! Almost as hard as the Doctor's, requiring skill and gentleness and firmness, and I know not what other rare qualities." '

The book was published in April and by the end of the year more than 11,000 copies had been sold. It was reprinted many times and J. J. Findlay, whose biography of Arnold was published in 1897, maintained that with the exception of Pestalozzi's *Leonard and Gertrude*, *Tom Brown* was the only work of fiction which had exercised a world-wide influence upon education. It was, however, a work of fiction written fifteen years after Arnold's death and, while its influence cannot be denied, as a picture of life at Rugby and as evidence of Arnold's attitude to games it must be treated with great reserve.

Tom Brown's Schooldays was certainly popular, but it did not escape criticism. Fitzjames Stephen in the *Edinburgh Review* for January 1858 attacked not only this novel but the whole movement towards 'muscular Christianity', a movement in which both Charles Kingsley, the author of *Westward Ho!* and Thomas Hughes were leaders. Stephen claimed that these writers were, by implication, casting a slur upon intellectual ability. Within the Public Schools themselves some headmasters saw and feared

186

the direction in which games were moving. Dr. Moberly, head-master of Winchester, who was no enemy of physical education as such, and even arranged for boys with stooping backs to have corrective exercises, yet saw that games which were in theory *play* were becoming an enthralling *business*. Preparation for inter-school matches was interfering with school work and Moberly put a stop to the annual cricket match against Eton at Lords. He did not, however, administer more than a temporary check to the growth of the games cult.

During the latter part of the century there were many other critics of organized games. Wilkie Collins used the medium of a novel, *Man and Wife* (1870), to offer a counterblast to the exaggerated emphasis put upon physical prowess by the press and the public. An article with a similar attack was contributed to the *Nineteenth Century* by Edward Lyttelton in 1880,[15] and the tyranny of organized games was the subject of a lengthy correspondence in *The Times* in 1889. The letters which were contributed brought out an interesting and significant change that had taken place in the recreations of Public Schoolboys. Early in the century the boys had indulged in hunting, stalking, fishing and other open-air pursuits without the need of compulsion, and at that time the Eton boys were mainly the sons of country gentlemen. By the latter part of the century the clientele of Eton and other Public Schools had changed. An increasing number of the new upper middle class had found their way in. The boys' recreations had changed too, to football and cricket and other games. In Matthew Arnold's terminology the Philistines had imposed upon the Public Schools not only their own clientele but also their own physical culture.

The critics had little effect upon the growth of athleticism which perhaps reached its peak at Eton under the headmaster-ship of Edmund Warre (1884–1905). Warre had been assistant master at Eton since 1860, had coached the Eight from his arrival and had taken a keen interest in games, so much so that in the year of his appointment as Headmaster a letter appeared in *The Times* to the effect that he had made no mark as scholar, preacher or man of letters and that his claim to fame was 'as the best rowing coach in England and as an able field officer of Volunteers.'[16] As headmaster it was his settled policy to glorify games and to make it impossible for boys to escape the

meshes of compulsion. In 1888 he wrote a letter to his colleagues expressing alarm that on a given afternoon there might be as many as 300 boys not occupied in games or rowing. Athleticism was probably more marked at Eton than elsewhere during the last decade of the nineteenth century, but in other Public Schools too, organized games were the accepted form of physical education.

A number of features of the system, as it then was, call for remark. The Games Master has already been mentioned. He was appointed to the staff and had the same status as any other master; he had a degree obtained at Oxford or Cambridge University and he taught in the classroom, but his primary task was to help with one or more school game and his qualification for appointment was his own prowess in those games. In the early years of the century when games had not won the active support of authority the boys might themselves, as at Harrow in 1821, obtain the services of a professional player to coach them, and 'professionals' continued to be appointed to a number of Public Schools. The Games Master, however, was a later feature of school life and, far from being a 'professional', he was in social status a gentleman and in athletic status an amateur. One of the earliest Games Masters was R. A. H. Mitchell who was appointed to Eton in 1866, and took an absorbing interest in cricket. He guided, advised, coached and criticized but he did not organize the game. Organization and much else to do with games remained in the hands of the boys. The demand for Games Masters was heavy as is shown by the story told in the *Contemporary Review* for 1900 of a university 'blue' who, on completing his century in the university cricket match, received five telegrams from as many headmasters offering him posts in their schools.

A second feature of athleticism was its close connection with military training. There had long been a belief in the efficacy of the prefect–fagging system in preparing boys for future service as officers in the army. From 1860, after the shocks of the Crimean War, 1854–6, and the Indian Mutiny, 1857–9, games were felt to be insufficient training and in many schools volunteer corps were established to give training in drill and manoeuvre and the use of arms. Nevertheless the real qualities that made a good officer, as distinct from the military techniques

188

which he needed, were still thought to emanate from the playing field, not the barrack square. Two verses of Henry Newbolt's poem *Vitai Lampada* serve to illustrate the close connection between playing field and battle field.

> There's a breathless hush in the Close tonight
> Ten to make and the match to win—
> A bumping pitch and a blinding light,·
> An hour to play and the last man in.
> And it's not for the sake of a ribboned coat,
> Or the selfish hope of a season's fame
> But his captain's hand on his shoulder smote—
> Play up! Play up! and play the game.
>
> The sand of the desert is sodden and red—
> Red with the wreck of a square that broke—
> The Gatling's jammed and the Colonel dead,
> And the regiment blind with dust and smoke.
> The river of death has brimmed his banks
> And England's far and Honour a name,
> But the voice of a schoolboy rallies the ranks;
> Play up! Play up! and play the game.

The distinction between major and minor games was implied in the conversation between Tom Brown and his master, in which hare and hounds was compared unfavourably with cricket and football, and it became an accepted part of the games system. Team games which fostered team spirit and group loyalty, held pride of place and took precedence; other games, however difficult or fascinating they might be, were relegated to a subordinate place. Gymnastics which in some other countries was the be-all and end-all of physical education was, in the Public Schools, a minor sport along with fives, swimming, track and field athletics and many others. Nothing, as Matthew Arnold said to the Taunton Commission, would make an ex-Public Schoolboy regard the gymnastics of a foreign school without a slight feeling of wonder and compassion, so much more animating and interesting did the games of his remembrance seem to him.

From an educational standpoint a significant feature of nineteenth-century athleticism was the ideal of sportsmanship which was bound up with it. Games were played according to rules which were carefully worked out and refined over the

189

years, but more powerful and binding even than the rules was the concept of the 'spirit of the game'. 'It's not cricket' became a colloquialism for the infringement of the code of fair play between honourable opponents in any sphere.[17] The ideal of sportsmanship was never more succintly expressed than in the Harrow school song 'Forty Years On' written in 1872. 'Strife without anger and art without malice' was shown by Public Schools to be a worthy and an attainable ideal. The early history of Association Football gave striking examples of how the ideal was extended beyond the Public School community and how Public Schoolmen resisted changes because they were contrary to the spirit of the game. For many years 'soccer', which was played under rules devised and formulated by Public School and University men, was played without umpires or referee. It was assumed that any infringement of a rule was unintentional and all disputes were settled by the two opposing captains on the field. For an even longer period the game was played without the 'penalty kick'. After this had been introduced by the Football Association in 1891 the teams of ex-Public Schoolboys playing in the Arthur Dunn Cup Competition some years later thought it such an insult to their sportsmanship that they decided to ignore the new rule. The continued inclusion of the phrase 'ungentlemanly conduct' in the laws of soccer is a reminder of an ideal of behaviour which was an intrinsic part of Public School physical education in the nineteenth century.

Public Schools were entirely independent of central and local government. Physical education in schools which did not enjoy such independence took on a very different pattern from organized games and athleticism. This is the more curious because it was not until the twentieth century, after the merits of organized games had been clearly recognized, that the Government could be said to have had a positive and constructive policy upon physical education in state-aided schools. When it finally formulated such a policy, the system imposed upon schools was the Swedish gymnastic system inspired as it still was by the pioneer work of P. H. Ling eighty years earlier. An easy explanation is that the games which were played in the Public Schools were developed by, and most suitable for older adolescents, while the vast majority of children for whom the state was responsible

190

left school at a younger age. The Education Department and, later, the Board of Education were forced therefore to devise or encourage a system which was suited to younger boys. This, however, is too easy an explanation since even for secondary schools where games would have been suitable and were in fact being played, the Board stressed the desirability of the Swedish system while many elementary schoolboys and girls were given opportunities to take part in games and sports through the initiative and voluntary work of devoted teachers outside the set curriculum. The reasons for the sharp difference between the physical education of the Public Schoolboy and the elementary and secondary schoolboy are complex.

At the beginning of the nineteenth century there was in Britain no comprehensive system of elementary education such as there had been in Prussia since the early eighteenth century and such as was enacted in Sweden in 1842. Compulsory education in England did not become law until the Education Acts of 1876 and 1880 were passed. At the beginning of the century the government did not consider education to be within its province. Elementary education for the poorer classes was provided parochially. When the industrial revolution brought about a great increase of the population, schools were provided by the National Society of the Church of England founded for this purpose in 1811, and by the British and Foreign School Society, a dissenting body set up in 1814. These bodies, depending, as they did, upon voluntary subscriptions and meagre fees from parents, concerned themselves with the basic needs of education, instruction in reading, writing and arithmetic, the three R's. They did not cater for the physical needs of pupils, although individual teachers in some schools did conduct classes of children in exercises, either 'elementary movements' or 'more complex combinations'. The exercises were probably derived from GutsMuths, whose book *Gymnastics for Youth* had appeared translated into English, in 1800.

In 1833 Parliament made a first grant of £20,000 in aid of elementary education and it was laid down that payments should be made only through one or other of these two Societies. In 1839 a committee of the Privy Council was set up to 'superintend the application of any sums voted by Parliament for public education'. The Vice-President of the Committee of

Council on Education was responsible to Parliament and under him was the Education Department. In addition, two inspectors of aided schools were appointed. To ensure their impartiality they received their appointment from the Queen not from the Education Department and they and their successors have ever since been known as Her (or His) Majesty's Inspectors of Schools.

At first the Education Department took an active interest in physical education. Inspectors were instructed to encourage the provision of facilities for recreation and exercise at new and existing schools and to report on the competence of pupil teachers to take classes in physical exercise. The Committee itself passed a lengthy minute to encourage the provision of physical training. However, between 1840 and 1870 when the Forster Education Act was passed, very little was done for the physical education of elementary school children. There were two reasons for this.

First, as the reports of the Inspectors came in during those early years they made very gloomy reading. The appalling physical conditions of the school rooms, the lack of books and equipment, the poor quality of the teachers and the abysmal ignorance of the children many of whom were poverty-stricken and some in a state of semi-starvation presented problems more pressing than the lack of physical training. Had the children been fit and the teachers competent, physical training would still have been restricted by the absence of school playgrounds. Of 35 schools provided by the British Society in the Metropolitan District of London only three were found to have playgrounds of any kind. Reports from elsewhere revealed a similar situation. Urban development had far outstripped the provision of schools and similar facilities.

Lack of facilities made it difficult to give even elementary physical education, and the Government's attitude was discouraging not to say obstructive. From time to time representations were made to the government urging that physical training should be provided. None was more pressing than that of Lord Elcho who, on 8th July 1862, brought this motion before the House of Commons: 'That it is expedient for the increase of bodily as well as mental aptitudes of children for civil, industrial as well as for possible military service that encouragement and

192

aid should be given for the extension of the practice of systematized gymnastic training, and for the teaching of military and naval drill . . .' Robert Lowe, the Vice-President of the Committee of the Council on Education opposed the motion partly on the ground of the expense involved, but he added most significantly that Lord Elcho's proposals 'embodied an idea— the idea that it was the duty of the Privy Council to devise means in addition to the existing grant to promote the teaching of anything because it might be deemed useful—which he must altogether repudiate.'[18] Physical education which, in the form of organized games, was viewed by the Clarendon Commission at this time as a valuable and essential feature of the Public School system was regarded by the Government as an unnecessary frill to public elementary education.

The Government, however, certainly did not have the backing of the whole country in its attitude and, since the publication of GutsMuths book in English, gymnastics had appealed to a number of people as a valuable means of physical education. P. H. Clias, a Swiss Army Officer and disciple of GutsMuths, published an abridged version of his master's work with his own additions in 1823, and at one time was a visiting instructor at Charterhouse School. In 1825 Jeremy Bentham had supported the German exile Carl Voelke when he opened a Turnplatz, after the manner of Jahn, near Regent's Park. At Oxford Archibald MacLaren opened a gymnasium in 1858 and, with gymnastics as a basis, he developed a comprehensive system of physical education. In 1861 he was invited to reorganize physical training in the army where his influence was very extensive. In schools it was less so. Gymnasia with equipment similar to MacLaren's were built at Public Schools, Harrow Wellington and Winchester among them, but gymnastics never dislodged team games from their pride of place and, because they were put in the hands of non-commissioned officers who held an inferior social status both in the schools and in public opinion, gymnastics tended to be regarded as inferior by association. In the 'fifties and 'sixties Herbert Spencer, John Ruskin and Matthew Arnold all wrote for the cause of physical education, but Matthew Arnold's argument that physical education should take the form of gymnastics because, if boys had to work long hours, or if they worked hard, gymnastics would do more

193

for their physical health in the comparatively short time allotted to recreation than anything else could do,[19] is in marked contrast to his testimony about games to the Taunton Commission. It suggests that he assumed that there should be one type of physical education for the ruling classes and a different one for the masses.

This class difference in physical education was a tacit assumption in many quarters. Later, in 1895, it was explicitly stated by Wallace MacLaren in the preface to a new edition of his father's book *Physical Education*, '. . . On the one side we have to deal with the upper and middle classes, in fact with all that large class who are sent to private and Public Schools or training colleges for their education, and proceed to the army, to the universities or to business life. On the other side is the still larger class of those whom the nation educates, a class which the subject of gymnastics may be thought to touch more nearly, in as much as, after an early age, they have little or no time for recreation like those socially above them, and the gymnasium is therefore to them a vital source of health.

'The requirements of these two classes physically are in themselves distinct, and must be dealt with from an altogether different standpoint.'[20]

In the event the public elementary schools experienced an even more limited form of physical education than that advocated by Matthew Arnold and the MacLarens. When Mr. Forster's Education Bill was put before Parliament in 1870 'to fill up gaps' in the educational system of the country, it made no mention of physical education, but the revised code of regulations which followed the passing of the Act stated that 'attendance at drill under a competent instructor for not more than two hours per week and twenty weeks in the year may be counted as school attendance' for purposes of financial grant from the government. Arrangements were made by the Education Department with the War Office for instruction to be given by drill sergeants at the rate of sixpence a day and a penny a mile marching money. It was hoped that these exercises 'would be sufficient to teach boys habits of sharp obedience, smartness and cleanliness.' This 'drill' continued to be the only officially approved form of physical education until 1890, although several School Boards and many individual teachers managed

194

to provide their children with instruction in gymnastics and even in swimming and team games, in spite of very limited facilities and opportunities.

A significant event in the development of a gymnastic form of physical education was the invitation sent by the London School Board in 1878 to Miss Concordia Löfving to come from Sweden and take up an appointment as Lady Superintendent of Physical Education. This was significant because it marked the real beginning of the steady rise of the Swedish system to dominate physical education in state aided schools. It was also significant as a pointer to the influence which women were to have in the future development of physical education in England. Women pioneers, both as individuals, and acting through their colleges and professional organization, were largely responsible for ousting military drill from elementary schools and for showing that even with the poor facilities that then existed there was a better and more scientific alternative.

The Swedish system had been introduced into England long before Miss Löfving arrived, but Ling's gymnastics had been used for the most part in their medical application. Several admirers of the system had advocated its wider use in schools and Dr. Matthias Roth, who had pursued a course of study at the Central Gymnastic Institute, Stockholm, had, since 1851, been tireless in his efforts to secure the adoption of the Swedish system in schools and colleges. He had written books and pamphlets, he had approached Members of Parliament, he had written an open letter to Mr. Forster at the time that his Education Bill was published and he had trained a number of teachers at his own expense. Little progress was made until he persuaded Mrs. Westlake, a member of the London School Board, to propose the invitation to Miss Löfving.

When she arrived her duty was to conduct courses for women teachers in the Board's schools. Within a year there were 600 applications to attend these courses. In 1881, Miss Löfving's place was taken by Miss Martina Bergman who later became Madam Bergman Österberg. In 1882 the Swedish system was extended to boys' schools. Men, however, were not so wholeheartedly in favour of the Swedish system and for some years an English system, as well as the Swedish system, was employed. In 1893 the Swedish system was officially dropped

195

by the London School Board as far as boys were concerned and the services of Allan Broman, who had run courses in the Swedish system, were dispensed with.

Miss Bergman, however, saw that there was a great future for the Swedish system for girls not only in elementary schools but in secondary schools, and in 1885, while continuing to work for the London School Board, she started her own college in Hampstead.

The secondary education of girls was making great progress at this time. It had received a great impetus in the 'sixties from the work of two headmistresses, Miss Dorothea Beale at Cheltenham Ladies' College, and Miss Frances Mary Buss at the North London Collegiate School. The Girls' Public Day School Trust was formed by a number of schools which were providing for girls the type of education which old and new Public Schools were providing for their brothers. Boarding schools were founded, and after the passing of the Endowed Schools Act in 1869, many girls' grammar schools were started as sister schools to existing grammar schools for boys.

The demand for secondary education for girls was tremendous, and their physical education presented a problem. Earlier in the century the education of girls had been said by Herbert Spencer to be calculated to produce 'a certain delicacy of strength and a fastidious appetite joined with that timidity which commonly accompanies feebleness'.[21] Some schools had provided croquet and callisthenics for their pupils. Miss Beale and Miss Buss thought them quite inadequate. A few schools in London had adopted the musical gymnastics of Dio Lewis. Other schools employed visiting army sergeants to drill the girls. But, by the 1880's, most girls' schools neglected physical education for want of a reliable system rather than for want of interest in the subject. The fact that several schools, Wycombe Abbey and Sheffield High School among them, appointed gymnastic mistresses direct from the Central Gymnastic Institute in Stockholm merely emphasized the great need for English teachers trained in a reliable system.

It was this need which Miss Bergman, later Madame Bergman Österberg, was steadily meeting, first in Hampstead and then from 1895 at Dartford in Kent where she founded her own college. With an eye to their future careers she insisted on girls

196

having a sound educational and social background before she would accept them as students. Thus she ensured that her students, when trained, could meet their colleagues on terms of equality. The demand for her students was pressing and they were almost invariably appointed to schools before they finished their training.

Although Madame Bergman Österberg based her training on Ling's Gymnastics and had little knowledge of, and perhaps not much use for games, she could not afford to neglect them. In some respects girls' schools imitated boys' Public Schools. Many of them like St. Leonards, Wycome Abbey and Roedean, introduced games as soon as they were founded. If Madame Österberg's students were to conduct the physical education of girls in these schools they must be competent to teach games. The students themselves were keen to incorporate games in their training. So it was that cricket, hockey, tennis and other games were included in the two years' course, and the game of Netball was adapted from Basket Ball. The original rules for the new game were drawn up by a group of Madame Österberg's students in 1900 and were designed to meet the need for an outdoor winter game occupying a small space and suitable for girls. Madame's students also devised the knee-length gym tunic with its three box pleats in front and at the back to replace the very full ankle length skirt which, together with straw hat, was *de rigeur* for games at that time.

Madame Österberg and her students were pioneers in more than dress. They opened up a new career to girls from middle-class families. Careers for these girls were restricted. An Act of Parliament passed in 1875 had permitted universities to confer degrees on women, and another had forbidden the Royal College of Surgeons to exclude them, yet the Universities of Oxford and Cambridge continued to refuse to admit women to examinations in medicine, theology and law. Teaching, however, had been open to women throughout the centuries and as the Public Schools and High Schools increased in number so did the opportunities to teach for women from the middle classes. Physical education was a new career within the teaching profession.

Towards the end of the nineteenth century and at the beginning of the next, other colleges for training women specialists in

197

physical education were started. Chelsea College was started in 1898 as part of the South Western Polytechnic, and Miss Rhoda Anstey founded her own college for women near Birmingham in 1899. Other colleges sprang up near Liverpool, at Dunfermline in Scotland, in Bedford, Bournemouth, and Manchester. Not all favoured the Swedish system yet all adopted it sooner or later. They could not afford to do otherwise. Public Schools and High Schools, in advertising their vacant posts, began to stipulate that applicants must be able to teach the Swedish system. Madame Österberg's insistence on a sound educational background for her students was justifying itself. What the schools really wanted in their gym mistresses was sound education and a college training. Madame Österberg's college had a well established reputation by the end of the century and because the training there was in the Swedish system the better schools began to insist upon this qualification. Other colleges felt bound to follow Madame Österberg's lead.

The movement towards the Swedish system was reinforced when, on 9th January 1899, thirty-one old students of Madame Österberg's College met and formed an association which came to be known as the Ling Association. Its purpose was to band together teachers trained in the Swedish system, to protect and improve their status and to arrange meetings and holiday courses. At first membership was confined to former members of Madame Österberg's College and of the Central Institute in Stockholm. Later, membership was extended to women trained at other gymnastic colleges provided that the gymnastic syllabus had been exclusively Swedish. An application from Irene Marsh's College near Liverpool for affiliation was turned down because, as well as the Swedish system, musical drill was used, and Miss Marsh refused to give it up.

A further pioneer effort by the women teachers was the starting of a professional journal. In 1908 one of Madame Österberg's former students, Mrs. E. Adair Impey, assisted by three gifts of £5 from Chelsea and Dunfermline Old Students' Associations and from Dorette Wilkie, principal of Chelsea College, produced the first number of the Journal of Scientific Physical Training. The journal was produced from then on once a term. While it provided a forum for discussion and gave

198

assistance to the many men and women teaching physical exercises who had neither the education nor the technical training of the new women specialists, it nevertheless propagated the Swedish system in preference to any other.

Madame Österberg died at her college in Dartford in 1915. Shortly before her death she had offered her college as a gift to the Nation. The offer was declined but arrangements were made for the college to be governed by a board of trustees which included the Chief Medical Officer of the Board of Education. She had trained some 500 students since she had founded her college 30 years before and had profoundly influenced the course of physical education in England. The achievements of women in the spheres of secondary education and teacher training, contrasted strongly with those of the men. One or two Public Schools, notable Eton and Bedales had gone some way to developing a comprehensive scheme of physical education based on the Swedish system. A one-year's course in educational gymnastics for men was started at the South Western Polytechnic in 1908 and was directed by Lieutenant Braae Hansen who came from the Central Gymnastic Institute in Copenhagen, and Allan Broman opened a Central Institute for Swedish Gymnastics in London in 1911. He, too, offered a one-year's course for men. Apart from these courses, specialist training in physical education could be obtained by men only in foreign countries, and, after 1911, at Dunfermline in Scotland.

In elementary schools, as well as in teacher training and in secondary schools, the influence of the women pioneers was profound. Madame Österberg, although holding a post under the London School Board, had not confined her activities to its teachers. She was responsible for introducing the Swedish system into Whitelands Training College, and for a year she travelled to Bristol on Friday nights, after finishing her work for the London School Board, to run courses for teachers in the West. The value of her work was recognized by the Royal Commission on Elementary Education which reported in 1888. While the Commission recommended for boys nothing more imaginative than a form of military drill, it referred specifically to Madame Bergman Österberg's evidence 'for an interesting account of the Swedish system of exercises for girls based on the study of physiology'[22] and expressed the hope that it would

o   199

be gradually introduced into elementary schools. This hope was to be fulfilled.

Six years after the Cross Commission reported, the Education Department gave official approval to the Swedish system and stated that 'after 31st August 1895 the higher grant for Discipline and Organization will not be paid to any school in which provision is not made for instruction in Swedish or other drill or suitable physical exercises'.[23] In this way physical education was brought within the system of 'payment by results' and furthermore the official attitude to the subject was underlined: physical education was primarily for discipline. Nevertheless the Swedish system had been recognized, and it was the only system which was mentioned by name.

In 1899 the Education Department was replaced by the Board of Education, the President of the Board being a member of the government of the day. The Gilbertian system, whereby for many years the Vice-President of the Committee of the Privy Council on Education had also been responsible for the importation and movement of cattle throughout the country, was certainly due for overhaul, and in 1902 a new Education Act, the Balfour Act, became law. The Act did not deal specifically with physical education but its reform of the administration of the educational system made possible the next steps forward.

In 1900 and again in 1906 organized games received tardy recognition as a possible means of physical education and were officially allowed by the Board to be a suitable alternative to Swedish drill or physical exercises. The hard realities of the situation prevented a very large number of children from benefiting from this innovation of policy. As recently as 1895 Her Majesty's Inspector for the Metropolitan division had estimated that there were 25,000 schoolchildren within a mile of Charing Cross who had no playground at all and very few playgrounds worth the name were to be found in the whole of London.

At the end of the nineteenth century, then, physical education in elementary schools was moving steadily away from military drill and equally steadily towards the Swedish system. The Boer War, which broke out in 1899, temporarily stopped this movement. Public opinion was greatly shocked by the vast number of recruits who were rejected by the army as physically

200

unfit, and in response to the general outcry a number of measures were taken, some of which directly affected physical education. In 1902 the Board of Education in consultation with the War Office published a 'Model Course of Physical Training', consisting mainly of military drill, and directly encouraged schools to appoint Army instructors. Colonel Malcolm Fox was appointed Inspector of Physical Training and introduced a system of drill taken by N.C.O. instructors who went from school to school.

This policy was resisted by the National Union of Teachers and was anathema to the women specialist teachers. It meant the abandonment of the Swedish system in favour of an unscientific drill and it further meant that physical education was being handed over to men who had not the same educational or social background as teachers of other subjects. The Ling Association drew up a Memorial to the Board of Education attacking the Model Course, and collected 1,408 signatures from teachers, doctors, professors and others. In addition, individual members of the Association went to the House of Commons and protested to their members of Parliament. The government responded to the protests and appointed an Interdepartmental Committee to examine the Model Course. The Committee reported that the Model Course was unsatisfactory and produced its own Syllabus of Physical Exercises in 1904. This syllabus, priced ninepence, incorporated a number of the features of the gymnastics which were being done in the women's colleges of physical education.

It was not so easy, however, to put into reverse Colonel Malcolm Fox's policy of employing army instructors in schools. Once appointed they could not easily be dismissed. Nor were the supporters of military drill silenced. Another Interdepartmental Committee, on Physical Deterioration, reported in 1904 in favour of compulsory physical training whereby, 'without recourse being had to any suggestion of compulsory military service, the male adolescent population might undergo a species of training that would befit them to bear arms with very little supplementary discipline'.[24] This was strongly resisted by teachers and an open debate was conducted by the *Manchester Guardian* in which a number of people argued that adequate feeding was more relevant to physical fitness than physical

o* 201

training and that the Swedish system was far superior to English military drill. The Swedish system now had a number of advocates outside the women's ranks. Commander N. C. Palmer and Lieutenant F. H. Grenfell had introduced it into the Navy in 1902. Grenfell then left the Navy to introduce it into preparatory schools and was assisted by Lieutenant B. T. Coote, R.N. Another vocal advocate was R. E. Roper, M.A., who through his training in Stockholm was one of the very few Englishmen who could join the Ling Association.

From 1904 to 1914 military drill lost ground steadily and support for the Swedish drill grew. In 1907 Colonel Malcolm Fox was sent to Sweden and in 1908 Miss L. M. Rendal, who had been trained at Chelsea College was appointed the first woman inspector of physical exercises. In the same year an even more significant step was taken when the medical department of the Board of Education was set up under Dr. (later Sir George) Newman and was given the oversight of physical training. Almost at once Dr. Newman secured the appointment of three more inspectors, Lieut.-Commander F. H. Grenfell, to supersede Colonel Malcolm Fox, and Mr. Veysey and Miss Koetter. In 1909 a new *Syllabus of Physical Training* was issued. Some games and recreative activities were included but the bulk of the book was concerned with an exposition of the Swedish system and contained seventy-one tables of exercises. At this time the Swedish system was excessively rigid and even minor departures were regarded with disapproval. The syllabus therefore came in for criticism from the *Journal of Scientific Physical Training* where the statement was made that emphasis on the recreative side was always at the expense of due emphasis on the educational effect of exercise.[25] The Swedish system, however, together with games and swimming was now the official policy of the government for physical education. When, in 1909 also, physical training was made a compulsory and examinable subject in training colleges the seal was also set upon the policy of requiring from teachers of physical education the same educational background that was thought necessary for teaching other subjects.

Not all advocates of physical education approved of these developments. The British College of Physical Education founded in 1891, the Gymnastic Teachers Institute founded in

202

1897 and the National Society for Physical Education founded in the same year had all aimed to develop a British System, but had in fact propounded modifications of German gymnastics. Many of their members who were not at all well educated saw their future in jeopardy. Nor was the exclusive use of the Swedish system to their liking. In 1905 they had negotiated with the Ling Association with a view to amalgamation in order to gain more definite recognition from the Board of Education. However, the negotiations had broken down upon the Ling Association's insistence upon high technical and educational qualifications. It was indeed the insistence upon these tenets by the women's colleges together with the intense loyalty of former students to their own Ling Association which enabled them to achieve so much in the early years of the twentieth century. Moreover, as there was a great dearth, almost a complete absence, of men teachers with any specialist training, it was the women teachers who provided the necessary support for the policy of physical education which Dr. Newman and Commander Grenfell began to build in 1908.

The 1914–18 war once more awakened people's concern for physical fitness. There was a danger that physical education might relapse into military training, but the voices in support of such a policy were much fainter than they had been in the Boer War. Dr. Newman was quick to see that the situation was not so much fraught with danger as full of new opportunities for physical education. Supported by a national concern for the fitness of the younger generation he pressed forward with a number of measures especially the appointment of organizers of physical education by local education authorities. Some authorities had made such appointments many years previously but it was not until 1917 that the Board was enabled to pay grants to local authorities in aid of expenditure on the appointments. Within twelve months forty new organizers were appointed. The number continued to grow after the war and the standard of teaching in schools rose in consequence. The following year the Fisher Education Act enabled local authorities to provide holiday and school camps, centres and equipment for physical training, playing fields, swimming baths and other facilities for physical training. This legislation was merely permissive but during the next two decades many authorities availed them-

203

selves of the opportunity provided by the act and, advised and encouraged by the Board of Education, constructed good gymnasia, playing fields and swimming baths. In 1919 a new syllabus was published and, while still relying mainly upon the Swedish system and upon therapeutic exercises with specific effects, the syllabus also included many suggestions on games and a special chapter upon the physical training of children under seven.

The close link between physical education and medicine which was reflected in administrative arrangements at the Board of Education whereby the Chief Medical Officer was responsible for physical education, was emphasized after the war when, in 1922, the Ling Association made arrangements with the Chartered Society of Massage and Medical Gymnastics for all students at colleges recognized by the Association to be examined by the Chartered Society. The emphasis upon the therapeutic value of physical education was a notable feature of developments during the 1920's and '30's and it led to some curious results.

In the first place it enabled physical education to escape the most serious consequences of the 'Geddes Axe' in 1922. When this economy campaign was launched the Board of Education pointed out that an efficient system of physical training was a potent auxiliary in the prevention of debility and disease among school children, and local authorities were asked to explore every other avenue of economy in order to retain or appoint organizers of physical training. From time to time the annual report of the Medical Department, *The Health of the School Child*, overstated the case for therapeutic exercise, and certainly the statement that 'Good posture indicates health and soundness, bad posture the reverse',[26] ignored difficulties of measuring posture and even differences of opinion on the nature of good posture. Posture became, during the 1930's, the yardstick of gymnastics. The emphasis on the scientific and therapeutic nature of artificial exercises also led to the neglect and even the denigration of games by some physical education teachers who thought of games as recreation not education. Some governing bodies of sport such as the Amateur Athletic Association and the Football Association ran coaching courses which helped to raise the standard of teaching of games and

204

sports and to redress the balance which was so much in favour of gymnastics. Official policy, with its emphasis on 'physical training' led Labour politicians such as Mr. Bevan and Mr. Maxton in the debate on the Physical Training and Recreation Bill in 1937, to accuse the government of providing physical education for the masses on the cheap, while the upper classes enjoyed lavish facilities at their Public Schools. This charge was not without foundation but ignored the fact that since the end of the 1914–18 war there had been a steady improvement in the provision of facilities and in the quality of teaching. If the Board's policy was more aptly called physical training than physical education there were nevertheless a number of teachers who had a wider vision than this and who established a more comprehensive programme of physical education than the Board officially laid down. Dr. L. P. Jack's condemnation of 'physical illiteracy' and his advocacy of the 'education of the whole man' and 'education through recreation' were powerful propaganda for liberal physical education, while M. L. Jacks, headmaster of Mill Hill School, appointed a Director of Physical Education there and showed how the 'education of the whole man' might be achieved in an English Public School.

During the 1920's the women's colleges came to adhere less closely to the Swedish system of former days although they maintained their enthusiasm for gymnastics. They were strongly influenced by Elli Björksten and Elin Falk who had broken away from the rigid positional gymnastics of Ling. The Ling Association itself both organized visits to Scandinavia and arranged for Niels Bukh to give demonstrations of his system of Danish gymnastics in this country. A new *Syllabus of Physical Training* published by the Board in 1933, like its predecessors, showed Scandinavian influence. It contained fresh exercises and new teaching methods 'with a view to the special encouragement of good posture and flexibility of muscles and joints',[27] but a large number of simple games were described and many free and vigorous 'activity' exercises were included. Its popularity as a handbook among teachers led to a great improvement in the physical education of children.

The Ling Association did valuable propaganda for physical education but its continued insistence on two years full time training as a condition of membership virtually excluded men.

205

From the end of the war until 1933 there was no college in England where men could obtain specialist training. The Board of Education ran vacation courses for men, but Secondary Schoolmasters, finding themselves excluded from the foremost professional organization, formed their own physical education association, ran their own courses and issued their own certificates.

At last in 1933 the Carnegie College of Physical Education was opened in Leeds and provided a year's course for men teachers who had already completed their two years' general training or who possessed a university degree. A similar course was started at Loughborough College in 1935 and at Goldsmiths' College London in 1937. These courses differed from those in the women's colleges in two important respects. First they were open only to teachers who were already qualified to teach other subjects; the Board had decided that specialist training in physical education for men must not exclude a general training as it had done in the women's colleges. Secondly many students who went to Carnegie College were grant-aided by the government. Women's colleges had all, except Chelsea College, been private enterprises which had had to pay their way on the fees of the students.

The isolation of the women's colleges from the general pattern of teacher training was not entirely to their liking, and in 1918 they had approached London University with a view to the examination of their students being undertaken by the University which would then grant a degree or diploma to successful candidates. After protracted negotiations the Senate of the University agreed to institute a diploma and the first examination was held in 1932. The high standard of work and training which had been guarded so jealously by the colleges was thus recognized and consolidated by association with the University.

In 1939 the centenary of P. H. Ling's death was celebrated with a gymnastic festival in Stockholm. Many troops of gymnasts from clubs and colleges in England made the journey to Sweden and the festival was a fitting end to a period of thirty years in which Swedish gymnastics had come to form the basis of physical education in state-aided schools. Hardly had the pilgrims returned home when war broke out and a new era in the development of physical education in Britain began.

206

REFERENCES

1. Report of Royal Commission on Public Schools 1864, p. 40.
2. *Edinburgh Review*, August 1810, Vol. 16, p. 326, 'Remarks on the System of Education in Public Schools.'
3. J. J. Findlay, *Arnold of Rugby*, p. 198. Cambridge 1897.
4. K. E. Kirk, *The Story of the Woodard Schools*, p. 28. London 1937.
5. Matthew Arnold, *Culture and Anarchy*, p. 65. London 1889.
6. G. W. Fisher, *Annals of Shrewsbury School*, p. 313. London 1899.
7. *Op. cit.*, p. 40.
8. *Op. cit.*, Minutes of Evidence. Written reply from Harrow III. 2.9.
9. *Op. cit.*, I, p. 56.
10. *Op. cit.*, I, p. 41.
11. W. H. G. Armytage, 'Thomas Arnold's Views on Physical Education', *Journal of Physical Education*, Vol. 47, No. 140, March 1955.
12. Frances J. Woodward, *The Doctor's Disciples*. Oxford 1954.
13. A. G. Bradley, *A History of Marlborough College*, p. 138. London 1893.
14. P. C. McIntosh, *Physical Education in England since 1800*, p. 36. London 1952.
15. Edward Lyttelton, 'Athletics in Public Schools', *Nineteenth Century*, January 1880.
16. C. R. L. Fletcher, *Edmund Warre*. pp. 106–107. London 1922.
17. *The Concise Oxford Dictionary*, 'Cricket'.
18. *Hansard*, 8 July 1862. Vol. 168, Col. 22.
19. Report of the Schools Inquiry Commission (Taunton Commission) 1868, Vol. VI, pp. 589–590.
20. A. MacLaren, *Physical Education*. Oxford 1895. Preface by W. MacLaren, p. vi.
21. Herbert Spencer, *Education: Intellectual, Moral and Physical*, pp. 152–153. London 1859. Ed. 1891.
22. Final Report of the Cross Commission on Elementary Education 1888, p. 145.
23. Annual Report of the Education Department 1893–4, p. 333.
24. Report of the Interdepartmental Committee on Physical Deterioration 1904, Minute 2430.
25. *Journal of Scientific Physical Training*, Nov. 1909. Vol. II, No. 1.

207

26. *The Health of the School Child* 1932, p. 81. Annual Report of the Chief Medical Officer 1932, p. 79.

27. *Ibid.* 1932, p. 79.

See also

Adamson, J. W. *English Education 1789–1902.* Cambridge 1930.

Archer, R. L. *Secondary Education in the Nineteenth Century.* Cambridge 1921.

Barnard, H. C. *A Short History of English Education from 1760 to 1944.* London 1947.

Hughes, T. *Tom Brown's Schooldays.* London 1857.

Mack, E. C. *Public Schools and British Opinion 1780–1860.* London 1938.

Mack, E.C. *Public Schools and British Opinion from 1860.* New York 1941.

Wordsworth, C. *Annals of My Early Life.* London 1891.

Worsley, T. C. *Barbarians and Phillistines.* London 1940.

Wymer, Norman. *Dr. Arnold of Rugby.* London 1953.

Young, G. M. *Early Victorian England.* London 1934.

A fuller bibliography will be found in *Physical Education in England since 1800* by P. C. McIntosh, London 1952.

208

INDEX

Index

211

Index

216

Index

217

Index

218